GRAND CANYON

AN ANTHOLOGY

On Grandview Trail. Guide in the foreground is Louis Boucher.
William Jennings Bryan at the rear.

GRAND CANYON

AN ANTHOLOGY

A Selection of Outstanding
Writings Compiled by

BRUCE BABBITT

Foreword by Dr. Robert C. Euler

NORTHLAND PRESS FLAGSTAFF, ARIZONA

Cover Photo: Zoroaster and Brahma Temple
FRONTISPIECE: Tourists guided down the Grandview Trail, 1904
Emery Kolb Collection, Photographs Copyright © 1976 by Edith Lehnert
Permission to reproduce any of the photographs must
be obtained in writing from the Director of Libraries,
Northern Arizona University.

SECOND PRINTING, 1981
ISBN 0-87358-283-7 softcover
ISBN 0-87358-180-6 hardcover
Library of Congress Catalog Card Number 78-58470
Composed and Printed in the United States of America

Contents

Foreword

IN SHEER NUMBERS, there probably have been more pictures taken than words written about Grand Canyon, but not much more. This torrent of verbosity began in the 1880s after the first tourists and what then passed for travel agents had "discovered" the canyon. Indeed, a recent bibliography of nineteenth-century magazine articles about Grand Canyon listed 119 items.

Today it almost seems as though anyone with an eye toward a quick dollar must take pen in hand and attempt prose or verse or photo caption about this incomparable scene. Books with such inspiring titles as *This Is Grand Canyon, Grand Canyon Country,* and *South Rim Grand Canyon* flow from the presses. The depth of understanding with which many historical and contemporary works treat the canyon is shallow indeed. As the compiler of this anthology has so aptly said: "Even today, the canyon has not been synthesized in our history, art or literature; its only enduring place on paper is an endless succession of color postcards and slick photographs."

Yet, during the past century, and even rarely before, some excellent treatises were written about a number of aspects of Grand Canyon. Perhaps of the hundreds of books and articles, not more than thirty fall into this enduring category. Unfortunately, the bulk of these are out of print or generally unavailable to those who might profit from reading them. Now, for the first time, many of these have been brought together and nicely introduced by a person who, like a number of us, has long carried on a literary love affair with Grand Canyon.

Bruce Babbitt, governor of Arizona, has ample qualifications as editor and compiler of the articles he has selected for this anthology. The first and perhaps the most important of these is that he is, in my opinion, a well-educated person.

Trained at Notre Dame, Harvard, and the University of Newcastle in Britain, he is grounded in the social and political sciences, law, geology, and the humanities. Couple that with his long interest in all facets of Grand Canyon, including backpacking and river running, and his expertise becomes clear.

While any individual similarly familiar with the literature of the canyon might not have made the precise same selections, those that Governor Babbitt has chosen are representative and well written, and range widely through history, science, art, and personal impression. They are uniquely organized in five segments, each preceded by an explanatory commentary by the compiler.

The history and exploration of the canyon are portrayed by accounts dating from the sixteenth century, when Spaniards became the first Europeans to view the gorge, through Powell's and Stanton's noted river surveys in the late 1800s, to those of early residents of the south rim such as John Hance and the Kolb brothers.

Three beautifully written views of the canyon follow in the second part. Mary Austin, John Van Dyke, and Clarence Dutton have, in the opinion of many, penned the most descriptive passages of the impacts they felt when looking at Grand Canyon.

Lesser known perhaps are articles authored by such luminaries as Irvin Cobb, J. B. Priestly, Wallace Stegner, and Haniel Long describing their visits to the canyon. Here we have the impressions of tourists, but tourists who could also turn a phrase.

Scientific studies of the canyon have been included in a fourth section. These include geology, natural history, and archaeology. All are written clearly and are intended to give the reader a base line from which a deeper and more holistic understanding may be gained.

Finally, there is a selection of articles describing several personal experiences in Grand Canyon. Early lion hunting by Theodore Roosevelt long before the national park was established; solitary backpacking through the gorge by Colin Fletcher; a river trip and a visit to Havasu by Edward Abbey; and, yes, even some exciting passages from Zane Grey's novel, *Heritage of the Desert,* are included.

There are undoubtedly some who will fail to see the value of an anthology such as this. They would rather read, if they read at all, something condensing all these variegated themes of Grand Canyon; something written today rather than in the past, and with the emphasis on illustration rather than text. After all, they are in a hurry and have time for but a quick glimpse. "They" are the average visitors to the canyon, many of whom fly in from Las Vegas in the morning, take in a few viewpoints, and are back in the glitter of the gaming tables that night. It has been estimated that some sixty percent of the three million persons who visit Grand Canyon each year never stay overnight. And what of those who but briefly, and seemingly reluctantly, only leave their recreational vehicles or the television set in the lobby of El Tovar to "see" the canyon on foot?

There may be many ways to enjoy and profit from a visit to Grand Canyon, but any of these can be improved if one would take a bit more time to read. Take this book out to some spot on the rim. Sit down and leisurely read, and look, and read again. Your own impressions will be heightened and deepened by understanding and contemplating what has gone before.

ROBERT C. EULER

Grand Canyon, Arizona
May 14, 1978

The Kolbs
and Their Photographs

DURING MY LIFETIME the Kolb brothers and their photography studio were a splendid anachronism. The Kolb home and studio, a tidy frame house pinned incongruously under the canyon lip, resembled a scene from an old wet plate negative. The battered river boat displayed outside under a rock ledge looked like a museum piece.

Inside that studio you paid a small fee, climbed down creaking stairs and sat on folding chairs arranged on a polished hardwood floor. Emery Kolb, small of stature, ancient, gentle of manner, then came on stage and narrated his faded, flickering motion pictures telling of exploits half a century old.

I went back many times to see that show, irresistibly drawn, curious to learn the Kolb secrets and understand the drawing power of this archaic side show, this cameo of sepia prints, glass negatives, antique Pathé cameras and sputtering silent films.

As the decades went by the show never changed. The Kolbs refused to modernize their studio, and they showed little enthusiasm for color photography and other modern inventions. They were frozen in the past, oblivious to the changes around them, still living and reliving their adventures and the great river trips of 1911 and 1923.

However archaic the show, there were always plenty of tourists, eager to step into the heroic past to share the excitement of discovery and the dangers of the river.

The lure of the Kolb Studio, then, was not as a museum of ancient photography. What beckoned was the spirit of the inhabitants, two ancient mariners who had ventured into the face of danger, won the contest, and returned to serve as inspiration to others. Tourists came to see not their photos, but to hear of their personal exploits, to measure not the photography but the men.

Their river book, *Through the Grand Canyon from Wyoming to Mexico,* remains popular for many of the same reasons. Others were first, others could write better, and some explained more clearly the meaning of the river and its canyons. But no other river runners were so uniquely American: average mid-western youths with no special education, no wealthy sponsors, just endowed with a big idea, plenty of persistence, naiveté and courage. Any daydreaming kid or would-be adventurer could relate to these two brothers and their exploits.

The Kolb photographs from which the selections in this anthology are taken were willed to Northern Arizona University upon Emery's death in 1976. The heart of the collection consists of several thousand dry plate glass negatives made in the early years of this century. Most of the photographs have never been published, although some have appeared over the years—in *Through the Grand Canyon from Wyoming to Mexico,* in a 1914 *National Geographic* article featuring the brothers, and in a now rare photographic album published by Kolb Studios in 1911.

In the long run, the memory of the men, their character, and their exploits may well outshine their photographs. However that may be, the Kolbs were talented photographers. If some of the photography seems contrived (one of the brothers dangling in mid-air or poking his head through the side of a battered boat) it reflects the spontaneous enthusiasm of two people engaged in a passionate encounter with the river and the canyon. Owen Wister, in his preface to *Through the Grand Canyon from Wyoming to Mexico,* described their affair with the canyon:

> Is much wonder to be felt that its beckoning enchantment should have drawn two young men to dwell beside it for many years; to give themselves wholly to it; to descend and ascend among its buttressed pinnacles; to discover caves and waterfalls hidden in its labyrinths; to climb, to creep, to hang in mid-air, in order to learn more and more of it, and at last to gratify wholly their passion in the great adventure of this journey through it from end to end?

The Kolb brothers were not addicted to the panoramic photography so popular at the time. Their best photographs are selective, carefully composed views that take in a river bend, an alcove, a small piece of the great panorama. They knew that a little less tells a lot more at Grand Canyon, a fact being rediscovered by contemporary photographers.

The Kolbs also perceived and used the secrets of desert light. They stayed away from the harsh, flat light of mid-day. Almost uniformly, Kolb photographs are carefully modeled in the oblique, contrasting light of early morning and late afternoon.

When the Kolb collection is definitively studied and cataloged there will be time enough for final judgment. Meanwhile it seems safe to predict that both the exploits and the photographs will remain an indelible part of canyon history.

THE PHOTOGRAPHS

DISCOVERY
AND
EXPLORATION

The final portage over icy rocks through Separation Rapid, January, 1912.
Bert Lauzon at the bow, Ellsworth Kolb behind.

GRAND CANYON is still a remote, alien and unassimilated place, like a landscape from a lifeless planet. Coronado's men located it in 1540. They tried to cross, but after several days without water they were forced to turn back. The canyon was then forgotten for centuries. Lieutenant Ives, the first official American explorer, didn't do much better than Coronado. After much hardship Ives got to the bottom, but, unable to get across, he too turned back, thirsty and frustrated. Upon leaving he wrote: "The region is altogether valueless. It can be approached only from the south, and after entering it there is nothing to do but leave."

Only in the last century has the canyon been thoroughly explored and put indelibly on the map of world tourism. Three million persons now come each year to marvel at a sight that was virtually unknown scarcely a hundred years ago. Even today, the canyon has not been synthesized in our history, art or literature; its only enduring place on paper is an endless succession of color postcards and slick photographs.

The literature of Grand Canyon has been slow to develop. No regional writer of the stature of Washington Irving or Mark Twain has yet come along to blend the canyon, its history and its people into enduring regional literature. Nonetheless, over the years a good number of talented writers have seen the canyon, paused to look carefully and written of their experiences.

The first writers were the early explorers. Starting with Coronado, many of them recorded their experiences, understandably emphasizing their hardships and suffering rather than the quality of the scenery. The first selections of this anthology chronicle three high points of early exploration: Coronado's discovery, the first organized American exploration by Lieutenant Ives, and the epic river voyage by John Wesley Powell.

The discovery and looting of Mexico by Cortes in 1520 ignited the greatest treasure hunt in the history of the world. One of those treasure hunters, a thirty-year-old patrician named Francisco Vásquez de Coronado, was selected by the viceroy to explore northward into the present-day American Southwest.

Coronado's southwestern entrada, searching for the fabled cities of gold, lasted from 1540 to 1542. In August of 1540, his men reached the Hopi villages, disappointed, but still hopeful that the golden cities would be found. The Hopis told them of a great river to the west that sounded promising, and Coronado promptly dispatched another detachment under Cárdenas to locate and explore the river. The official account of that exploration, written for Coronado, has never been discovered. However, two narratives written by members of the Coronado expedition do contain a description of the discovery of Grand Canyon, presumably obtained from either the original written report or verbal descriptions by soldiers who accompanied Cárdenas. The best-known narrative, that of Castañeda, is reprinted here, as is the pertinent portion of the other narrative, the *Relacion del Suceso,* whose author remains unknown to this day.

Reading the two accounts in translation, four hundred years later, there is no suggestion that the thirteen Spanish discoverers beheld anything of beauty. They were searching not for esthetic values, but for tangible riches. And they were eager to get across only to see if anything more promising lay on the other side. The explorers tried unsuccessfully for three days to find a way to the bottom. Suffering for lack of water, "even though they had the river before their eyes," the party gave up, returned to the Hopi villages, and rejoined the main expedition for another two years of fruitless wandering upon the plains of New Mexico, Texas, and Kansas.

Coronado's great scenic discovery was likewise of no interest to anyone in Mexico City or Madrid. His reports were filed and forgotten. The Spanish treasure hunts were over, at least in this region.

Some two centuries later another Spaniard, a wandering Franciscan missionary named Francisco Garcés, happened upon the canyon in the year 1776. He made his way down a precipitous trail into Havasu Canyon and spent five days enjoying Indian hospitality and preaching the gospel. But he too moved on, eventually to become a martyr at the hands of the Yuma Indians.

The next canyon visitors were American mountain men searching for beaver. From about 1820, trappers invaded the Southwest, defying Mexican orders to stay out and working every wet stream for beaver pelts. Fur trappers didn't read or write, and most of their exploits went unrecorded. But one of the more colorful southwestern trappers, James Ohio Pattie, was persuaded to dictate his memoirs to an Ohio publisher. The resulting book, *The Personal Narrative of James O. Pattie,* published in 1831, is a curious blend of hard fact and airy fantasy, including a journey by Pattie along the canyon rim on his way up the Colorado River from southern Arizona to Wyoming. Pattie's narrative is so unreliable that scholars are still arguing whether he actually saw the canyon. Pattie's disputed description reads: "At last we reached the place where the river emerges from these horrid mountains which so cage it up as to deprive all human beings of the ability to descend to its banks and make use of its waters." That brief narrative, if indeed it describes Grand Canyon, is its first known description by an American.

In 1857 the United States Army took up canyon exploration just about where Coronado's army had left off three hundred years earlier in 1540. The exploring party, led by Lieutenant Joseph Christmas Ives, assembled on the muddy tidal flats of the Colorado River Delta, bolted together an iron steamboat shipped in pieces from Philadelphia, and steamed upriver hoping to reach the Mormon settlements in Utah. Navigating the Colorado upstream was not exactly a new idea; one Hernando Alarcon had tried and failed to sail upstream in 1540 in an attempt to connect with Coronado's overland party. The Ives steamboat expedition did not do much better. In Black Canyon the steamer crashed and nearly foundered upon a submerged rock, bringing the navigation effort to an inglorious end.

Undaunted by his failure as a navigator, Ives struck out overland with a mule train to explore along the canyon south rim toward the Utah Mormon settlements. After much hardship, Ives reached Cataract Creek and the Havasupais. There he made a major miscalculation. Concluding that the main course of the Colorado River turned north through Kanab Canyon, he decided to terminate his efforts since he could not cross the gorge to continue in that direction.

Plagued by lack of water, extremes of temperature, runaway mules and unreliable Indian guides, Ives left the region greatly discouraged and far short of his objective, after penning one of the least prophetic valedictories in southwestern history:

Ours has been the first, and doubtless will be the last party of whites to visit this profitless locality. It seems intended by nature that the Colorado River along the greater part of its lonely and majestic way, shall be forever unvisited and undisturbed.

For all his failures, Ives did leave one major geographic contribution: he descended Diamond Creek to the banks of the Colorado River—the first recorded descent to the canyon bottom. In the selection printed here, Ives describes that trip down Diamond Creek. The selection begins with negotiations by Ives and his trusted Mohave Indian guide, Ireteba, for the services of several rather reluctant Hualapais Indians to guide them down into the canyon. Ives's description is taken from his official publication, *Report upon the Colorado River of the West,* published in 1861.

The first explorer to meet the canyon head on and come to terms with its reality was John Wesley Powell. His 1869 river journey, with four boats and just ten men, ranks with the great western explorations of Lewis and Clark, Coronado, Jedediah Smith, and Escalante.

Powell made two summer fields trips to study the upper river and its canyons in 1867 and 1868. He planned carefully and made one basic and fateful choice—there could be no half commitments to overland approaches or upstream navigation from the quiet reaches of the lower river. He would commit himself to the rushing torrent and ride it out wherever it might lead. It was a dangerous gamble but, given his methodical preparation and total commitment, the chances of success were probably quite high.

Powell's personal account of the trip was written in 1874 for serial publication by *Scribner's Monthly*. Over the years a scholarly and sometimes pedantic debate has developed over the accuracy of detail and amount of literary license indulged by the author. Nonetheless, Powell's account is fresh and vivid, and it has all the elements of an exciting adventure story. The selection printed here begins on August 14, 1869, as the party, already three months on the river, prepares to start through Grand Canyon proper. The first short paragraphs of the August 14 entry are perhaps the most eloquent and moving lines in all the literature of Grand Canyon.

Several elements of hardship pervade the pages of Powell's journal. Short of food, finally reduced to a subsistence diet of musty flour, dried apples and coffee, the party moved against a starvation deadline, a "race to dinner" Powell termed it. The most exhausting work was alternately portaging the heavy oak boats and lining them through the worst rapids. August of 1869 was an unusually rainy season; the party was continuously soaked by chilling rains that made working miserable and extinguished campfires as fast as they could be kindled.

Powell's account reaches a high point with the desertion of three men at Separation Rapid, one day before the party emerged from the canyon depths into the quiet waters of Grand Wash. Powell wrote, "Each party thought the other to be taking the more dangerous course." Some months later he received the ironic news that the three men who had deserted to avoid the dangers of the river had been killed by Shivwits Paiute Indians on the north rim.

Powell's trip put both him and Grand Canyon on the map of America forever. With his canyon adventure as a springboard, Powell went on to a brilliant career in government, science and reclamation politics. Powell never really left the canyon country; he returned personally for several years to direct the geological surveys, and the men he recruited, Dutton, Gilbert and Walcott, laid the foundations of modern scientific knowledge of the canyon.

After Powell opened the country, the focus of activity shifted from exploration to commercial exploitation. Prospectors, homesteaders, surveyors, railway engineers and cattlemen swarmed throughout the southwestern region. Grand Canyon was no exception, however unlikely a place it might seem for building railroads or developing mineral riches.

The inevitable western railroad speculation got off to an early start. Today it seems, by any measure, a wildly improbable, quixotic adventure. But the nineteenth century was an age of gilded optimism and headlong expansion. Anything was possible.

The man who dreamed it up was a Denver capitalist named Frank Brown. He interested a talented railway engineer, Robert Brewster Stanton. Brown organized the Denver Railway Company, hired Stanton as chief engineer, and together they started down the river to survey a "water level" railroad through the Colorado's canyons from the Rocky Mountains to California.

The Brown-Stanton survey party was ill prepared for the river: the boats were constructed of brittle, light cedar and there were no life preservers. In Marble Canyon, President Brown was spilled into a whirlpool below Soap Creek Rapid and drowned. Six days later, two more men drowned in another upset, and the party gave up.

But Stanton would not quit. A year later he returned to the river with new, improved boats and life preservers. After an initial mishap, he completed the railway survey without further incident.

Stanton spent much of his remaining life promoting Colorado River development projects and arguing the feasibility of his railroad. There were no takers. Stanton was a grandiose dreamer. In his account of the second river trip, he reveals his thoughts during a quiet stretch below Hance Rapid. "I dreamed one of my daydreams and saw each cove with its picturesque Swiss chalet, and its happy mountain people with their herds of sheep and mountain goats, developing local business for our future railroad." Today one can stand in utter solitude at the banks of the Colorado River on Bass Trail where Stanton planned a railroad switchyard and marvel at both the man and the spirit of that time.

Stanton's personal account of the disasters of the first voyage, the decision to abandon the river, and the retreat northward out of the canyon to Mormon settlements is reprinted here from the original article written for *Scribner's* magazine in 1890.

The prospectors were not far behind. After 1870 they swarmed through the canyon, staking out claims and working bodies of silver, lead, asbestos and copper. Many of the aboriginal canyon trails were improved so that horses and burros could be used at mineral claims: Hance's Trail led to an asbestos claim, Berry's Grand View Trail was built to bring out copper ore by mule train, and the Bass Trail also led to copper claims. Most of the prospectors were just as unlucky as Coronado, and several lost their lives. Henry Ashurst, a pioneer homesteader and father of Senator Henry Fountain Ashurst, died an agonized death in the canyon, trapped beneath a boulder he had dislodged while prospecting. James Mooney fell to his death near the falls that bear his name while working a silver deposit in the sheer face of a cliff. The Kolb brothers photographed the bleached skeleton of a nameless prospector in Granite Gorge in 1906.

Perhaps the most audacious and flamboyant of all the early prospectors and promoters was Ralph Henry Cameron. At one time or another he promoted schemes for the development of mining claims, dams for electric power, a scenic railway along the rim and a tourist hotel. Fighting to control the canyon as a commercial venture, Cameron brazenly staked fraudulent mining claims at strategic locations to control trail access and springs and to frustrate the development plans of the Santa Fe Railway. In 1920 he was elected to the United States Senate where he spent most of his one and only term promoting his claims and trying unsuccessfully to do in his rivals, the National Park Service and the Santa Fe. With Cameron's demise the era of unrestrained commercial exploitation came to an end.

In the final selection of this part, Edwin Corle, a popular historian and novelist of the Southwest, traces the process by which early prospectors like John Hance and Pete Berry, defeated by the overwhelming costs of taking copper out of the canyon, gradually accepted reality and became innkeepers, tour guides and the legendary folk heroes of canyon history. After all else failed, the tourists finally arrived to provide an economic rationale for Grand Canyon. The selection presented here is taken from Corle's book, *Listen, Bright Angel*.

The Colorado River below Havasu Canyon, 1914

The Coronado Expedition

CASTAÑEDA'S HISTORY OF THE EXPEDITION

THE PROVINCE is governed like Cíbola, by an assembly of the oldest men. They have their chosen governor and captains. Here information was obtained of a large river and that several days down the river there were people with very large bodies.

As Don Pedro de Tovar had no other commission, he returned from Tusayán and gave his report to the general. The latter at once dispatched Don García López de Cárdenas there with about twelve men to explore this river. When he reached Tusayán he was well received and lodged by the natives. They provided him with guides to proceed on his journey. They set out from there laden with provisions, because they had to travel over some uninhabited land before coming to settlements, which the Indians said were more than twenty days away. Accordingly when they had marched for twenty days they came to the gorges of the river, from the edge of which it looked as if the opposite side must have been more than three or four leagues away by air. This region was high and covered with low and twisted pine trees; it was extremely cold, being open to the north, so that, although this was the warm season, no one could live in this canyon because of the cold.

The men spent three days looking for a way down to the river; from the top it looked as if the water were a fathom across. But, according to the infor-

From *Narratives of the Coronado Expedition,* by George P. Hammond and Agapito Rey. The University of New Mexico Press, 1940.

mation supplied by the Indians, it must have been half a league wide. The descent was almost impossible, but, after these three days, at a place which seemed less difficult, Captain Melgosa, a certain Juan Galeras, and another companion, being the most agile, began to go down. They continued descending within view of those on top until they lost sight of them, as they could not be seen from the top. They returned about four o'clock in the afternoon, as they could not reach the bottom because of the many obstacles they met, for what from the top seemed easy, was not so; on the contrary, it was rough and difficult. They said that they had gone down one-third of the distance and that, from the point they had reached, the river seemed very large, and that, from what they saw, the width given by the Indians was correct. From the top they could make out, apart from the canyon, some small boulders which seemed to be as high as a man. Those who went down and who reached them swore that they were taller than the great tower of Seville.

The party did not continue farther up the canyon of the river because of the lack of water. Up to that time they had gone one or two leagues inland in search of water every afternoon. When they had traveled four additional days the guides said that it was impossible to go on because no water would be found for three or four days, that when they themselves traveled through that land they took along women who brought water in gourds, that in those trips they buried the gourds of water for the return trip, and that they traveled in one day a distance that took us two days.

This was the Tízon river, much closer to its source than where Melchior Díaz and his men had crossed it. These Indians were of the same type, as it appeared later. From there Cárdenas and his men turned back, as that trip brought no other results. On the way they saw a waterfall which came down a rock. They learned from the guides that some clusters which hung like fine crystals were salt. They went thither and gathered quantities of it which they brought and distributed when they returned to Cíbola.

RELACION DEL SUCESO

WHEN DON PEDRO DE TOVAR returned and gave an account of those pueblos, the general at once sent Don García de López de Cárdenas, maestre de campo, over the same route by which Don Pedro had come, for the purpose of going west beyond that province of Tuzán. He allotted him eighty days for the round trip of exploration. He went beyond Tuzán with native guides who said that there were settlements ahead, although quite far. After going fifty leagues west from Tuzán, and eighty from Cíbola, he came to the canyon of a river where it was utterly impossible to find a way down, either for horses or on foot, except at a very difficult descent where it was almost two leagues down. The canyon was so lined with rock that one could hardly see the river, although it is said to be as large or much larger than the one at Seville. From the top it looked like an arroyo. Although the men sought diligently in many places for a crossing, none was found.

Here they spent a good number of days, suffering from lack of water which they could not obtain even though they had the river before their eyes. For this reason Don García López was compelled to go back until they found some. This river flows from the northeast and turns south southwest, so it can not fail to be the one reached by Melchior Díaz.

Mojave Valley to Big Cañon

IRETEBA, AT MY REQUEST, again went in search of some Hualpais tractable enough to enlist for a few days in our service. After an absence of several hours he came back and reported that he had discovered two who were willing to go. In a little while, from the top of a neighboring hill, a discordant screaming was heard, proceeding from two Indians who were suspiciously surveying camp. It was some time before our Mojaves could persuade them to approach, and when they did they looked like men who had screwed up their courage to face a mortal peril. They were squalid, wretched-looking creatures, with splay feet, large joints, and diminutive figures, but had bright eyes and cunning faces, and resembled a little the Chemehuevis. Taking them into the tent occupied by Lieutenant Tipton and myself, with many misgivings as to how many varieties of animal life were being introduced there, I brought out some pipes and tobacco and told Ireteba to proceed with the negotiations. These were not soon arranged. The sententiousness belonging to Mr. Cooper's and other story-book Indians is not a gift of the tribes that one encounters in travelling. Our old guides and the two new candidates talked all at once, and with amazing volubility; they seemed to be recounting their personal histories from birth to the present date. The conclusion arrived at was that they knew nothing about the country—neither a good road nor the localities of grass and water; that they were out hunting and had lost their way, and had no idea of the direction even of their own villages. This very probable statement I correctly supposed to be a hint that they were

From *Report Upon the Colorado River of the West,* by Lieutenant Joseph C. Ives. Washington, D.C.: Government Printing Office, 1861.

not to be approached empty-handed; for when Ireteba had been authorized to make a distinct offer of beads and blankets, one of them recollected where he was, and also that there were watering places ahead to which he could guide us. It was thought advisable to again lie over for a day; and they went away, agreeing to be in camp on the day but one following.

A third Hualpais turned up this morning; he had features like a toad's, and the most villainous countenance I ever saw on a human being. Mr. Mollhausen suggested that we should take him and preserve him in alcohol as a zoological specimen; and at last he became alarmed at the steadfast gaze he was attracting, and withdrew to the edge of a rock overhanging the cook's fire, where he remained till dark, with his eyes fixed in an unbroken stare upon the victuals. The Hualpais are but little removed from the Diggers. They present a remarkable contrast to our tall and athletic Mojaves. The latter, as I discovered to-day for the first time, have suspected that the object of the expedition was to make war upon the others; and I had some trouble in convincing Ireteba that this was not the case. That we have come out to fight somebody he has fully made up his mind.

Deer and antelope are now frequently seen, but they are shy and hard to approach. A single antelope one of the Mexicans succeeded in killing; they are just in season, and the flesh was tender and delicately flavored.

Camp 67, Big cañon of the Colorado, April 3.—The two Hualpais preserved the credit of the Indian employés by being punctual to their engagement, and led off in company with the Mojaves as we ascended the ravine from Peacock's spring. It was a cool lovely morning, and a favorable day for travel. After proceeding a mile or two we issued from the hills and entered a region totally different from any that had been seen during the expedition. A broad tableland, unbroken by the volcanic hills that had overspread the country since leaving Fort Yuma, extended before us, rising in a gradual swell towards the north. The road became hard and smooth, and the plain was covered with excellent grass. Herds of antelope and deer were seen bounding over the slopes. Groves of cedar occurred, and with every mile became more frequent and of larger size. At the end of ten miles the ridge of the swell was attained, and a splendid panorama burst suddenly into view. In the foreground were low table-hills, intersected by numberless ravines; beyond these a lofty line of bluffs marked the edge of an immense cañon; a wide gap was directly ahead, and through it were beheld, to the extreme limit of vision, vast plateaus, towering one above the other thousands of feet in the air, the long horizontal bands broken at intervals by wide and profound abysses, and extending a hundred miles to the north, till the deep azure blue faded into a light cerulean tint that blended with the dome of the heavens. The famous "Big cañon" was before us; and for a long time we paused in wondering delight, surveying this stupendous formation through which the Colorado and its tributaries break their way.

Our guides, becoming impatient of the detention, plunged into a narrow and precipitous ravine that opened at our feet, and we followed as well as we could, stumbling along a rough and rocky pathway. The Hualpais were now of great assistance, for the ravines crossed and forked in intricate confusion; even Ireteba, who had hitherto led the train, became at a loss how to proceed, and had to put the little Hualpais in front. The latter, being perfectly at home, conducted us rapidly down the declivity. The descent was great and the trail blind and circuitous. A few miles of difficult travelling brought us into a narrow valley flanked by steep and high slopes; a sparkling stream crossed its centre, and a gurgling in some tall grass near by announced the presence of a spring. The water was delicious. The grass in the neighborhood was sparse, but of good quality.

This morning we left the valley and followed the course of a creek down a ravine, in the bed of which the water at intervals sank and rose for two or three miles, when it altogether disappeared. The ravine soon attained the proportions of a cañon. The bottom was rocky and irregular, and there were some jump-offs over which it was hard to make the pack animals pass. The vegetation began to disappear, leaving only a few stunted cedars projecting from the sides of the rugged bluffs. The place grew wilder and grander. The sides of the tortuous cañon became loftier, and before long we were hemmed in by walls two thousand feet high. The scenery much resembled that in the Black cañon, excepting that the rapid descent, the increasing magnitude of the colossal piles that blocked the end of the vista, and the corresponding depth and gloom of the gaping chasms into which we were plunging, imparted an unearthly character to a way that might have resembled the portals of the infernal regions. Harsh screams issuing from aerial recesses in the cañon sides and apparitions of goblin-like figures perched in the rifts and hollows of the impending cliffs, gave an odd reality to this impression. At short distances other avenues of equally magnificent proportions came in from one side or the other; and no trail being left on the rocky pathway, the idea suggested itself that were the guides to desert us our experience might further resemble that of the dwellers in the unblest abodes —in the difficulty of getting out.

Huts of the rudest construction, visible here and there in some sheltered niche or beneath a projecting rock, and the sight of a hideous old squaw, staggering under a bundle of fuel, showed that we had penetrated into the domestic retreats of the Hualpais nation. Our party being, in all probability, the first company of whites that had ever been seen by them, we had anticipated producing a great effect, and were a little chagrined when the old woman, and two or three others of both sexes that were met, went by without taking the slightest notice of us. If pack-trains had been in the habit of passing twenty times a day they could not have manifested a more complete indifference.

Seventeen miles of this strange travel had now been accomplished. The road was becoming more difficult, and we looked ahead distrustfully into the dark and apparently interminable windings, and wondered where we were to find a camping place. At last we struck a wide branch cañon coming in from the south, and saw with joyful surprise a beautiful and brilliantly clear stream of water gushing over a pebbly bed in the centre, and shooting from between the rocks in sparkling jets and miniature cascades. On either side was an oasis of verdure—young willows and a thick patch of grass. Camp was speedily formed, and men and mules have had a welcome rest after their fatiguing journey.

A hundred yards below camp the cañon takes a turn; but as it was becoming very dark, all further examinations were postponed till to-morrow. In the course of the evening Ireteba came into my tent, and I asked him how far we had still to travel before reaching the great river. To my surprise he informed me that the mouth of the creek is only a few yards below the turn, and that we are now camped just on the verge of the Big Cañon of the Colorado.

Camp 69, Cedar Forest, April 5.—A short walk down the bed of Diamond river, on the morning after we had reached it, verified the statement of Ireteba, and disclosed the famous Colorado cañon. The view from the ridge, beyond the creek to which the Hualpais had first conducted us, had shown that the plateaus further north and east were several thousand feet higher than that through which the Colorado cuts at this point, and the cañons proportionally deeper; but the scene was sufficiently grand to well repay for the labor of the descent. The cañon was similar in character to others that have been mentioned, but on a larger scale, and thus far unrivalled in grandeur. Mr. Mollhausen has taken a sketch, which gives a better idea of it than any description. The course of the river could be traced for only a few hundred yards, above or below, but what had been seen from the table-land showed that we were at the apex of a great southern bend. The walls, on either side, rose directly out of the water. The river was about fifty yards wide. The channel was studded with rocks, and the torrent rushed through like a mill-race.

The day was spent in an examination of the localities. Dr. Newberry has had opportunities for observation seldom afforded to the geologist. This plateau formation has been undisturbed by volcanic action, and the sides of the cañons exhibit all of the series that compose the table-lands of New Mexico, presenting, perhaps, the most splendid exposure of stratified rocks that there is in the world.

A few of the Hualpais paid us a visit, but their intelligence is of so low an order that it is impossible to glean information from them, and their filthiness makes them objectionable. Our new guides seemed to think we should have difficulty in ascending to the portion of the plateau which they traverse on the way to higher points upon the river. The route they ordinarily pursue follows the cañon of Diamond creek, but this they pronounced impracticable for mules, and said that we must retrace our course for several miles in order to strike a more circuitous, but easier trail, that ascended one of the branch cañons.

Following their advice and guidance, yesterday morning we toiled up the rough road by which we had come, for six miles, when they struck off into a side ravine that led towards the southeast. Half a mile from the mouth, the Hualpais told Ireteba that our camping place was just ahead, and scrambling over the summit of a hill, in a minute were both out of sight. For a mile we kept on, every few moments coming to a fork, where the selection of the right road was left to chance. There was a network of cañons, and the probabilities were that nine out of ten would lead to an impassable precipice. The ascent became so rough that it was already almost impracticable for the mules, and at last the Mojaves stopped, declaring that they had lost their way, and had no idea how to find the camping place or the water, and that the Hualpais were a very bad set. This opinion no one was inclined just then to dispute. I however asked one of the Indians to go back and endeavor to find the deserters or some other member of their tribe. We waited impatiently half an hour, and then the order was given to countermarch, for I intended to search for the route by which we had come; but before going far, the little Hualpais came back. He seemed amused that we should not have been able to find the water, and again took his place at the head of the column. He conducted us for two miles through a difficult and intricate maze of ravines, and then climbed a side hill, and in a most unexpected place pointed out a little spring. There was a sufficiency of water, and tolerable grass near by. The second Hualpais came back during the evening, and seemed also to be astonished that we should have had trouble in finding what to him was so familiar. They both professed a determination to accompany the train, and Ireteba told me that it was time for himself and companions to return.

This morning the Mojaves left us. I gave them three mules, and a large part of the remaining stock of Indian goods. Ireteba in particular was loaded with presents, every one being desirous to give him something. He is the best Indian that I have ever known. He is perfectly unobtrusive, and is the only one that has never begged for anything. He has proved to me, as he did to Lieutenant Whipple, a faithful guide. He seemed sorry to separate from us, but informed me, in a confidential way, that the Hualpais were great scoundrels, and that it would not be safe for himself and friends to go further from their own tribe. He said that they would certainly be watched during their return; and if not vigilant, would lose both their presents and their lives, and that they were going to travel, for two days, without rest or sleep. I gave them a bag of provisions and some cooking utensils, and packing all of their presents upon the mules they departed, much gratified with the termination of their expedition.

Maud Powell (center), Major Powell's niece, riding with other tourists
on Bright Angel Trail, 1910

CHAPTER
THREE

The Grand Cañon
of the Colorado

AUGUST 13.—We are now ready to start on our way down the Great Unknown. Our boats, tied to a common stake, are chafing each other, as they are tossed by the fretful river. They ride high and buoyant, for their loads are lighter than we could desire. We have but a month's rations remaining. The flour has been resifted through the mosquito net sieve; the spoiled bacon has been dried, and the worst of it boiled; the few pounds of dried apples have been spread in the sun, and reshrunken to their normal bulk; the sugar has all melted, and gone on its way down the river; but we have a large sack of coffee. The lighting of the boats has this advantage: they will ride the waves better, and we shall have but little to carry when we make a portage.

We are three-quarters of a mile in the depths of the earth, and the great river shrinks into insignificance, as it dashes its angry waves against the walls and cliffs, that rise to the world above; they are but puny ripples, and we but pigmies, running up and down the sands, or lost among the boulders.

We have an unknown distance yet to run; an unknown river yet to explore. What falls there are, we know not; what rocks beset the channel, we know not; what walls rise over the river, we know not. Ah, well! we may conjecture many things. The men talk as cheerfully as ever; jests are bandied about freely this morning; but to me the cheer is somber and the jests are ghastly.

With some eagerness, and some anxiety, and some misgiving, we enter the cañon below, and are carried along by the swift water through walls which rise

From *Exploration of the Colorado River of the West and Its Tributaries,* by John Wesley Powell. Washington, D.C.: Government Printing Office, 1875.

from its very edge. They have the same structure as we noticed yesterday—tiers of irregular shelves below, and, above these, steep slopes to the foot of marble cliffs. We run six miles in a little more than half an hour, and emerge into a more open portion of the cañon, where high hills and ledges of rock intervene between the river and the distant walls. Just at the head of this open place the river runs across a dike; that is, a fissure in the rocks, open to depths below, has been filled with eruptive matter, and this, on cooling, was harder than the rocks through which the crevice was made, and, when these were washed away, the harder volcanic matter remained as a wall, and the river has cut a gateway through it several hundred feet high, and as many wide. As it crosses the wall, there is a fall below, and a bad rapid, filled with boulders of trap; so we stop to make a portage. Then on we go, gliding by hills and ledges, with distant walls in view; sweeping past sharp angles of rock; stopping at a few points to examine rapids, which we find can be run, until we have made another five miles, when we land for dinner.

Then we let down with lines, over a long rapid, and start again. Once more the walls close in, and we find ourselves in a narrow gorge, the water again filling the channel, and very swift. With great care, and constant watchfulness, we proceed, making about four miles this afternoon, and camp in a cave.

August 14.—At daybreak we walk down the bank of the river, on a little sandy beach, to take a view of a new feature in the cañon. Heretofore, hard rocks have given us bad river; soft rocks, smooth water; and a series of rocks harder than any we have experienced sets in. The river enters the granite!

We can see but a little way into the granite gorge, but it looks threatening.

After breakfast we enter on the waves. At the very introduction, it inspires awe. The cañon is narrower than we have ever before seen it; the water is swifter; there are but few broken rocks in the channel; but the walls are set, on either side, with pinnacles and crags; and sharp, angular buttresses, bristling with wind and wave polished spires, extend far out into the river.

Ledges of rocks jut into the stream, their tops sometimes just below the surface, sometimes rising few or many feet above; and island ledges, and island pinnacles, and island towers break the swift course of the stream into chutes, and eddies, and whirlpools. We soon reach a place where a creek comes in from the left, and just below, the channel is choked with boulders, which have washed down this lateral cañon and formed a dam, over which there is a fall of thirty or forty feet; but on the boulders we can get foothold, and we make a portage.

Three more such dams are found. Over one we make a portage; at the other two we find chutes, through which we can run.

As we proceed, the granite rises higher, until nearly a thousand feet of the lower part of the walls are composed of this rock.

About eleven o'clock we hear a great roar ahead, and approach it very cautiously. The sound grows louder and louder as we run, and at last we find ourselves above a long, broken fall, with ledges and pinnacles of rock obstructing the river. There is a descent of, perhaps, seventy-five or eighty feet in a third of a mile, and the rushing waters break into great waves on the rocks, and lash themselves into a mad, white foam. We can land just above, but there is no foothold on either side by which we can make a portage. It is nearly a thousand feet to the top of the granite, so it will be impossible to carry our boats around, though we can climb to the summit up a side gulch, and, passing along a mile or two, can descend to the river. This we find on examination; but such a portage would be impracticable for us, and we must run the rapid, or abandon the river. There is no hesitation. We step into our boats, push off and away we go, first on smooth but swift water, then we strike a glassy wave, and ride to its top, down again into the trough, up again on a higher wave, and down and up on waves higher and still higher, until we strike one just as it curls back, and a breaker rolls over our little boat. Still, on we speed, shooting past projecting rocks, till the little boat is caught in a whirlpool, and spun around several times. At last we pull out again into the stream, and now the other boats have passed us. The open compartment of the "Emma Dean" is filled with water, and every breaker rolls over us. Hurled back from a rock, now on this side, now on that, we are carried into an eddy, in which we struggle for a few minutes, and are then out again, the breakers still rolling over us. Our boat is unmanageable, but she cannot sink, and we drift down another hundred yards, through breakers; how, we scarcely know. We find the other boats have turned into an eddy at the foot of the fall, and are waiting to catch us as we come, for the men have seen that our boat is swamped. They push out as we come near, and pull us in against the wall. We bail our boat, and on we go again.

The walls, now, are more than a mile in height—a vertical distance difficult to appreciate. Stand on the south steps of the Treasury building, in Washington, and look down Pennsylvania Avenue to the Capitol Park, and measure this distance overhead, and imagine cliffs to extend to that altitude, and you will understand what I mean; or, stand at Canal street, in New York, and look up Broadway to Grace Church, and you have about the distance; or, stand at Lake street bridge, in Chicago, and look down to the Central Depot, and you have it again.

A thousand feet of this is up through granite crags, then steep slopes and perpendicular cliffs rise, one above another, to the summit. The gorge is black and narrow below, red and gray and flaring above, with crags and angular projections on the walls, which, cut in many places by side cañons, seem to be a vast wilderness of rocks. Down in these grand, gloomy depths we glide, ever listening, for the mad waters keep up their roar; ever watching, ever peering ahead, for the narrow cañon is winding, and the river is closed in so that we can see but a few hundred yards, and what there may be below we know not; but we listen for falls, and watch for rocks, or stop now and then, in the bay of a recess, to admire the gigantic scenery. And ever, as we go, there is some new pinnacle or tower, some crag or peak, some distant view of the upper plateau, some strange-shaped rock, or some deep, narrow side cañon. Then we come to another broken fall, which appears more difficult than the one we ran this morning.

A small creek comes in on the right, and the first fall of the water is over the boulders, which have been carried down by this lateral stream. We land at its mouth, and stop for an hour or two to examine the fall. It seems possible to let down with lines, at least a part of the way, from point to point, along the right-hand wall. So we make a portage over the first rocks, and find footing on some boulders below. Then we let down one of the boats to the end of her line, when she reaches a corner of the projecting rock, to which one of the men clings, and steadies her, while I examine an eddy below. I think we can pass the other boats down by us, and catch them in the eddy. This is soon done and the men in the boats in the eddy pull us to their side. On the shore of this little eddy there is about two feet of gravel beach above the water. Standing on this beach, some of the men take the line of the little boat and let it drift down against another projecting angle. Here is a little shelf on which a man from my boat climbs, and a shorter line is passed to him, and he fastens the boat to the side of the cliff. Then the second one is let down, bringing the line of the third. When the second boat is tied up, the two men standing on the beach above spring into the last boat, which is pulled up alongside of ours. Then we let down the boats, for twenty-five or thirty yards, by walking along the shelf, landing them again in the mouth of a side cañon. Just below this there is another pile of boulders, over which we make another portage. From the foot of these rocks we can climb to another shelf, forty or fifty feet above the water.

On this bench we camp for the night. We find a few sticks, which have lodged in the rocks. It is raining hard, and we have no shelter, but kindle a fire and have our supper. We sit on the rocks all night, wrapped in our ponchos, getting what sleep we can.

August 15.—This morning we find we can let down for three or four hundred yards, and it is managed in this way: We pass along the wall, by climbing from projecting point to point, sometimes near the water's edge, at other places fifty or sixty feet above, and hold the boat with a line, while two men remain aboard, and prevent her from being dashed against the rocks, and keep the line from getting caught on the wall. In two hours we have brought them all down, as far as it is possible, in this way. A few yards below, the river strikes with great violence against a projecting rock, and our boats are pulled up in a little bay above. We must now manage to pull out of this, and clear the point below. The little boat is held by the bow obliquely up the stream. We jump in, and pull out only a few strokes, and sweep clear of the dangerous rock. The other boats follow in the same manner, and the rapid is passed.

It is not easy to describe the labor of such navigation. We must prevent the waves from dashing the boats against the cliffs. Sometimes, where the river is swift, we must put a bight of rope about a rock, to prevent her being snatched from us by a wave; but where the plunge is too great, or the chute too swift, we must let her leap, and catch her below, or the undertow will drag her under the falling water, and she sinks. Where we wish to run her out a little way from shore, through a channel between rocks, we first throw in little sticks of driftwood, and watch their course, to see where we must steer, so that she will pass the channel in safety. And so we hold, and let go, and pull, and lift, and ward, among rocks, around rocks, and over rocks.

And now we go on through this solemn, mysterious way. The river is very deep, the cañon very narrow, and still obstructed, so that there is no steady flow of the stream; but the waters wheel, and roll, and boil, and we are scarcely able to determine where we can go. Now, the boat is carried to the right, perhaps close to the wall; again, she is shot into the stream, and perhaps is dragged over to the other side, where, caught in a whirlpool, she spins about. We can neither land nor run as we please. The boats are entirely unmanageable; no order in their running can be preserved; now one, now another, is ahead, each crew laboring for its own preservation. In such a place we come to another rapid. Two of the boats run it perforce. One succeeds in landing, but there is no foothold by which to make a portage, and she is pushed out again into the stream. The next minute a great reflex wave fills the open compartment; she is waterlogged, and drifts unmanageable. Breaker after breaker rolls over her, and one capsizes her. The men are thrown out; but they cling to the boat, and she drifts down some distance, alongside of us, and we are able to catch her. She is soon bailed out, and the men are aboard once more; but the oars are lost, so a pair from the "Emma Dean" is spared. Then for two miles we find smooth water.

Clouds are playing in the cañon today. Sometimes they roll down in great masses, filling the gorge with gloom; sometimes they hang above, from wall to wall, and cover the cañon with a roof of impending storm; and we can peer long distances up and down this cañon corridor, with its cloud roof overhead, its walls of black granite, and its river bright with the sheen of broken waters. Then, a gust of wind sweeps down a side gulch, and, making a rift in the clouds, reveals the blue heavens, and a stream of sunlight pours in. Then, the clouds drift away into the distance, and hang around crags, and peaks, and pinnacles, and towers, and walls, and cover them with a mantle, that lifts from time to time, and sets them all in sharp relief. Then, baby clouds creep out of side cañons, glide around points, and creep back again, into more distant gorges. Then, clouds, set in strata, across the cañon, with intervening vista views, to cliffs and rocks beyond. The clouds are children of the heavens, and when they play among the rocks, they lift them to the region above.

It rains! Rapidly little rills are formed above, and these soon grow into brooks, and the brooks grow into creeks, and tumble over the walls in innumerable cascades, adding their wild music to the roar of the river. When the rain ceases, the rills, brooks, and creeks run dry. The waters that fall, during a rain, on these steep rocks, are gathered at once into the river; they could scarcely be poured in more suddenly, if some vast spout ran from the clouds to the stream itself. When a storm bursts over the cañon, a side gulch is dangerous, for a sudden flood may come, and the inpouring waters will raise the river, so as to hide the rocks before your eyes.

Early in the afternoon, we discover a stream, entering from the north, a clear, beautiful creek, coming down through a gorgeous red cañon. We land, and camp on a sand beach, above its mouth, under a great, overspreading tree, with willow-shaped leaves.

August 16.—We must dry our rations again today, and make oars.

The Colorado is never a clear stream, but for the past three or four days it has been raining much of the time, and the floods, which are poured over the walls, have brought down great quantities of mud, making it exceedingly turbid now. The little affluent, which we have discovered here, is a clear, beautiful creek, or river, as it would be termed in this western country, where streams are not abundant. We have named one stream, away above, in honor of the great chief of the "Bad Angels," and, as this is in beautiful contrast to that, we conclude to name it "Bright Angel."

Early in the morning, the whole party starts up to explore the Bright Angel River, with the special purpose of seeking timber, from which to make oars. A couple of miles above, we find a large pine log, which has been floated down from the plateau, probably from an altitude of more than six thousand feet, but not many miles back. On its way, it must have passed over many cataracts and falls, for it bears scars in evidence of the rough usage which it has received. The men roll it on skids, and the work of sawing oars is commenced.

This stream heads away back, under a line of abrupt cliffs, that terminates the plateau, and tumbles down more than four thousand feet in the first mile or two of its course; then runs through a deep, narrow cañon, until it reaches the river.

Late in the afternoon I return, and go up a little gulch, just above this creek, about two hundred yards from camp, and discover the ruins of two or three old houses, which were originally of stone, laid in mortar. Only the foundations are left, but irregular blocks, of which the houses were constructed, lie scattered about. In one room I find an old mealing stone, deeply worn, as if it had been much used. A great deal of pottery is strewn around, and old trails, which in some places are deeply worn into the rocks, are seen. . . .

August 17.—Our rations are still spoiling; the bacon is so badly injured that we are compelled to throw it away. By an accident, this morning, the saleratus is lost overboard. We have now only musty flour sufficient for ten days, a few dried apples, but plenty of coffee. We must make all haste possible. If we meet with difficulties, as we have done in the cañon above, we may be compelled to give up the expedition, and try to reach the Mormon settlements to the north. Our hopes are that the worst places are passed, but our barometers are all so much injured as to be useless, so we have lost our reckoning in altitude, and know not how much descent the river has yet to make.

The stream is still wild and rapid, and rolls through a narrow channel. We make but slow progress, often landing against a wall, and climbing around some point, where we can see the river below. Although very anxious to advance, we are determined to run with great caution, lest, by another accident, we lose all our supplies. How precious that little flour has become! We divide it among the boats, and carefully store it away, so that it can be lost only by the loss of the boat itself.

We make ten miles and a half, and camp among the rocks, on the right. We have had rain, from time to time, all day, and have been thoroughly drenched and chilled; but between showers the sun shines with great power, and the mercury in our thermometers stands at 115°, so that we have rapid changes from great extremes, which are very disagreeable. It is especially cold in the rain tonight. The little canvas we have is rotten and useless; the rubber ponchos, with which we started from Green River City, have all been lost; more than half the party is without hats, and not one of us has an entire suit of clothes, and we have not a blanket apiece. So we gather driftwood, and build a fire; but after supper the rain, coming down in torrents, extinguishes it, and we sit up all night, on the rocks, shivering, and are more exhausted by the night's discomfort than by the day's toil. . . .

August 25.—We make twelve miles this morning, when we come to monuments of lava, standing in the river; low rocks, mostly, but some of them shafts more than a hundred feet high. Going on down, three or four miles, we find them increasing in number. Great quantities of cooled lava and many cinder-cones are seen on either side; and then we come to an abrupt cataract. Just over the fall, on the right wall, a cinder-cone, or extinct volcano, with a well-defined crater, stands on the very brink of the cañon. This, doubtless, is the one we saw two or three days ago. From this volcano vast floods of lava have been poured down into the river, and a stream of the molten rock has run up the cañon, three or four miles, and down, we know not how far. Just where it poured over the cañon wall is the fall. The whole north side, as far as we can see, is lined with the black basalt, and high up on the opposite wall are patches of the same material, resting on the benches, and filling old alcoves and caves, giving to the wall a spotted appearance.

The rocks are broken in two, along a line which here crosses the river, and the beds, which we have seen coming down the cañon for the last thirty miles, have dropped 800 feet, on the lower side of the line, forming what geologists call a fault. The volcanic cone stands directly over the fissure thus formed. On the side of the river opposite, mammoth springs burst out of this crevice, one or two hundred feet above the river, pouring in a stream quite equal in volume to the Colorado Chiquito.

This stream seems to be loaded with carbonate of lime, and the water, evaporating, leaves an incrustation on the rocks; and this process has been continued for a long time, for extensive deposits are noticed, in which are basins, with bubbling springs. The water is salty.

We have to make a portage here, which is completed in about three hours, and on we go.

We have no difficulty as we float along, and I am able to observe the wonderful phenomena connected with this flood of lava. The cañon was doubtless filled to a height of twelve or fifteen hundred feet, perhaps by more than one flood. This would dam the water back; and in cutting through this great lava bed, a new channel has been formed, sometimes on one side, sometimes on the other. The cooled lava, being of firmer texture than the rocks of which the walls are composed, remains in some places; in others a narrow channel has been cut, leaving a line of basalt on either side. It is possible that the lava cooled faster on the sides against the walls, and that the center ran out; but of this we can only conjecture. There are other places, where almost the whole of the lava is gone, patches of it only being seen where it has caught on the walls. As we float down, we can see that it ran out into side cañons. In some places this basalt has a fine, columnar structure, often in concentric prisms, and masses of these concentric columns have coalesced. In some places, when the flow occurred, the cañon was probably at about the same depth as it is now, for we can see where the basalt has rolled out on the sands, and, what seems curious to me, the sands are not melted or metamorphosed to any appreciable extent. In places the bed of the river is of sandstone or limestone, in other places of lava, showing that it has all been cut out again where the sandstones and limestones appear; but there is a little yet left where the bed is of lava.

What a conflict of water and fire there must have been here! Just imagine a river of molten rock, running down into a river of melted snow. What a seething and boiling of the waters; what clouds of steam rolled into the heavens!

Thirty-five miles today. Hurrah!

August 26.—The cañon walls are steadily becoming higher as we advance. They are still bold, and nearly vertical up to the terrace. We still see evidence of the eruption discovered yesterday, but the thickness of the basalt is decreasing, as we go down stream; yet it has been reinforced at points by streams that have come down from volcanoes standing on the terrace above, but which we cannot see from the river below.

Since we left the Colorado Chiquito, we have seen no evidences that the tribe of Indians inhabiting the plateaus on either side ever come down to the river; but about eleven o'clock today we discover an Indian garden, at the foot of the wall on the right, just where a little stream, with a narrow flood-plain, comes down through a side cañon. Along the valley, the Indians have planted corn, using the water which burst out in springs at the foot of the cliff, for irrigation. The corn is looking quite well, but is not sufficiently advanced to give us roasting ears; but there are some nice, green squashes. We carry ten or a dozen of these on board our boats, and hurriedly leave, not willing to be caught in the robbery, yet excusing ourselves by pleading our great want. We run down a short distance, to where we feel certain no Indians can follow; and what a kettle of squash sauce we make! True, we have no salt with which to season it, but it makes a fine addition to our unleavened bread and coffee. Never was fruit so sweet as these stolen squashes.

After dinner we push on again, making fine time, finding many rapids, but none so bad that we cannot run them with safety, and when we stop, just at dusk, and foot up our reckoning, we find we have run thirty-five miles again.

What a supper we make; unleavened bread, green squash sauce, and strong coffee. We have been for a few days on half rations, but have no stint of roast squash.

A few days like this, and we are out of prison.

August 27.—This morning the river takes a more southerly direction. The dip of the rocks is to the north, and we are rapidly running into lower formations. Unless our course changes, we shall very soon run again into the granite. This gives us some anxiety. Now and then the river turns to the west, and excites hopes that are soon destroyed by another turn to the south. About nine o'clock we come to the dreaded rock. It is with no little misgiving that we see the river enter these black, hard walls. At its very entrance we have to make a portage; then we have to let down with lines past some ugly rocks. Then we run a mile or two farther, and then the rapids below can be seen.

About eleven o'clock we come to a place in the river where it seems much worse than any we have yet met in all its course. A little creek comes down from the left. We land first on the right, and clamber up over the granite pinnacles for a mile or two, but can see no way by which we can let down, and to run it would be sure destruction. After dinner we cross to examine it on the left. High above the river we can walk along on the top of the granite, which is broken off at the edge, and set with crags and pinnacles, so that it is very difficult to get a view of the river at all. In my eagerness to reach a point where I can see the roaring fall below, I go too far on the wall, and can neither advance nor retreat.

I stand with one foot on a little projecting rock, and cling with my hand fixed in a little crevice. Finding I am caught here, suspended 400 feet above the river, into which I should fall if my footing fails, I call for help. The men come, and pass me a line, but I cannot let go of the rock long enough to take hold of it. Then they bring two or three of the largest oars. All this takes time which seems very precious to me; but at last they arrive. The blade of one of the oars is pushed into a little crevice in the rock beyond me, in such a manner that they can hold me pressed against the wall. Then another is fixed in such a way that I can step on it, and thus I am extricated.

Still another hour is spent in examining the river from this side, but no good view of it is obtained, so now we return to the side that was first examined, and the afternoon is spent in clambering among the crags and pinnacles, and carefully scanning the river again. We find that the lateral streams have washed boulders into the river, so as to form a dam, over which the water makes a broken fall of eighteen or twenty feet; then there is a rapid, beset with rocks, for two or three hundred yards, while, on the other side, points of the wall project into the river. Then there is a second fall below; how great, we cannot tell. Then there is a rapid, filled with huge rocks, for one or two hundred yards. At the bottom of it, from the right wall, a great rock projects quite half-way across the river. It has a sloping surface extending up stream, and the water, coming down with all the momentum gained in the falls and rapids above, rolls up this inclined plane many feet, and tumbles over to the left. I decide that it is possible to let down over the first fall, then run near the right cliff to a point just above the second, where we can pull out into a little chute, and, having run over that in safety, we must pull with all our powers across the stream, to avoid the great rock below. On my return to the boat, I announce to the men that we are to run it in the morning. Then we cross the river, and go into camp for the night on some rocks, in the mouth of the little side cañon.

After supper Captain Howland asks to have a talk with me. We walk up the little creek a short distance, and I soon find that his object is to remonstrate against my determination to proceed. He thinks that we had better abandon the river here. Talking with him, I learn that his brother, William Dunn, and himself have determined to go no farther in the boats. So we return to camp. Nothing is said to the other men.

For the last two days, our course has not been plotted. I sit down and do this now, for the purpose of finding where we are by dead reckoning. It is a clear night, and I take out the sextant to make observations for latitude, and find that the astronomic determination agrees very nearly with that of the plot—quite as closely as might be expected, from a meridian observation on a planet. In a direct line, we must be about forty-five miles from the mouth of the Rio Virgen. If we can reach that point, we know that there are settlements up that river about twenty miles. This forty-five miles, in a direct line, will probably be eighty or ninety in the meandering line of the river. But then we know that there is comparatively open country for many miles above the mouth of the Virgen, which is our point of destination.

As soon as I determine all this, I spread my plot on the sand, and wake Howland, who is sleeping down by the river, and show him where I suppose we are, and where several Mormon settlements are situated.

We have another short talk about the morrow, and he lies down again; but for me there is no sleep. All night long, I pace up and down a little path, on a few yards of sand beach, along by the river. Is it wise to go on? I go to the boats again, to look at our rations. I feel satisfied that we can get over the danger immediately before us; what there may be below I know not. From our outlook yesterday, on the cliffs, the cañon seemed to make another great bend to the south, and this, from our experience heretofore, means more and higher granite walls. I am not sure that we can climb out of the cañon here, and, when at the top of the wall, I know enough of the country to be certain that it is a desert of rock and sand, between this and the nearest Mormon town, which, on the most direct line, must be seventy-five miles away. True, the late rains have been favorable to us, should we go out, for the probabilities are that we shall find water still standing in holes, and, at one time, I almost conclude to leave the river. But for years I have been contemplating this trip. To leave the exploration unfinished, to say that there is a part of the cañon which I cannot explore, having already almost accomplished it, is more than I am willing to acknowledge, and I determine to go on.

I wake my brother, and tell him of Howland's determination, and he promises to stay with me; then I call up Hawkins, the cook, and he makes a like promise; then Sumner, and Bradley, and Hall, and they all agree to go on.

August 28.—At last daylight comes, and we have breakfast, without a word being said about the future. The meal is as solemn as a funeral. After breakfast, I ask the three men if they still think it best to leave us. The elder Howland thinks it is, and Dunn agrees with him. The younger Howland tries to persuade them to go on with the party, failing in which, he decides to go with his brother.

Then we cross the river. The small boat is very much disabled, and unseaworthy. With the loss of hands, consequent on the departure of the three men, we shall not be able to run all of the boats, so I decide to leave my "Emma Dean."

Two rifles and a shot gun are given to the men who are going out. I ask them to help themselves to the rations, and to take what they think to be a fair share. This they refuse to do, saying they have no fear but that they can get something to eat; but Billy, the cook, has a pan of biscuits prepared for dinner, and these he leaves on a rock.

Before starting, we take our barometers, fossils, the minerals, and some ammunition from the boat, and leave them on the rocks. We are going over this place as light as possible. The three men help us lift our boats over a rock twenty-five or thirty feet high, and let them down again over the first fall, and now we are all ready to start. The last thing before leaving, I write a letter to my wife, and give it to Howland. Sumner gives him his watch, directing that it be sent to his sister, should he not be heard from again. The records of the expedition have been kept in duplicate. One set of these is given to Howland, and now we are ready. For the last time, they entreat us not to go on, and tell us that it is madness to set out in this place; that we can never get safely through it; and, further, that the river turns again to the south into the granite, and a few miles of such rapids and falls will exhaust our entire stock of rations, and then it will be too late to climb out. Some tears are shed; it is rather a solemn parting; each party thinks the other is taking the dangerous course.

My old boat left, I go on board of the "Maid of the Cañon." The three men climb a crag, that overhangs the river, to watch us off. The "Maid of the Cañon" pushes out. We glide rapidly along the foot of the wall, just grazing one great rock, then pull out a little into the chute of the second fall, and plunge over it. The open compartment is filled when we strike the first wave below, but we cut through it, and then the men pull with all their power toward the left wall, and swing clear of the dangerous rock below all right. We are scarcely a minute in running it, and find that, although it looked bad from above, we have passed many places that were worse.

The other boat follows without more difficulty. We land at the first practicable point below and fire our guns, as a signal to the men above that we have come over in safety. Here we remain a couple of hours, hoping that they will take the smaller boat and follow us. We are behind a curve in the cañon, and cannot see up to where we left them, and so we wait until their coming seems hopeless, and push on.

And now we have a succession of rapids and falls until noon, all of which we run in safety. Just after dinner we come to another bad place. A little stream comes in from the left, and below there is a fall, and still below another fall. Above, the river tumbles down, over and among the rocks, in whirlpools and great waves, and the waters are lashed into mad, white foam. We run along the left, above this, and soon see that we cannot let down on this side, but it seems possible to let down on the other. We pull up stream again, for two or three hundred yards, and cross. Now there is a bed of basalt on this northern side of the cañon, with a bold escarpment, that seems to be a hundred feet high. We can climb it, and walk along its summit to a point where we are just at the head of the fall. Here the basalt is broken down again, so it seems to us, and I direct the men to take a line to the top of the cliff, and let the boats down along the wall. One man remains in the boat, to keep her clear of the rocks, and prevent her line from being caught on the projecting angles. I climb the cliff, and pass along to a point just over the fall, and descend by broken rocks, and find that the break of the fall is above the break of the wall, so that we cannot land; and that still below the river is very bad, and that there is no possibility of a portage. Without waiting further to examine and determine what shall be done, I hasten back to the top of the cliff, to stop the boats from coming down. When I arrive, I find the men have let one of them down to the head of the fall. She is in swift water, and they are not able to pull her back; nor are they able to go on with the line, as it is not long enough to reach the higher part of the cliff, which is just before them; so they take a bight around a crag. I send two men back for the other line. The boat is in very swift water, and Bradley is standing in the open compartment, holding out his oar to prevent her from striking against the foot of the cliff. Now she shoots out into the stream, and up as far as the line will permit, and then, wheeling, drives headlong against the rock, then out and back again, now straining on the line, now striking against the rock. As soon as the second line is brought, we pass it down to him; but his attention is all taken up with his own situation, and he does not see that we are passing the line to him. I stand on a projecting rock, waving my hat to gain his attention, for my voice is drowned by the roaring of the falls. Just at this moment, I see him take his knife from its sheath, and step forward to cut the line. He has evidently decided that it is better to go over with the boat as it is, than to wait for her to be broken to pieces. As he leans over, the boat sheers again into the stream, the stem post breaks away, and she is loose. With perfect composure Bradley seizes the great scull oar, places it in the stern rowlock, and pulls with all his power (and he is an athlete) to turn the bow of the boat down stream, for he wishes to go bow down, rather than to drift broadside on. One, two strokes he makes, and a third just as she goes over, and the boat is fairly turned, and she goes down almost beyond our sight, though we are more than a hundred feet above the river. Then she comes up again, on a great wave, and down and up, then around behind some great rocks, and is lost in the mad, white foam below. We stand frozen with fear, for we see no boat. Bradley is gone, so it seems. But now, away below, we see something coming out of the waves. It is evidently a boat. A moment more, and we see Bradley standing on deck, swinging his hat to show that he is all right. But he is in a whirlpool. We have the stem post of his boat attached to the line. How badly she may be disabled we know not. I direct Sumner and Powell to pass along the cliff, and see if they can reach him from below. Rhodes, Hall, and myself run to the other boat, jump aboard, push out, and away we go over the falls. A wave rolls over us, and our boat is unmanageable. Another great wave strikes us, the boat rolls over, and tumbles and tosses, I know not how. All I know is that Bradley is picking us up. We soon have all right again, and row to the cliff, and wait until Sumner and Powell can come. After a difficult climb they reach us. We run two or three miles farther, and turn again to the northwest, continuing until night, when we have run out of the granite once more.

August 29.—We start very early this morning. The river still continues swift, but we have no serious difficulty, and at twelve o'clock emerge from the Grand Cañon of the Colorado.

We are in a valley now, and low mountains are seen in the distance, coming to the river below. We recognize this as the Grand Wash.

A few years ago, a party of Mormons set out from St. George, Utah, taking with them a boat, and came down to the mouth of the Grand Wash, where they divided, a portion of the party crossing the river to explore the San Francisco Mountains. Three men—Hamblin, Miller, and Crosby—taking the boat, went on down the river to Callville, landing a few miles below the mouth of the Rio Virgen. We have their manuscript journal with us, and so the stream is comparatively well known.

Tonight we camp on the left bank, in a *mesquite* thicket.

The relief from danger, and the joy of success, are great. When he who has been chained by wounds to a hospital cot, until his canvas tent seems like a dungeon cell, until the groans of those who lie about, tortured with probe and knife, are piled up, a weight of horror on his ears that he cannot throw off, cannot forget, and until the stench of festering wounds and anæsthetic drugs has filled the air with its loathsome burthen, at last goes out into the open field, what a world he sees! How beautiful the sky; how bright the sunshine; what "floods of delirious music" pour from the throats of birds; how sweet the fragrance of earth, and tree, and blossom! The first hour of convalescent freedom seem rich recompense for all—pain, gloom, terror.

Something like this are the feelings we experience tonight. Ever before us has been an unknown danger, heavier than immediate peril. Every waking hour passed in the Grand Cañon has been one of toil. We have watched with deep solicitude the steady disappearance of our scant supply of rations, and from time to time have seen the river snatch a portion of the little left, while we were ahungered. And danger and toil were endured in those gloomy depths, where ofttimes the clouds hid the sky by day, and but a narrow zone of stars could be seen at night. Only during the few hours of deep sleep, consequent on hard labor, has the roar of the waters been hushed. Now the danger is over; now the toil has ceased; now the gloom has disappeared; now the firmament is bounded only by the horizon; and what a vast expanse of constellations can be seen!

The river rolls by us in silent majesty; the quiet of the camp is sweet; our joy is almost ecstasy. We sit till long after midnight, talking of the Grand Cañon, talking of home, but chiefly talking of the three men who left us. Are they wandering in those depths, unable to find a way out? are they searching over the desert lands above for water? or are they nearing the settlements?

CHAPTER
FOUR

Through the Grand Cañon
of the Colorado

FROM THE MOUNTAIN PEAKS above, many have looked down into the almost unknown depths of the Grand Cañon of the Colorado River of the West, and while wrapt in admiration and amazement at the picture spread out before them, have longed for a nearer view of the foaming waters and roaring cataracts of what appeared to them as but a silver thread winding its silent way among the caverns, so many thousands of feet below.

It has, however, been the good fortune of but few to be able to journey at the bottom of these cañons, along the only path that is yet open to man—the raging waters of the river itself—and to look up at the beauties and wonders that nature has formed, piled one upon the other, seemingly to the blue of the sky above; or to live among the stupendous gorges and caverns that have been cut out of the very bowels of the earth, as this mightiest of rivers has carved for itself a pathway from the Rocky Mountains to the sea.

When, in the spring of 1889, I took charge of the survey for a railway line along this river, from Grand Junction, Col., to the Gulf of California, I considered myself favored. Previous to this time no party had traversed these cañons, except that of Major J. W. Powell, in 1869, and no one had ever made a continuous trip along the waters of this river from its head to its mouth.

With a naturally sanguine disposition, I had no conception of the dangers and hardships to be encountered in a journey by boat down a river that has a descent of over four thousand two hundred feet, and in a distance of

"Through the Grand Cañon of the Colorado," by Robert Brewster Stanton. *Scribner's Magazine,* 1890.

less than five hundred miles contains five hundred and twenty rapids, falls, and cataracts. . . .

Our first expedition was organized by, and under the immediate charge of, Mr. Frank M. Brown, the President of the Railroad Company. When I took charge of the engineering work, the preparations were all complete, the boats bought and shipped to the river. We started from Green River Station, Utah, May 25th, with a party of sixteen men and six boats. The story of our journey as far as Lee's Ferry has been told, and I shall not repeat it.

Cataract Cañon, in its 41 miles, has 75 rapids and cataracts, and 57 of these are crowded into 19 miles, with falls in places of 16 to 20 feet. Being thrown into the water bodily almost every day, and working in water almost up to one's armpits for weeks at a time, guiding the boats through whirlpools and eddies, and when not thus engaged, carrying sacks of flour and greasy bacon on one's back over bowlders half as high as a house, is not the most pleasant class of engineering work to contemplate—except as a "backsight."

We had lost much of our store of provisions by the upsetting of our boats while running the rapids, boats that were too light and too frail to stand the rough usage of such waters. It was necessary to go upon short rations. With a party of five I was ahead, pushing on the survey, while the rest of the men brought on the boats and supplies. On the evening of June 15th, we reached a portion of the river where it was impossible for us to run our line without the assistance of the boats, and we turned back to meet them. That very afternoon another accident had sunk to the bottom of the river all our provisions, except a sack and a half of flour, a little coffee, sugar, and condensed milk.

The flour was immediately baked into bread, without either salt or yeast of any kind, and the whole of the food divided equally among the men. Arrangements were made for one boat's crew to go with President Brown down to the placer mines at Dandy Crossing, some thirty-five miles, for supplies.

The scarcity of food, and the separating of the party, alarmed the men, and nearly all of them wished to abandon the work at once. Knowing that if we abandoned the survey then, we could not return to it, and feeling sure that we could carry on the work to Dandy Crossing with what we had, I determined not to leave without an effort to complete the survey, if enough men would remain to assist me. My first assistant engineer, John Hislop, and C. W. Potter, together with our colored cook, G. W. Gibson, and colored steward, H. C. Richards, volunteered to remain.

The next morning eleven of the party started down river, leaving five of us and one boat. For six days we toiled on, continuing the survey at the rate of four miles per day, with one small piece of bread, a little coffee and milk for our morning and evening meal, and three lumps of sugar and as much river water as we wished at noon. Under such circumstances the true nobleness of men's characters comes out. The men worked on without a murmur, carrying the survey over the rocks and cliffs, on the side of the cañon, and handling the boat through the rapids of the river. At night, when they laid down on the sand to sleep, after a meal that was nine-tenths water and hope, and one-tenth bread and coffee, it was without a complaint. Those who could stand the privations best divided their scanty store with those who suffered most. At the end of the sixth day we were met by a boat, towed up the river, with provisions. Our suffering was over, except from the effects of eating too much at the first meal.

We soon reached Dandy Crossing, and with new provisions pushed on to Lee's Ferry, a party under Mr. W. H. Bush being left to bring on the survey. We reached Lee's Ferry, 150 miles below Dandy Crossing, July 2d. The next day President Brown started on horseback for Kanab, Utah, for supplies to take us through the remainder of the trip; for it was decided that Mr. Brown and myself, together with six others, Hislop, McDonald, Hansbrough, Richards, Gibson, and Photographer Nims, should go on and make an examination of the lower cañons, take notes and photographs, but without an instrumental survey.

On the morning of July 9th, Mr. Brown and the supplies having arrived, we started into the unknown depths of Marble Cañon, with three boats and our little party of eight.

The first day's run of ten miles was made without danger, making two heavy portages around the rapids at Badger and Soap Creeks. That night we camped at the lower end of the Soap Creek rapid. President Brown seemed lonely and troubled, and asked me to sit by his bed and talk. We sat there late, smoking and talking of our homes and our journey on the morrow. When I awoke in the morning Mr. Brown was up, and as soon as he saw me said, "Stanton, I dreamed of the rapids last night, the first time since we started." After breakfast we were again on the river in very swift water. Mr. Brown's boat, with himself and McDonald, was ahead, my boat, getting out from shore with some difficulty, was a little distance behind. In two minutes we were at the next rapid. Just as we dashed into the head of it, I saw McDonald running up the bank waving both arms. We had, for a few moments, all we could do to manage our own boat. It was but a moment. We were through the rapid, and turning out into the eddy. I heard McDonald shout, "Mr. Brown is in there." I looked to the right, but saw nothing. As our boat turned around the whirlpool on the left, the note-book which Mr. Brown always carried shot up on top of the water, and we picked it up as we passed.

Mr. Brown's boat was about one-half minute ahead of mine. His boat went safely through the worst part of the rapid, but in turning out into the eddy an upshooting wave, so common in that river between the current and the whirl-pools and eddies on the side, upset it without a moment's warning. Brown was thrown into the whirlpool, while McDonald was thrown into the current. Mc-Donald as he came up saw Brown on the side of the current, and shouted to him, "Come on." He answered with a cheerful "All right." McDonald, carried down by the stream, "was three times thrown under by the terrific tossings of the mad waters," and with great effort reached the left bank, where the current rushed upon the shore at a sudden turn to the right. As soon as he recovered himself he saw Brown still in the whirlpool, swimming round and round. Rushing up the bank he shouted to us for help. In that whirlpool poor Brown battled for his life, till exhausted in the fight he sank, a hero and a martyr to what some day will be a successful cause.

A noble man, and a true friend, he had won the love of everyone associated with him. We sat that whole day watching the ever-changing waters of that rapid—its whirlpools and eddies; but we did not realize, till the darkness gathered around us and we turned away to go to our camp, that we should never again see the face of our noble-hearted leader.

In this world we are left but little time to mourn. We had work to do, and I determined if possible to complete the whole of that work. With this intention we started out next morning. Thursday, Friday, and Saturday we pushed on with our usual work, shooting through or portaging round twenty-four bad rapids, getting deeper and deeper between the marble walls. After a quiet rest on Sunday, Monday morning found us at the head of two very rough and rocky rapids. We portaged both of them. While the photographer and myself took our notes and pictures, the boats were to go on through the lower end of the second rapid to a sand-bar, a half-mile below. It was easy walking for us along the bank. The first boat got down with difficulty, as the current beat hard against the left cliff. My boat was the next to start. I pushed it out from shore myself with a cheerful word to the men, Hansbrough and Richards. It was the last they ever heard. The current drove them against the cliff, under an overhanging shelf. In trying to push away from the cliff the boat was upset. Hansbrough was never seen to rise. Richards, a powerful man, swam some distance down stream. The first boat started out to the rescue, but he sank before it reached him.

Two more faithful and good men gone! Astonished and crushed by their loss, our force too small to portage our boats, and our boats entirely unfit for such work, I decided to abandon the trip, with then and there a determination, as soon as a new outfit could be secured, to return and complete our journey to the Gulf.

From then our only object was to reach a side cañon leading to the north, through which to make our retreat.

Just above Vasey's Paradise, in the deepest part we had seen, we camped for our last night in the cañon. The sad thoughts of the past few days crowded in upon us. A great storm was gathering over our heads. The rain was falling in a steady shower. No shelter below; not a dry blanket or a coat. About forty feet up on the side of the marble cliff I saw a small cave, with a marble shelf projecting over it. With some difficulty I climbed up to it. It was hardly large enough for my body, and not long enough for me to stretch fully out; but I crawled in, and, worn out by the work and excitement of the day, soon fell asleep.

About midnight I was awakened by a terrific peal of thunder, and around me and over me raged one of the most awful storms it has been my fate to witness. I have seen the lightning play and heard the thunder roll among the summit peaks of the Rocky Mountains, as I have stood on some rocky point far above the clouds, but nowhere has the awful grandeur equalled that night in the lonesome depths of what was to us death's cañon.

The lightning's flash lit up the dark recesses of the gorge, and cast ghastly shadows upon cliffs and sloping hillsides; and again all was shut in by darkness thicker than that of Egypt. The stillness was only broken by the roar of the river as it rushed along beneath me. Suddenly, as if the mighty cliffs above were rolling down against each other, there was peal after peal of thunder striking against the marble cliffs below, and, mingling with their echoes, bounding from cliff to cliff. Thunder with echo, echo with thunder, crossed and recrossed from wall to wall of the cañon, and rising higher and higher, died away among the side gorges and caverns thousands of feet above my head. For hours the tempest raged. Tucked away as a little worm in a cleft in the rock, the grandeur of the storm spoke as to the Psalmist of old; and out of the stillness came a voice mightier than the tempest, and said, "Be still and know that I am God."

On the 18th of July we took up our retreat. Preparing even then for our return, we cached our large stock of provisions and supplies in a marble cave. By

2 P.M. we were out of the cañon, and on the plateau 2,500 feet above. That night, favored by the rains of the past few days, we camped by a pool of water on what is usually a dry waste. Next day we came to a cattle ranch. With a team from there, and the kindness of the Mormon settlers, we soon reached Kanab. Through the extreme courtesy of Bishop Mariger, of Kanab, we were enabled in a few days to be once more at our homes.

On reaching Denver I immediately set about preparing for a new expedition to complete our survey to the Gulf. But it was not till November 25th that we again started for the river. I had learned a lesson during the summer. Our second outfit was vastly different from the first. It consisted of three boats twenty-two feet long, four and one-half feet beam, and twenty-two inches deep. These were built of oak, from plans of my own, with ribs one and one-half by three-quarters of an inch, placed four inches apart, and planked with one-half inch oak, all riveted together with copper rivets. Each boat had ten separate air-tight compartments running all round the sides. The best cork life-preservers were provided for all the men, and they were required to wear them whenever they were upon the water. All stores and provisions were packed in water-tight rubber bags made expressly for the purpose.

We started from the mouth of Crescent Creek, just above Dandy Crossing, December 10th, having hauled the boats and supplies by wagon one hundred and twenty miles from the railroad. From there we had two hundred miles of the old journey to go over again. That through Glen Cañon was the easiest of the river, and was good training for the new men. The party consisted of twelve men, four of whom had been on the first expedition. My boat, No. 1, the Bonnie Jean, had for crew Harry McDonald. Langdon Gibson, and Elmer Kane; No. 2, the Lillie, Assistant Engineer John Hislop, Photographer Nims, Reginald Travers, and W. H. Edwards; No. 3, the Marie, A. B. Twining, H. G. Ballard, L. G. Brown, and James Hogue, the cook.

Our trip through Glen Cañon was like a pleasure trip on a smooth river in autumn, with beautiful wild flowers and ferns at every camp. At Lee's Ferry we ate our Christmas dinner, with the table decorated with wild flowers picked that day.

On December 28th we started to traverse once more that portion of Marble Cañon made tragic by the death of three of our companions the summer before. On the next Tuesday we reached the spot where President Brown lost his life. What a change in the waters! What was then a roaring torrent, now, with the water some nine feet lower, seemed from the shore like the gentle ripple upon a quiet lake. We found, however, in going through it with our boats, there was the same swift current, the same huge eddy, and between them the same whirl-pool, with its ever-changing circles.

Marble Cañon seemed destined to give us trouble. On January 1st our photographer, Mr. Nims, fell from a bench of the cliff, some twenty-two feet, on to the sand beach below, receiving a severe jar, and breaking one of his legs just above the ankle. Having plenty of bandages and medicine, we made Nims as comfortable as possible till the next day, when we loaded one of the boats to make him a level bed, and constructing a stretcher of two oars and a piece of canvas, put him on board and floated down river a couple of miles—running two small rapids—to a side cañon which led out to the Lee's Ferry road.

The next day, after finding a way out on top, I walked thirty-five miles back to Lee's Ferry for a wagon to take Nims where he could be cared for. But then came the tug of war—the getting of Nims up from the river, one thousand seven hundred feet to the mesa above. Eight of the strongest men of the party started with him early Saturday morning, and reached the top at 3:30 P.M., having carried him four miles in distance and one thousand seven hundred feet up hill, the last half-mile being at an angle of forty-five degrees up a loose rock slide.

In two places the stretcher had to be hung by ropes from above, while the men slid it along a sloping cliff too steep to stand upon, and in two places it was lifted up with ropes over perpendicular cliffs ten and fifteen feet high. The party reached the top, however, without the least injury to themselves or the sick man.

Late on Sunday we bade Nims goodby, leaving him in charge of Mr. W. M. Johnson, of Lee's Ferry, and we returned to our camp in the cañon below. Nims's departure was a great loss to the expedition. His work fell to me, and the remainder of the photographic work (some seven hundred and fifty views) was done without preparation or previous experience.

We continued our journey over the same part of the river that we had travelled last summer, till January 13th, when we reached Point Retreat, where we left the cañon on our homeward march just six months before. We found our supplies, blankets, flour, sugar, coffee, etc., which we had cached in the marble cave, all in good condition. From the head of the Colorado to Point Retreat we had encountered one hundred and forty-four rapids, not counting small draws, in a distance of two hundred and forty miles. From Lee's Ferry to Point Retreat there are forty-four rapids, in a distance of thirty miles. With our new boats we ran nearly all of these, and portaged but few; over many of them our boats had danced and jumped at the rate of fifteen miles an hour and over some, by actual measurement, at the rate of twenty miles per hour. To stand in the bow of one of these boats as she dashes through a great rapid, with first the bow and then the stern jumping into the air, and the spray of the breakers splashing over one's head, is an excitement the fascination of which can only be understood through experience.

We stopped two days to complete our railway survey around a very difficult point, and on January 15th our boats were repacked, and we were ready to start down into the "Great Unknown."

This part of Marble Cañon, from Point Retreat for thirty-five miles down to the Little Colorado, is by far the most beautiful and interesting cañon we have yet passed through. At Point Retreat the marble walls stand perpendicularly 300 feet from the water's edge, while the sandstone above benches back in slopes and cliffs to 2,500 feet high. Just below this the cañon is narrowest, being but a little over 300 feet from wall to wall. As we go on, the marble rapidly rises till it stands in perpendicular cliffs 700 to 800 feet high, colored with all the tints of the rainbow, but mostly red. In many places toward the top it is honeycombed with caves, arches, and grottoes, with here and there a natural bridge left from one crag to another over some sidewash, making a grotesque and wonderful picture as our little boats glide along this quiet portion of the river, so many hundred feet below.

At the foot of these cliffs, in many places, are fountains of pure sparkling water gushing from the rock—in one place, Vasey's Paradise, several hundred feet up the wall—and dropping among shrubbery, ferns, and flowers, some of which even at this time of year are found in bloom.

Ten miles below Point Retreat, as we went into camp one evening, we discovered the body of Peter M. Hansbrough, one of the boatmen drowned on our trip last summer. His remains were easily recognized from the clothing that was still on them. The next morning we buried them under an overhanging cliff. The burial service was brief and simple. We stood around the grave while one short prayer was offered, and we left him with a shaft of pure marble for his headstone, seven hundred feet high, with his name cut upon the base; and in honor of his memory we named a magnificent point opposite—Point Hansbrough.

From Point Hansbrough to the Little Colorado the cañon widens, the marble benches retreat, new strata of limestone, quartzite, and sandstone come up from the river, and the débris forms a talus equal to a mountain slope. Here the bottoms widen into little farms covered with green grass and groves of mesquite, making a most charming summer picture, in strong contrast with the dismal narrow cañons above. And as we pass the valleys of the Nan-co-weap and the Kwagunt the contrast is more strongly brought out. Here, among green grass and summer flowers, yonder, far up the valley on the lofty mountains covered with their winter mantle of pure white snow for a background, stand out sharp points of scarlet sandstone, and the darker green of the cedar and pine is heightened in color by the rose-tinted light which the morning sun flashes over the eastern walls of the cañon.

We reached the end of Marble Cañon, at the mouth of the Little Colorado, January 20th, and slept that night in the Grand Cañon.

Copper miners at Peter Berry's "Last Chance" mine. The photograph was probably taken in the early 1900s after Berry had sold out to the Grand Canyon Copper Company.

And Those Who Came Later

BY "MONEYMAKERS" the Hopis mean, of course, the wealthy tourists. Actually they are the money *spenders* who make the rim resorts possible and support the Hopi and Navajo Indian crafts by their purchases at Hopi House on the South Rim.

Those who really wanted to become the moneymakers at the Grand Canyon came before the tourists, and some of these have stayed on. After the aborigines came the soldier, the priest, and the scientist; but between this latter group and the contemporary tourist there was another group which did not fit into any of the above categories. They were all manner of men and might be called the Utilitarians or the Pragmatists since they came to make a practical thing of the canyon: miners, ranchers, hermits, free-lance explorers, nature-lovers, professional liars, and William Randolph Hearst.

One of the first of these to arrive was John Hance, sometimes known as Captain John Hance, but he was captain not of a company or a ship; he was instead a captain of mendacity. Hance is supposed to have arrived at the South Rim about 1881. Nobody could say where he came from or just what his previous profession had been. In those days of the West, it was not good taste to inquire too specifically into a man's past. It was a vital country; only the present mattered. If questioned, Hance replied, "I do not like ancient history." But he said it with a smile and he was a warm outgoing man and apparently everyone who knew him liked him.

From *Listen, Bright Angel,* by Edwin Corle. Duell, Sloan & Pearce, 1946. Copyright 1946 by Edwin Corle. Reprinted by permission of Hawthorn Books, Inc.

John Hance loved the Grand Canyon. Its mysticism touched him and once that happened he was destined to live on the rim and in the bottom for the remainder of his life. It was a shrine and he had come to it; it was a sanctuary and he devoted himself to it; it was his pet and he liked to have it perform for strangers while he told tall tales about it. Hance was not a religious man. One of his friends once said, "Oh, he believed in God—I guess. But he believed mostly in the canyon and John Hance." If he had been told that the canyon had appealed to his latent sense of teleological inquiry he would have been nonplused and would have countered with some remark intended to astound his visitor and put him on the defensive.

His excuse for living on the South Rim was a mine. It was an asbestos mine deep down in the bottom where the second geological era had fused and pressed its elementary constitutents some billion years ago until it had created this heat-resistant mineral. Asbestos mines are not common. Hance thought that he had a good thing, and he had. But like most other mineralogical efforts to make the Grand Canyon pay dividends, it failed because the cost of getting the product out of the canyon was prohibitive. Hance came, in time, to understand that his mine was impractical. But he never quite gave it up. It remained his excuse for living at the South Rim, although the real reason was his love for the canyon itself.

The first few tourists began to arrive in the late eighteen eighties. They came by stagecoach from Flagstaff over rough roads and there were no accommodations at the South Rim once they arrived. Naturally, they met Hance as his camp offered the only place to spend the night. Some of the more intrepid tourists wanted to go down into the canyon, and the only way to do that was to be guided by John Hance who had built a trail down to his asbestos mine. So, inadvertently and accidentally, John Hance found himself forced into the tourist business.

It was a happy incident.

It was worth more to him than his mine. He became the unofficial receptionist, guide, host, and storyteller to his unexpected visitors. And for these offices he was well qualified.

The Hance cabin was just east of Grand View Point, or about eighteen miles east of the present Grand Canyon village. Hance lived on the rim in the summer, and when winter snows made survival too hazardous, he descended his trail and lived below for months in the warmer Lower-Sonoran life zone of the canyon's depths. Thus by going up and down his trail he could select his climate at will. Hance never had any great amount of money (except for one windfall of ten thousand dollars for a mining claim—and with this he went to San Francisco where he spent the money in ten days) and there were times when the food problem was difficult. All supplies had to come from Flagstaff and in the eighteen eighties that was two days away. So, while life was glorious, life was not easy, and there were times when Hance literally did not have enough to eat. The tourist business corrected that condition, and by 1892 other men, ostensibly miners but destined to be drawn into the tourist trade as was Hance, had settled along the South Rim.

One of these was Pete Berry and he built the first hotel at Grand View Point in 1892. It was made of native logs and was supplemented by tents and the little settlement was at the head of what Berry called the Grand View Trail. Berry's Trail, like Hance's was built by himself and led down to some mines. Hance had asbestos, Berry had copper, but the Grand Canyon had them both.

Like Hance, Berry became a "dude wrangler" and three years later the Grand Canyon Copper Company, which was made up of Pete Berry and Ralph and Miles Cameron, constructed a three-story building at Grand View Point and went in for the tourist business, as well as copper mining.

The history of the Grand Canyon Copper Company is worth a brief examination. Although it never became a great corporation, its life was an index to American business organization and the eventual concentrating of control in the hands of one tycoon. Pete Berry found copper. Then a group of Arizona men formed a company. The company functioned but needed more capital to develop the natural resources. The original Arizona organizers sold control of the company to a group of Eastern men. The Grand Canyon Copper Company was reincorporated in New England. The president became John H. Page and the general manager was Harold Smith, neither of whom had anything to do with the immediate scene at the South Rim or the mines in the bottom, and the Grand Canyon Copper Company found itself a Vermont corporation with all records in Montpelier, Vermont. When the company failed to operate at a profit the men in control were no longer interested in keeping it a going concern. It cost twelve thousand dollars a year to keep the Grand View Trail open so that ten mules a day could each carry two hundred pounds of ore from the mines to the rim. The price of copper collapsed in 1907, and it was not worth the expense of getting the ore out of the mines. The company had other assets, notably the Grand View Hotel, but the Eastern promoters were interested in mining and not tourists. Just when the corporate superstructure began to topple over on the little fellows underneath, notably Pete Berry who now worked for the company that his strike had brought into being, William Randolph Hearst appeared on the scene and bought the entire property—mines, trail, mules, hotel, equipment, fixtures, and whatever future prospects there might be. Hearst was now the Grand Canyon Copper Company personified in one individual. He had no intention of operating the mines; he saw the rich tourist trade that was bound to come to the South Rim. He was going to exploit the Grand Canyon. The pattern might have run on along this line until it became Grand Hearst Canyon, but fortunately Washington stepped in and the area, after a long struggle, was made a National Park.

With all these elements seething about him, John Hance and his hit-or-miss tourist camp was left out in the cold. His gift was lying, not promotion. So following Ben Franklin's advice that if you can't defeat your rival you'd better join hands with him, John Hance became a fixture around the Grand View Hotel. For the next twenty-five years, he was a kind of privileged guest of the South Rim resorts. He had no official position but he was a "character" to the strangers and he entertained them with his adventures which he fabricated as he went along. He graduated to a kind of court fool or canyon clown, and in later years the Fred Harvey Company gave him room and board so that he would always be present to interest and astound their guests. And of this Hance never wearied. His method was to answer questions tirelessly and to begin a perfectly plausible story and let it drift into the impossible and fantastic while still holding the listeners' credulity. Then, when the tale had stretched far beyond reason, he would let it snap into absurdity and the tourists either loved it and enjoyed the joke, or pointed him out as a madman. At least they never forgot him.

Children loved John Hance, and to them he always explained how the canyon came into being. "I dug it," he would say simply. This story worked well for years until one little four-year-old girl asked seriously, "And where did you put the dirt?" Hance had no ready answer; he never used the story again. But it bothered him the rest of his life, and when he was dying he whispered to his waiting friends, "Where do you suppose I could have put that dirt?"

One of Hance's favorite stories was the fog yarn. At rare times the canyon will be filled with clouds. Both rims will be clear, but the depths will be concealed by a sea of fog temporarily locked within the walls. Hance would then bring out his snowshoes and causally approach whatever tourists might be at the rim.

"Well," he'd say to himself, "she's just about right to cross."

Inevitably somebody would ask him what he meant.

"Oh, don't you know? Strangers here, eh? Well, say, too bad I haven't got another pair of snowshoes or you could join me."

"What are you going to do?"

"Whenever she fogs up good and solid like this, I always put on my snowshoes and take a walk across to the North Rim."

The startled visitors looked aghast, but hesitated to call the bluff for Hance was busy strapping on his snowshoes. He'd test them gingerly and add, "Yep, just right," and before the bewildered audience he would walk to the rim, stick a foot into space, and say, "Ah, that's just fine!" Then he'd stroll along the rim and call back to his audience, "It's a lot shorter if I start from Yaki Point. You just keep watching and tonight when you see a fire over on the North Rim you'll know I made it." And off he would go, disappearing along the rim walk in the direction of Yaki Point.

The next day he would be "back."

"See my fire last night?" he'd ask.

Once in a while somebody would say yes, and Hance would merely nod matter-of-factly. But as the answer was usually in the negative, he would say, "Well, the danged fog rose and blotted it out for you. I couldn't see your lights over here either. You know that blasted fog pretty near fooled me? It was good and thick goin' over but when I come back it was so thin that I sagged with every step. Once I thought I was goin' to hit bottom. Just like walkin' on a featherbed only worse. Plumb wore myself out gettin' back. You want to try it some time. Stay around a while and I'll lend you my snowshoes next time she fogs good and solid."

Other men, more famous in Arizona history than John Hance, also belonged to this pre-tourist era. One was William Owen O'Neill, better known as Bucky O'Neill, who died with his boots on during the charge of Colonel Roosevelt's Rough Riders at San Juan Hill. O'Neill had a series of exciting adventures in Tombstone and Prescott during the formative period of the West and it was because of his efforts that the Grand Canyon was at last served by a railroad. To this day it remains the only National Park with that distinction.

O'Neill had copper interests on the Coconino Plateau near the South Rim. A railroad was built north from Williams to the Anita Mine. Later this road was taken over by the Santa Fe, regraded, and extended to the South Rim. No longer was the jolting stagecoach journey necessary, and visitors began to arrive in great numbers. The Fred Harvey Company, in conjunction with the Santa

Fe, built the popular El Tovar Hotel in 1904 and it became famous the world over for its unique location and its sumptuous (for 1904) accommodations. It is still functioning and while the years have somewhat dimmed its luster, it is not at all eclipsed by the more modern Bright Angel Lodge.

After 1904 the commercial aspect of the Grand Canyon was pretty much in the control of the Santa Fe and Fred Harvey. And as is customary in the tradition of both of these institutions, they did a fine job. The Park Service took over administrative reins in 1919 and the Grand Canyon is now under the supervision of the Department of the Interior.

People who resent the doctrine of socialism often overlook the fact that a form of socialism has worked in the guise of the Park Service for years. All National Parks are natural phenomena socialized for the use and benefit of everybody. The Grand Canyon is run by the government and this socialization has prevented its belonging to any individual from Vasquez de Coronado to William Randolph Hearst. It belongs to you.

Perhaps the last of the "practical" ventures at Grand Canyon, and one that is not without irony, occurred as late as 1937. It was not a moneymaking scheme. In fact, it was costly. But if those who backed it were able to declare their expenditures in their income tax as legitimate deductions in the interest of the advancement of science, they may have put their money to legitimate use after all.

From the South Rim at Grand Canyon village, looking off to the northwest, there is a large flat-topped formation known as Shiva Temple. Once it is identified for you it is unmistakable. Thousands of years of erosion have contrived to isolate a large section of what was once a part of the Kaibab Plateau of the North Rim. It is 7,650 feet above sea level, contains a forested area of six square miles, and up to 1937, it had never been explored because of its presumably unscalable walls. Here was an area that had been cut off from the rest of the plateau country for thousands of years, perhaps as many as fifty thousand. A scientific expedition led by Dr. Harold E. Anthony of the American Museum of Natural History, determined to scale Shiva and set foot on a part of the globe where no man, and certainly no white man, had ever set foot before. Because of its fifty thousand years of isolation it was expected that the flat top of Shiva Temple would yield specimens of plant and animal life of a forgotten world. If the animals that lived on this lone mesa had been cut off from their fellow creatures for all those centuries, they might conceivably be evolutionary freaks. Here was a section where time might have stood still, or even evolved in some unexpected manner. Anything could have happened on Shiva.

News of the expedition got abroad. Apparently the project was being very well done. Nothing was overlooked, and supplies which could not be transported up the sheer walls were to be dropped by parachute from an airplane. In September, 1937, the ascent began. It was extremely difficult and dangerous. And it was a thrill indeed to the members of the party who finally made the neck-breaking climb when they clambered over the rim and stood—the first human beings—on a part of the earth that had never been trod before, six square miles of virgin soil which no man had ever seen, six square miles that had been as remote through the centuries as if they had been six square miles on the moon or Mars.

And then things began to happen.

One of the party found a pair of deer horns. They all looked at each other blankly. Those deer horns were new. They had been dropped within the last year. How had the deer got up to this place? Nobody could say. Had they been here for fifty thousand years? Most unlikely.

They explored a little farther.

The next find was truly startling. It was a small yellow oblong box made of cardboard and printed on it in red letters were the words, "Eastman Kodak—panchromatic."

The jig was up. And while the daring explorers waited for their parachute-dropped supplies they almost hesitated to look farther. And finally, down from the skies, floated their sealed tins of water and food. It all became a bit ridiculous; and as one of the party declared, they would not have been surprised to find, in this place where man had never set foot, a movie company on location. The expedition had one satisfaction, however. They proved the practicality of being supplied in inaccessible places by air. A carton of eggs, among other things, came down by parachute and not an egg was broken.

But the expedition, no matter how bad the dent put in its prestige, did explore and record a section of the Grand Canyon terrain which had never been formally explored before. And as far as the fifty-thousand-year inaccessibility of Shiva was concerned, that myth was destroyed forever. Animals of all kinds seemed to have no trouble in making yearly ascents and descents. There was no difference whatever between the species on the isolated Shiva and those of the Kaibab Plateau. This was not the conclusion that the party had hoped to reach, but in the interests of science they could arrive at no other.

The pre-exploration publicity which had been serious and sober became somewhat derisive when the party returned. This was not entirely fair. The expedition had set forth in good faith. They had no way to foretell that the deer roamed Shiva at will. And as for the person who tossed away that empty box of film when he reloaded his camera—well, you couldn't kill him for that. But who in the name of Shiva was he?

His identity has never been firmly established, but those who know the Grand Canyon and its permanent residents smile knowingly. Whoever went up there was a photographer; he was not a stranger to the area; and he was adept at canyon-climbing. Does that fit anybody we know? We can put two and two together and get four or twenty-two depending upon how we put them together. Now the news had been bruited about that Shiva was to be scientifically scaled. Any explorations of that nature would have been bound to interest one or both of two brothers who were photographers and who were not strangers to the area and who were adept at canyon-climbing. No names or inscriptions were found by the scientific party on Shiva, but they might well have been, and if they had, there are only two names that would be logical. They are Ellsworth Kolb and Emery Kolb. If you are still in doubt, why not ask one of the brothers the next time you visit the South Rim?

THE
VISUAL
IMAGE

A winter view across the canyon from just below the Kolb Studio

MOST EVERY WRITER starts by declaring that Grand Canyon is beyond description. Irvin Cobb complained: "Nearly everybody, on taking a first look at the Grand Canyon, comes right out and admits its wonders are absolutely indescribable, and then proceeds to write anywhere from two thousand to fifty thousand words giving the full details."

One writer, Edwin Corle, resisted the impulse to paint any visual images at all. Corle wrote an entire book describing the men and events that made Grand Canyon without once turning an adjective to describe the visual landscape. Many consider that book one of the best ever written about the canyon.

But most writers—and their readers—demand description, however short it may fall of reality. The tradition of descriptive Grand Canyon literature was slow getting started. The early Spaniards made no serious attempts at description for at least two reasons: first, the canyon was to them a nuisance and barrier to travel and, second, the whole concept of landscape as something to be admired for its own sake did not even develop until the nineteenth century.

The American scientific explorers of the nineteenth century initiated the trend toward literary description. Educated in a tradition of romantic literature and Hudson River landscape painters, these explorers traveled with fresh insight and a ready imagination. Lieutenant Ives began the process, but another army engineer, Clarence Edward Dutton, brought it to a high point.

A graduate of West Point, Dutton was detailed to work as a topographical engineer with the Powell survey in 1880. Dutton's real interest was geomorphology, the study of land forms, and by 1882 he had prepared a landmark study entitled *Tertiary History of the Grand Cañon District.*

The *Tertiary History* is a Jeffersonian blend of literary effort and sound scientific observation. In the chapter reprinted here, Dutton describes the canyon from a promontory on the north rim which he considered to be the best of all rim views and which he named "Point Sublime."

Dutton approaches canyon description like an engineer drawing a map: first he lays out the scale, then he draws in the topography—buttes, promontories, embayments and tributary courses. Finally, he provides a verbal overlay of colors in a vivid, highly charged description of day's end and the setting sun at Point Sublime.

Dutton's descriptions are heavy with architectural simile; half the monuments of the ancient world are dredged up as points of comparison. Dutton also initiated the practice of naming the canyon's temples and buttes after Oriental deities. Today, thanks to Dutton's initiative, one looks out at Brahma Temple, Buddha Temple, Cheops Pyramid, Confucius Temple, Hindu Amphitheater, Isis Temple, Manu Temple, Shiva Temple, Vishnu Temple, Wotan's Throne and Zoroaster Temple. Another canyon writer, John C. Van Dyke, launched a spirited attack on Dutton's architectural similes and Oriental nomenclature:

> It seems that years ago, when this country was young and defenseless, some people more or less in authority broke in on the Canyon and exhausted the pantheon of gods in giving names to the buttes and promontories; and now everyone who talks or writes about the Canyon from necessity uses architectural terms and mythological names to point his meaning. The result is that these enormous Canyon forms are dwarfed to the building plan of a Buddhist temple and the great goddess Nature is put out of countenance by the blinking little divinities of India and Egypt.

The debate over Dutton's style started by Van Dyke continues to this day. Whatever the critics may conclude, the debate itself emphasizes Dutton's role as initiator of a whole tradition of canyon descriptive literature. The concluding paragraphs of the Point Sublime chapter are perhaps the most quoted scenic descriptions in canyon literature.

After Dutton, canyon description gave way to a legion of moralizing, sermonizing Victorian writers given to overblown imagery. One characterized the canyon as a victim of "fluvial rape"; another called it a "sabre thrust in the rich red bosom of Mother Earth"; yet another wrote of "Nature wounded unto death and lying stiff and ghostly, with a gash 200 miles in length and a mile in depth in her bared breast. . . ." The best writings of this Victorian school were collected and published in 1906 by the Santa Fe Railway in a booklet entitled *The Grand Canyon of Arizona.*

More than anyone, John C. Van Dyke was responsible for bringing canyon writing back to reality, to style and imagination built upon the bedrock of good observation and knowledge of real places and real rock formations. Van Dyke made his first career as professor of art history at Rutgers University. Driven to the Southwest in search of good health, Van Dyke was soon studying and writing about the Sonoran Desert as a real-life art form. His early works brought the Arizona desert to public attention much as John Muir awakened the nation to the California Sierra. Like Muir, Van Dyke headed out on solitary hikes through the back country for weeks and months at a time. Van Dyke once encountered Muir in California; he was dismayed to find that his fifty-pound pack made him a dude compared to Muir who slept without blankets and travelled with only tea and dried bread.

In 1919, Van Dyke spent two months at Grand Canyon researching and writing a book with the bland title, *The Grand Canyon of the Colorado* and a slightly more revealing subtitle, *Recurrent Studies in Impressions and Appearances.* Van Dyke's book is one of only two generalized and descriptive Grand Canyon books that were printed in the early twentieth century. The other, by George Wharton James, had the wider circulation, was more in the nature of a guidebook and is of less lasting interest to a general audience.

Van Dyke's book owes an obvious debt to the work of Clarence Dutton. Like Dutton, Van Dyke starts off with a measured, objective approach to the canyon, first describing the whole and then dissecting the components—canyon walls, buttes, rock formations and the river in separate chapters.

In the chapter reprinted here, Van Dyke stations himself at Desert View near where Coronado's party first saw the canyon and gives an intricate and detailed description of the canyon from sunrise to sunset. Van Dyke goes beyond Dutton in the emphasis he gives to the flowing impressionistic colors over clinical description of the forms. His words paint a changing kaleidoscope of hues, tones and atmospheric effects as the day progresses from dawn to nightfall.

Frank Waters saw the Grand Canyon the same way, writing of "Color so rich and rampant that it floods the whole chasm; so powerful that it dissolves like acid all the shapes within it."

Joaquin Miller, a nineteenth-century writer, was also overwhelmed by the colors, but he only saw red. "It is old, old, this Grand Canyon, and yet so new it seems almost to smell of paint—red paint, pink, scarlet . . . every shade and hue of red, as far as the eye can compass. It is a scene of death-like silence, a dead land of red, a burning world."

Van Dyke reminds us that the early riser will see color effects equal to the better-known sunsets. He advises that midday is a good time to do other things (except when storm clouds are gathering). Finally, he explains how he learned to get the most out of a canyon sunset by lying on a rock to view the scene sideways. Van Dyke was opinionated and forceful, and he makes good reading.

Mary Austin first achieved recognition as an interpreter of the California desert, especially with the widely admired *Land of Little Rain*. Tiring of California, she eventually moved to Santa Fe in search of fresh landscapes and inspiration. She lived in New Mexico the rest of her life, writing of the Southwest, befriending young writers, quarreling with her literary enemies, and dominating the cultural life of Santa Fe.

Her impressions of Grand Canyon were included in the 1924 book, *Land of Journey's Ending,* a natural history and cultural interpretation of Arizona and New Mexico. Preparing to write the book, she travelled extensively through Arizona and New Mexico in 1923, travels which included a stay at Grand Canyon. The selection printed here is excerpted from that book.

In sharp contrast to the objective precision of both Dutton and Van Dyke, Austin ruminates upon the landscape in a more speculative, subjective mode, frequently lapsing into mythical allusion. She compresses all the red sunsets and glowing buttes into one memorable phrase: "Cliffs burning red from within; the magical, shifting shadows, the vast downthrow of Kaibab, grape-colored, with a bloom on it of refracted light . . ." Standing on the rim at dawn, she sees more than just a parade of colors: "The dawn came up, as it does in Navajo country, a turquoise horse, neighing jealously." From there she proceeds to view the canyon in a broad mythical and geographic framework, finally looking upward to a cloud-charged sky as the radiant source of the canyon's mystery.

Mary Austin saw and described the same canyon that Thomas Moran loved to paint: a dynamic, stormy panorama charged by conflict between sun and shadow. Major Powell had observed the same interplay between earth and sky on August 15, 1869. He wrote: "The clouds are children of the heavens, and when they play among the rocks, they lift them to the region above."

CHAPTER
SIX

The Panorama
from Point Sublime

WHEREVER WE REACH the Grand Cañon in the Kaibab it bursts upon the vision in a moment. Seldom is any warning given that we are near the brink. At the Toroweap it is quite otherwise. There we are notified that we are near it a day before we reach it. As the final march to that portion of the chasm is made the scene gradually develops, growing by insensible degrees more grand until at last we stand upon the brink of the inner gorge, where all is before us. In the Kaibab the forest reaches to the sharp edge of the cliff and the pine trees shed their cones into the fathomless depths below.

If the approach is made at random, with no idea of reaching any particular point by a known route, the probabilities are that it is first seen from the rim of one of the vast amphitheaters which set back from the main chasm far into the mass of the plateau. It is such a point to which the reader has been brought in the preceding chapter. Of course there are degrees in the magnitude and power of the pictures presented, but the smallest and least powerful is tremendous and too great for comprehension. The scenery of the amphitheaters far surpasses in grandeur and nobility anything else of the kind in any other region, but it is mere by-play in comparison with the panorama displayed in the heart of the cañon. The supreme views are to be obtained at the extremities of the long promontories, which jut out between these recesses far into the gulf. Towards such a point we now direct our steps. The one we have chosen is on the whole the most commanding in the Kaibab front, though there are several others

From *A Tertiary History of the Grand Canyon District,* by Clarence Dutton, 1882. Reprinted by Peregrine Smith, 1977.

which might be regarded as very nearly equal to it, or as even more imposing in some respects. We named it *Point Sublime*.

The route is of the same character as that we have already traversed—open pine forest, with smooth and gently-rolling ground. The distance from the point where we first touched the rim of the amphitheater is about 5 miles. Nothing is seen of the chasm until about a mile from the end we come once more upon the brink. Reaching the extreme verge the packs are cast off, and sitting upon the edge we contemplate the most sublime and awe-inspiring spectacle in the world.

The Grand Cañon of the Colorado is a great innovation in modern ideas of scenery, and in our conceptions of the grandeur, beauty, and power of nature. As with all great innovations it is not to be comprehended in a day or a week, nor even in a month. It must be dwelt upon and studied, and the study must comprise the slow acquisition of the meaning and spirit of that marvelous scenery which characterizes the Plateau Country, and of which the great chasm is the superlative manifestation. The study and slow mastery of the influences of that class of scenery and its full appreciation is a special culture, requiring time, patience, and long familiarity for its consummation. The lover of nature, whose perceptions have been trained in the Alps, in Italy, Germany, or New England, in the Appalachians or Cordilleras, in Scotland or Colorado, would enter this strange region with a shock, and dwell there for a time with a sense of oppression, and perhaps with horror. Whatsoever things he had learned to regard as beautiful and noble he would seldom or never see, and whatsoever he might see would appear to him as anything but beautiful and noble. Whatsoever might be bold and striking would at first seem only grotesque. The colors would be the very ones he had learned to shun as tawdry and bizarre. The tones and shades, modest and tender, subdued yet rich, in which his fancy had always taken special delight, would be the ones which are conspicuously absent. But time would bring a gradual change. Some day he would suddenly become conscious that outlines which at first seemed harsh and trivial have grace and meaning; that forms which seemed grotesque are full of dignity; that magnitudes which had added enormity to coarseness have become replete with strength and even majesty; that colors which had been esteemed unrefined, immodest, and glaring, are as expressive, tender, changeful, and capacious of effects as any others. Great innovations, whether in art or literature, in science or in nature, seldom take the world by storm. They must be understood before they can be estimated, and must be cultivated before they can be understood.

It is so with the Grand Cañon. The observer who visits its commanding points with the expectation of experiencing forthwith a rapturous exaltation, an ecstasy arising from the realization of a degree of grandeur and sublimity never felt before, is doomed to disappointment. Supposing him to be but little familiar with plateau scenery, he will be simply bewildered. Must he, therefore, pronounce it a failure, an overpraised thing? Must he entertain a just resentment towards those who may have raised his expectations too high? The answer is that subjects which disclose their full power, meaning, and beauty as soon as they are presented to the mind have very little of those qualities to disclose. Moreover, a visitor to the chasm or to any other famous scene must necessarily come there (for so is the human mind constituted) with a picture of it created by his own imagination. He reaches the spot, the conjured picture vanishes in an instant, and the place of it must be filled anew. Surely no imagination can construct out of its own material any picture having the remotest resemblance to the Grand Cañon. In truth, the first step in attempting a description is to beg the reader to dismiss from his mind, so far as practicable, any preconceived notion of it.

Those who have long and carefully studied the Grand Cañon of the Colorado do not hesitate for a moment to pronounce it by far the most sublime of all earthly spectacles. If its sublimity consisted only in its dimensions, it could be sufficiently set forth in a single sentence. It is more than 200 miles long, from 5 to 12 miles wide, and from 5,000 to 6,000 feet deep. There are in the world valleys which are longer and a few which are deeper. There are valleys flanked by summits loftier than the palisades of the Kaibab. Still the Grand Cañon is the sublimest thing on earth. It is so not alone by virtue of its magnitudes, but by virtue of the whole—its *ensemble*.

The common notion of a cañon is that of a deep, narrow gash in the earth, with nearly vertical walls, like a great and neatly cut trench. There are hundreds of chasms in the Plateau Country which answer very well to this notion. Many of them are sunk to frightful depths and are fifty to a hundred miles in length. Some are exceedingly narrow, as the cañons of the forks of the Virgen, where the overhanging walls shut out the sky. Some are intricately sculptured, and illuminated with brilliant colors; others are picturesque by reason of their bold and striking sculpture. A few of them are most solemn and impressive by reason of their profundity and the majesty of their walls. But, as a rule, the common cañons are neither grand nor even attractive. Upon first acquaintance they are curious and awaken interest as a new sensation, but they soon grow tiresome

for want of diversity, and become at last mere bores. The impressions they produce are very transient, because of their great simplicity, and the limited range
of ideas they present. But there are some which are highly diversified, presenting many attractive features. These seldom grow stale or wearisome, and their
presence is generally greeted with pleasure.

It is perhaps in some respects unfortunate that the stupendous pathway of
the Colorado River through the Kaibabs was ever called a cañon, for the name
identifies it with the baser conception. But the name presents as wide a range of
signification as the word house. The log cabin of the rancher, the painted and
vine-clad cottage of the mechanic, the home of the millionaire, the places where
parliaments assemble, and the grandest temples of worship, are all houses. Yet
the contrast between Saint Marc's and the rude dwelling of the frontiersman is
not greater than that between the chasm of the Colorado and the trenches in the
rocks which answer to the ordinary conception of a cañon. And as a great cathedral is an immense development of the rudimentary idea involved in the four
walls and roof of a cabin, so is the chasm an expansion of the simple type of
drainage channels peculiar to the Plateau Country. To the conception of its vast
proportions must be added some notion of its intricate plan, the nobility of its
architecture, its colossal buttes, its wealth of ornamentation, the splendor of its
colors, and its wonderful atmosphere. All of these attributes combine with infinite complexity to produce a whole which at first bewilders and at length
overpowers.

From the end of Point Sublime, the distance across the chasm to the nearest
point in the summit of the opposite wall is about 7 miles. This, however, does
not fairly express the width of the chasm, for both walls are recessed by wide
amphitheaters, setting far back into the platform of the country, and the promontories are comparatively narrow strips between them. A more correct statement of the general width would be from 11 to 12 miles. This must dispose at
once of the idea that the chasm is a narrow gorge of immense depth and simple
form. It is somewhat unfortunate that there is a prevalent idea that in some way
an essential part of the grandeur of the Grand Cañon is the narrowness of its
defiles. Much color has been given to this notion by the first illustrations of the
cañon from the pencil of Egloffstein in the celebrated report of Lieutenant Ives.
Never was a great subject more artistically misrepresented or more charmingly
belittled. Nowhere in the Kaibab section is any such extreme narrowness observ-
able, and even in the Uinkaret section the width of the great inner gorge is a
little greater than the depth. In truth, a little reflection will show that such a

character would be inconsistent with the highest and strongest effects. For it is obvious that some notable width is necessary to enable the eye to see the full extent of the walls. In a chasm one mile deep, and only a thousand feet wide, this would be quite impossible. If we compare the Marble Cañon or the gorge at the Toroweap with wider sections it will at once be seen that the wider ones are much stronger. If we compare one of the longer alcoves having a width of 3 or 4 miles with the view across the main chasm the advantage will be overwhelmingly with the latter. It is evident that for the display of wall surface of given dimensions a certain amount of distance is necessary. We may be too near or too far for the right appreciation of its magnitude and proportions. The distance must bear some ratio to the magnitude. But at what precise limit this distance must in the present case be fixed is not easy to determine. It can hardly be doubted that if the cañon were materially narrower it would suffer a loss of grandeur and effect.

The length of cañon revealed clearly and in detail at Point Sublime is about 25 miles in each direction. Towards the northwest the vista terminates behind the projecting mass of Powell's Plateau. But again to the westward may be seen the crests of the upper walls reaching through the Kanab and Uinkaret Plateaus, and finally disappearing in the haze about 75 miles away.

The space under immediate view from our standpoint, 50 miles long and 10 to 12 wide, is thronged with a great multitude of objects so vast in size, so bold yet majestic in form, so infinite in their details, that as the truth gradually reveals itself to the perceptions it arouses the strongest emotions. Unquestionably the great, the overruling feature is the wall on the opposite side of the gulf. Can mortal fancy create a picture of a mural front a mile in height, 7 to 10 miles distant, and receding into space indefinitely in either direction? As the mind strives to realize its proportions its spirit is broken and its imagination completely crushed. If the wall were simple in its character, if it were only blank and sheer, some rest might be found in contemplating it; but it is full of diversity and eloquent with grand suggestions. It is deeply recessed by alcoves and amphitheaters receding far into the plateau beyond, and usually disclosing only the portals by which they open into the main chasm. Between them the promontories jut out, ending in magnificent gables with sharp mitered angles. Thus the wall rambles in and out, turning numberless corners. Many of the angles are acute, and descend as sharp spurs like the forward edge of a plowshare. Only those alcoves which are directly opposite to us can be seen in their full length and depth. Yet so excessive, nay so prodigious, is the effect of foreshortening, that it is impossible to realize their full extensions. We have already noted this effect in the Vermilion Cliffs, but here it is much more exaggerated. At many points the profile of the façade is thrown into view by the change of trend, and its complex character is fully revealed. Like that of the Vermilion Cliffs, it is a series of many ledges and slopes, like a molded plinth, in which every stratum is disclosed as a line or a course of masonry. The Red Wall limestone is the most conspicuous member, presenting its vertical face eight hundred to a thousand feet high, and everywhere unbroken. The thinner beds more often appear in the slopes as a succession of ledges projecting through the scanty talus which never conceals them.

Numerous detached masses are also seen flanking the ends of the long promontories. These buttes are of gigantic proportions, and yet so overwhelming is the effect of the wall against which they are projected that they seem insignificant in mass, and the observer is often deluded by them, failing to perceive that they are really detached from the wall and perhaps separated from it by an interval of a mile or two.

At the foot of this palisade is a platform through which meanders the inner gorge, in whose dark and somber depths flows the river. Only in one place can the water surface be seen. In its windings the abyss which holds it extends for a short distance towards us and the line of vision enters the gorge lengthwise. Above and below this short reach the gorge swings its course in other directions and reveals only a dark, narrow opening, while its nearer wall hides its depths. This inner chasm is 1,000 to 1,200 feet deep. Its upper 200 feet is a vertical ledge of sandstone of a dark rich brownish color. Beneath it lies the granite of a dark iron-gray shade, verging towards black, and lending a gloomy aspect to the lowest deeps. Perhaps a half mile of the river is disclosed. A pale, dirty red, without glimmer or sheen, a motionless surface, a small featureless spot, inclosed in the dark shade of the granite, is all of it that is here visible. Yet we know it is a large river, a hundred and fifty yards wide, with a headlong torrent foaming and plunging over rocky rapids.

A little, and only a little, less impressive than the great wall across the chasm are the buttes upon this side. And such buttes! All others in the west, saving only the peerless Temples of the Virgen, are mere trifles in comparison with those of the Grand Cañon. In nobility of form, beauty of decoration, and splendor of color, the Temples of the Virgen must, on the whole, be awarded the palm; but those of the Grand Cañon, while barely inferior to them in those respects, surpass them in magnitude and fully equal them in majesty. But while the Valley of the Virgen presents a few of these superlative creations, the Grand Cañon presents them by dozens. In this relation the comparison would be analogous to one between a fine cathedral town and a metropolis like London or Paris. In truth, there is only a very limited ground of comparison between the two localities, for in style and effects their respective structures differ as decidedly as the works of any two well-developed and strongly contrasted styles of human architecture.

Whatsoever is forcible, characteristic, and picturesque in the rock-forms of the Plateau Country is concentrated and intensified to the uttermost in the buttes. Wherever we find them, whether fringing the long escarpments of terraces or planted upon broad mesas, whether in cañons or upon expansive plains, they are always bold and striking in outline and ornate in architecture. Upon their flanks and entablatures the decoration peculiar to the formation out of which they have been carved is most strongly portrayed and the profiles are most sharply cut. They command the attention with special force and quicken the imagination with a singular power. The secret of their impressiveness is doubtless obscure. Why one form should be beautiful and another unattractive; why one should be powerful, animated, and suggestive, while another is meaningless, are questions for the metaphysician rather than the geologist. Sufficient here is the fact. Yet there are some elements of impressiveness which are too patent to escape recognition. In nearly all buttes there is a certain *definiteness* of form which is peculiarly emphatic, and this is seen in their profiles. Their ground-plans are almost always indefinite and capricious, but the profiles are rarely so. These are usually composed of lines which have an approximate and sometimes a sensibly perfect geometrical definition. They are usually few and simple in their ultimate analysis, though by combination they give rise to much variety. The ledges are vertical, the summits are horizontal, and the taluses are segments of hyperbolas of long curvature and concave upwards. These lines greatly preponderate in all cases, and though others sometimes intrude they seldom blemish greatly the effects produced by the normal ones. All this is in striking contrast with the ever-varying, indefinite profiles displayed in mountains and hills or on the slopes of valleys. The profiles generated by the combinations of these geometric lines persist along an indefinite extent of front. Such variations as occur arise not from changes in the nature of the lines, but in the modes of combination and proportions. These are never great in any front of moderate extent, but are just sufficient to relieve it from a certain monotony which would otherwise prevail. The same type and general form is persistent.

Like the key-note of a song, the mind carries it in its consciousness wherever the harmony wanders.

The horizontal lines or courses are equally strong. These are the edges of the strata, and the deeply eroded seams where the superposed beds touch each other. Here the uniformity as we pass from place to place is conspicuous. The Carboniferous strata are quite the same in every section, showing no perceptible variation in thickness through great distances, and only a slight dip.

It is readily apparent, therefore, that the effect of these profiles and horizontal courses so persistent in their character is highly architectural. The relation is more than a mere analogy or suggestion; it is a vivid resemblance. Its failure or discordance is only in the ground plan, though it is not uncommon to find a resemblance, even in this respect, among the Permian buttes. Among the buttes of the Grand Cañon there are few striking instances of definiteness in ground plan. The finest butte of the chasm is situated near the upper end of the Kaibab division; but it is not visible from Point Sublime. It is more than 5,000 feet high, and has a surprising resemblance to an Oriental pagoda. We named it Vishnu's Temple.

On either side of the promontory on which we stand is a side gorge sinking nearly 4,000 feet below us. The two unite in front of the point, and, ever deepening, their trunk opens into the lowest abyss in the granite at the river. Across either branch is a long rambling mass, one on the right of us, the other on the left. We named them the Cloisters. They are excellent types of a whole class of buttes which stand in close proximity to each other upon the north side of the chasm throughout the entire extent of the Kaibab division. A far better conception of their forms and features can be gained by an examination of Mr. Holmes's panoramic picture than by reading a whole volume of verbal description. The whole prospect, indeed, is filled with a great throng of similar objects, which, as much by their multitude as by their colossal size, confuse the senses; but these, on account of their proximity, may be most satisfactorily studied. The infinity of sharply defined detail is amazing. The eye is instantly caught and the attention firmly held by its systematic character. The parallelism of the lines of bedding is most forcibly displayed in all the windings of the façades, and these lines are crossed by the vertical scorings of numberless waterways. Here, too, are distinctly seen those details which constitute the peculiar style of decoration prevailing throughout all the buttes and amphitheaters of the Kaibab. The course of the walls is never for a moment straight, but extends as a series of cusps and re-entrant curves. Elsewhere the reverse is more frequently seen; the projections of the wall are rounded and are convex towards the front, while the re-entrant portions are cusp-like recesses. This latter style of decoration is common in the Permian buttes and is not rare in the Jurassic. It produces the effect of a thickly set row of pilasters. In the Grand Cañon the reversal of this mode produces the effect of panels and niches. In the western Cloister may be seen a succession of these niches, and though they are mere details among myriads, they are really vast in dimensions. Those seen in the Red Wall limestone are over 600 feet high, and are overhung by arched lintels with spandrels.

As we contemplate these objects we find it quite impossible to realize their magnitude. Not only are we deceived, but we are conscious that we are deceived, and yet we cannot conquer the deception. We cannot long study our surroundings without becoming aware of an enormous disparity in the effects produced upon the senses by objects which are immediate and equivalent ones which are more remote. The depth of the gulf which separates us from the Cloisters cannot be realized. We crane over the brink, and about 700 feet below is a talus, which ends at the summit of the cross-bedded sandstone. We may see the bottom of the gorge, which is about 3,800 feet beneath us, and yet the talus seems at least half-way down. Looking across the side gorge the cross-bedded sandstone is seen as a mere band at the summit of the Cloister, forming but a very small portion of its vertical extent, and, whatever the reason may conclude, it is useless to attempt to persuade the imagination that the two edges of the sandstone lie in the same horizontal plane. The eastern Cloister is nearer than the western, its distance being about a mile and a half. It seems incredible that it can be so much as one-third that distance. Its altitude is from 3,500 to 4,000 feet, but any attempt to estimate the altitude by means of visual impressions is felt at once to be hopeless. There is no stadium. Dimensions mean nothing to the senses, and all that we are conscious of in this respect is a troubled sense of immensity.

Beyond the eastern Cloister, five or six miles distant, rises a gigantic mass which we named Shiva's Temple. It is the grandest of all the buttes, and the most majestic in aspect, though not the most ornate. Its mass is as great as the mountainous part of Mount Washington. That summit looks down 6,000 feet into the dark depths of the inner abyss, over a succession of ledges as impracticable as the face of Bunker Hill Monument. All around it are side gorges sunk to a depth nearly as profound as that of the main channel. It stands in the midst of a great throng of cloister-like buttes, with the same noble profiles and strong lineaments as those immediately before us, with a plexus of awful chasms between them. In such a stupendous scene of wreck it seemed as if the fabled "Destroyer" might find an abode not wholly uncongenial.

In all the vast space beneath and around us there is very little upon which the mind can linger restfully. It is completely filled with objects of gigantic size and amazing form, and as the mind wanders over them it is hopelessly bewildered and lost. It is useless to select special points of contemplation. The instant the attention lays hold of them it is drawn to something else, and if it seeks to recur to them it cannot find them. Everything is superlative, transcending the power of the intelligence to comprehend it. There is no central point or object around which the other elements are grouped and to which they are tributary. The grandest objects are merged in a congregation of others equally grand. Hundreds of these mighty structures, miles in length, and thousands of feet in height, rear their majestic heads out of the abyss, displaying their richly-molded plinths and friezes, thrusting out their gables, wing-walls, buttresses, and pilasters, and recessed with alcoves and panels. If any one of these stupendous creations had been planted upon the plains of central Europe it would have influenced modern art as profoundly as Fusiyama has influenced the decorative art of Japan. Yet here they are all swallowed up in the confusion of multitude. It is not alone the magnitude of the individual objects that makes this spectacle so portentious, but it is still more the extravagant profusion with which they are arrayed along the whole visible extent of the broad chasm.

The color effects are rich and wonderful. They are due to the inherent colors of the rocks, modified by the atmosphere. Like any other great series of strata in the Plateau Province, the Carboniferous has its own range of characteristic colors, which might serve to distinguish it even if we had no other criterion. The summit strata are pale grey, with a faint yellowish cast. Beneath them the cross-bedded sandstone appears, showing a mottled surface of pale pinkish hue. Underneath this member are nearly 1,000 feet of the lower Aubrey sandstones, displaying an intensely brilliant red, which is somewhat masked by the talus shot down from the grey, cherty limestones at the summit. Beneath the Lower Aubrey is the face of the Red Wall limestone, from 2,000 to 3,000 feet high. It has a strong red tone, but a very peculiar one. Most of the red strata of the west have the brownish or vermilion tones, but these are rather purplish-red, as if the pigment had been treated to a dash of blue. It is not quite certain that this may not arise in part from the intervention of the blue haze, and probably it is rendered more conspicuous by this cause; but, on the whole, the purplish cast seems to be inherent. This is the dominant color-mass of the cañon, for the expanse of rock surface displayed is more than half in the Red Wall group. It is less brilliant than the fiery red of the Aubrey sandstones, but is still quite strong and rich. Beneath are the deep browns of the lower Carboniferous. The dark iron-black of the hornblendic schists revealed in the lower gorge makes but little impression upon the boundless expanse of bright colors above.

The total effect of the entire color-mass is bright and glowing. There is nothing gloomy or dark in the picture, except the opening of the inner gorge, which is too small a feature to influence materially the prevailing tone. Although the colors are bright when contrasted with normal landscapes, they are decidedly less intense than the flaming hues of the Trias or the dense cloying colors of the Permian; nor have they the refinement of those revealed in the Eocene. The intense luster which gleams from the rocks of the Plateau Country is by no means lost here, but is merely subdued and kept under some restraint. It is toned down and softened without being deprived of its character. Enough of it is left to produce color effects not far below those that are yielded by the Jura-Trias.

But though the inherent colors are less intense than some others, yet under the quickening influence of the atmosphere they produce effects to which all others are far inferior. And here language fails and description becomes impossible. Not only are their qualities exceedingly subtle, but they have little counterpart in common experience. If such are presented elsewhere they are presented so feebly and obscurely that only the most discriminating and closest observers of nature ever seize them, and they so imperfectly that their ideas of them are vague and but half real. There are no concrete notions founded in experience upon which a conception of these color effects and optical delusions can be constructed and made intelligible. A perpetual glamour envelops the landscape. Things are not what they seem, and the perceptions cannot tell us what they are. It is not probable that these effects are different in kind in the Grand Cañon from what they are in other portions of the Plateau Country. But the difference in degree is immense, and being greatly magnified and intensified many characteristics become palpable which elsewhere elude the closest observation.

In truth, the tone and temper of the landscape are constantly varying, and the changes in its aspect are very great. It is never the same, even from day to day, or even from hour to hour. In the early morning its mood and subjective influences are usually calmer and more full of repose than at other times, but as the sun rises higher the whole scene is so changed that we cannot recall our first impressions. Every passing cloud, every change in the position of the sun, recasts the whole. At sunset the pageant closes amid splendors that seem more than earthly. The direction of the full sunlight, the massing of the shadows, the manner in which the side lights are thrown in from the clouds determine these modulations, and the sensitiveness of the picture to the slightest variations in these conditions is very wonderful.

The shadows thrown by the bold abrupt forms are exceedingly dark. It is almost impossible at the distance of a very few miles to distinguish even broad details in these shadows. They are like remnants of midnight unconquered by the blaze of noonday. The want of half tones and gradations in the light and shade, which has already been noted in the Vermilion Cliffs, is apparent here, and is far more conspicuous. Our thoughts in this connection may suggest to us a still more extreme case of a similar phenomenon presented by the half-illuminated moon when viewed through a large telescope. The portions which catch the sunlight shine with great luster, but the shadows of mountains and cliffs are black and impenetrable. But there is one feature in the cañon which is certainly extraordinary. It is the appearance of the atmosphere against the background of shadow. It has a metallic luster which must be seen to be appreciated. The great wall across the chasm presents at noonday, under a cloudless sky, a singularly weird and unearthly aspect. The color is for the most part gone. In place of it comes this metallic glare of the haze. The southern wall is never so poorly lighted as at noon. Since its face consists of a series of promontories projecting towards the north, these projections catch the sunlight on their eastern sides in the forenoon, and upon their western sides in the afternoon; but near meridian the rays fall upon a few points only, and even upon these with very great obliquity. Thus at the hours of greatest general illumination the wall is most obscure and the abnormal effects are then presented most forcibly. They give rise to strange delusions. The rocks then look nearly black, or very dark grey, and covered with feebly shining spots. The haze is strongly luminous, and so dense as to obscure the details already enfeebled by shade as if a leaden or mercurial vapor intervened. The shadows antagonize the perspective, and everything seems awry. The lines of stratification, dimly seen in one place and wholly effaced in another, are strangely belied, and the strata are given apparent attitudes which are sometimes grotesque and sometimes impossible.

Those who are familiar with western scenery have, no doubt, been impressed with the peculiar character of its haze—or atmosphere, in the artistic sense of the word—and have noted its more prominent qualities. When the air is free from common smoke it has a pale blue color which is quite unlike the neutral gray of the east. It is always apparently more dense when we look towards the sun than when we look away from it, and this difference in the two directions, respectively, is a maximum near sunrise and sunset. This property is universal, but its peculiarities in the Plateau Province become conspicuous when the strong rich colors of the rocks are seen through it. The very air is then visible. We see it, palpably, as a tenuous fluid, and the rocks beyond it do not appear to be colored blue as they do in other regions, but reveal themselves clothed in colors of their own. The Grand Cañon is ever full of this haze. It fills it to the brim. Its apparent density, as elsewhere, is varied according to the direction in which it is viewed and the position of the sun; but it seems also to be denser and more concentrated than elsewhere. This is really a delusion arising from the fact that the enormous magnitude of the chasm and of its component masses dwarfs the distances; we are really looking through miles of atmosphere under the impression that they are only so many furlongs. This apparent concentration of haze, however, greatly intensifies all the beautiful or mysterious optical defects which are dependent upon the intervention of the atmosphere.

Whenever the brink of the chasm is reached the chances are that the sun is high and these abnormal effects in full force. The cañon is asleep. Or is it under a spell of enchantment which gives its bewildering mazes an aspect still more bewildering. Throughout the long summer forenoon the charm which binds it grows in potency. At midday the clouds begin to gather, first in fleecy flecks, then in cumuli, and throw their shadows into the gulf. At once the scene changes. The slumber of the chasm is disturbed. The temples and cloisters seem to raise themselves half awake to greet the passing shadow. Their wilted, drooping, flattened faces expand into relief. The long promontories reach out from the distant wall as if to catch a moment's refreshment from the shade. The colors begin to glow; the haze loses its opaque density and becomes more tenuous. The shadows pass, and the chasm relapses into its dull sleep again. Thus through the midday hours it lies in fitful slumber, overcome by the blinding glare and withering heat, yet responsive to every fluctuation of light and shadow like a delicate organism.

As the sun moves far into the west the scene again changes, slowly and imperceptibly at first, but afterwards more rapidly. In the hot summer afternoons the sky is full of cloud-play and the deep flushes with ready answers. The banks of snowy clouds pour a flood of light sidewise into the shadows and light up the gloom of the amphitheaters and alcoves, weakening the glow of the haze and rendering visible the details of the wall faces. At length, as the sun draws near the horizon, the great drama of the day begins.

Throughout the afternoon the prospect has been gradually growing clearer. The haze has relaxed its steely glare and has changed to a veil of transparent blue. Slowly the myriads of details have come out and the walls are flecked with lines of minute tracery, forming a diaper of light and shade. Stronger and sharper becomes the relief of each projection. The promontories come forth from the opposite wall. The sinuous lines of stratification which once seemed meaningless, distorted, and even chaotic, now range themselves into a true perspective of graceful curves, threading the scallop edges of the strata. The colossal buttes expand in every dimension. Their long, narrow wings, which once were folded together and flattened against each other, open out, disclosing between them vast alcoves illumined with Rembrandt lights tinged with the pale refined blue of the ever-present haze. A thousand forms, hitherto unseen or obscure, start up within the abyss, and stand forth in strength and animation. All things seem to grow in beauty, power, and dimensions. What was grand before has become majestic, the majestic becomes sublime, and, ever expanding and developing, the sublime passes beyond the reach of our faculties and becomes transcendent. The colors have come back. Inherently rich and strong, though not superlative under ordinary lights, they now begin to display an adventitious brilliancy. The western sky is all aflame. The scattered banks of cloud and wavy cirrhus have caught the waning splendor, and shine with orange and crimson. Broad slant beams of yellow light, shot through the glory-rifts, fall on turret and tower, on pinnacled crest and winding ledge, suffusing them with a radiance less fulsome, but akin to that which flames in the western clouds. The summit band is brilliant yellow; the next below is pale rose. But the grand expanse within is a deep, luminous, resplendent red. The climax has now come. The blaze of sunlight poured over an illimitable surface of glowing red is flung back into the gulf, and, commingling with the blue haze, turns it into a sea of purple of most imperial hue—so rich, so strong, so pure that it makes the heart ache and the throat tighten. However vast the magnitudes, however majestic the forms, or sumptuous the decoration, it is in these kingly colors that the highest glory of the Grand Cañon is revealed.

At length the sun sinks and the colors cease to burn. The abyss lapses back into repose. But its glory mounts upward and diffuses itself in the sky above. Long streamers of rosy light, rayed out from the west, cross the firmament and converge again in the east, ending in a pale rosy arch, which rises like a low aurora just above the eastern horizon. Below it is the dead gray shadow of the world. Higher and higher climbs the arch, followed by the darkening pall of gray, and as it ascends it fades and disappears, leaving no color except the after-glow of the western clouds and the lusterless red of the chasm below. Within the abyss the darkness gathers. Gradually the shades deepen and ascend, hiding the opposite wall and enveloping the great temples. For a few moments the summits of these majestic piles seem to float upon a sea of blackness, then van-ish in the darkness, and, wrapped in the impenetrable mantle of the night, they await the glory of the coming dawn.

Bright Angel Trail and Canyon including Indian Gardens Camp and Plateau Point

CHAPTER
SEVEN

From Dawn to Dusk

DAYS AND WEEKS can be given to Desert View without exhausting the scene or the interest. You are away from the hotel and the crowd, and can see things like a lone eagle from your point of rock. Both the rock and the eagle are here (an eagle usually has a nest every summer not five hundred yards to the east of Desert View), so the allusion is not forced. If you watch the eagle you will see that she does her coming and going early in the morning and late in the evening, and, if you follow her example, you, too, will go out to your point of rock at dawn and at sunset.

Perhaps you will have noticed, as at Lincoln Point, that the Canyon here is happily disposed for morning and evening effects because it runs practically east and west, and the light strikes not so much across it as along its length. The sun comes up over the Painted Desert and drives its golden shafts down the Canyon for sixty miles or more; at evening the reddened beams drive back through the Canyon upon the mesas and ridges of this same Painted Desert. If there is anything unusual, any special spread of splendor coming from that

"Nebulous star we call the sun,"

you are sure to see it here.

The first gray half-light of the dawn has no effect on the Canyon. It is only when it turns pale yellow and begins to creep around the horizon that faint reflections appear upon the eastern faces of the Kaibab and Coconino. Often the

From *The Grand Canyon of the Colorado,* by John C. Van Dyke. Reprinted by permission of Charles Scribner's Sons. Copyright 1920 by Charles Scribner's Sons.

light from below the verge at first strikes high up on the zenith, making a white spot on the blue that in turn illumines the depth; and, often again, feathery cirrus clouds up there will catch the light and begin to redden, casting down pale pinks upon the walls below. As the light increases in the east the color brightens from silver and rose to pink and perhaps carmine. The face-walls make answer in grays, then silvers, then saffrons creeping into orange, followed by roses and heliotropes. They are wonderfully delicate colors.

One by one the tops of the buttes and points and promontories take up and carry on the light far down the Canyon. First one glows and shifts into a bright garb, and then another farther on repeats the litany of color. As the light increases, the color spreads down the walls from the high points. The local hue of the strata begins to come out, the purples of the depth awaken, the shadows turn ultramarine, the air becomes gray-blue, or sometimes pink over purple.

The reflected lights from sky and cloud arouse the Canyon to its inner depths. There is a shaking off of the night gloom, and if the sky in the east is a broad range of orange or fiery with red clouds, the reflecting walls will show very lively hues. When the sun itself comes over the horizon there is instant focussing of high lights on the rocky points and the forming of blue shadows behind every interposing tree, ridge, butte, and promontory. The change is swift and positive.

With the coming of the sun you can almost make yourself believe there is a faint music of the elements, or at least a trailing of wings. But no.

> "Not with the roll of thunder drums,
> But softly, soundless, as beseems
> The alchemist of color dreams,
> The Sun God comes."

The light falls on the Kaibab faces and changes them to light gold or warm orange, Wotan's Throne reddens, the tips of the buttes turn pink; but there is no sound to warn you of the change. Nor is there any permanence in the change. The colors shift and go, and as the sun lifts higher in the sky you notice that, while the local color is more pronounced, the reflected colors from the sky and cloud seem to grow fainter and duller. The splendor of the dawn soon goes out before the more commonplace color of the morning.

For as the sun continues to rise, the Canyon begins to lose not only in hue but in definiteness. This has already been alluded to in connection with the abnormal appearance of the buttes at noonday. The sun high in the heavens plays havoc with lines and surfaces. Planes begin to shut up bellows-like and perspective collapses. Drawing, too, fails. Objects do not project or recede, or give a sense of bulk or weight, but seem continuous or superimposed, one upon another. The long promontories running out from the Rim not only lose their thickness and resemble stage screens, but they lose their relative position. After nine o'clock in the morning even the isolated buttes do not seem isolated. The overhead light reflects rather than illumines, distorts the normal appearance, and makes everything uncertain, illusory, indefinite. A haze envelops the Canyon and a beautiful blur is upon it; but the effect is disappointing to those who would see the reality. You must turn to other things until the depth comes back to itself in the late afternoon.

The midday period is occasionally varied by flying cloud-shadows that chase each other across the platforms, or by sunbursts that fling down their search-lights into the Canyon, revealing hidden depths and dormant colors. Rain, of course, veils everything. Even the thunder-storms that let down trailing fringes of rain—let them down ten thousand feet—shut out the view temporarily. But they also often bring out the profiles of the buttes in relief and reveal their fine lines with great effect. In fact, one does not know what forceful contours these buttes and promontories possess until he sees them with a rain-veil behind them. They then begin to resemble sierra ridges in their outline drawing.

Often, again, after the rain has passed, the hot rocks will steam and the sunlight will flash on wet pinnacles with a glittering effect which, shown in relief against deep-blue shadows, and in connection perhaps with a rainbow and dark passing clouds, is very picturesque. The rainbow at the Canyon happens quite easily, and sometimes apparently without rain. I have already mentioned the appearance at noontime of the spectrum colors, waving like a flag, in the cirrus directly overhead. And with no other clouds in sight. It is a very strange phenomenon.

During the long summer afternoon the Canyon seems to doze in the sunlight. It has a blue-gray color without accent, tone, or quality. The tourist may think it wonderful but the artist knows its monotony. At five o'clock, however, a change begins to take place. The Canyon colors begin to revive faintly, the blue shadows draw a little behind buttes and promontories, the ledges and platforms and pinnacles begin to lengthen and lift, the walls become enormous in bulk and sharpen in contour. Gradually perspective and planes come back. As the sun slips down the western sky the whole Canyon continues to grow more intense in light and shadow, more acute in line and color. It is the dramatic hour.

The spectacle of a Canyon sunset is usually one of intense light and warmth, and the sky absorbs attention to the exclusion of everything else. Perhaps it should not. One may not wholly agree with Whistler in his jibe at those who admire "a foolish sunset," and yet still consider that the effect here, on Canyon and Painted Desert, is perhaps more beautiful than the cause itself. The effect is more subdued, more subtle in its mingling of local hues with the colors flashed by the sun. It is color filtered, strained, refined, and for that reason perhaps more acceptable as more purely sensuous.

The various hues that appear on the Canyon walls at sunset are akin to the evening glows of snow mountains. The very brilliant reflections are not usually from the sun itself, but from the sky or clouds that are set glowing with color by its light. The molten golds, scarlets, and carmines that surround the sun, or are above it, are the torches that fire the buttes with flame and turn the pinnacles into towers of golden light. Often they "glow like plated Mars," and occasionally the illusion of molten metal appears in pinnacles, resembling the red of hot iron that finally dies out in a beautiful ash gray.

From Desert View at sunset, tints and tones innumerable are seen, not only on Canyon walls, but on the mesas of the Painted Desert. The barrage of light seems to lift and lift, striking farther away as the sun sinks in the west. You can see it move along the ridges, spreading from cliff to cliff, and tingeing all the faces a bright vermilion. Far to the east it flies, growing fainter and fainter on butte and ridge, until it is lost in the thick violet air of distance. Navaho Mountain is too far away to respond in anything more pronounced than a rosy tone. It is the last echo.

These sun-shafts and rock reflections on the Desert are just as remarkable as those in the Canyon. The background of the Desert, with its thick, dust-laden air, makes possible a perfect blend. At sundown the general tone of the whole flat basin is golden with a rose tinge in it, and through this envelope you see the red of the Echo Cliffs glowing like the fire of a bright opal. The jewel quality of desert light and color are never so apparent as just then and there.

Occasionally at sunset a wind will pass over the Desert's face, raising great clouds of dust that reach up almost to the zenith. This dust-veil is, generally speaking, rosy red, but like the dawn and the sunset sky, it also shows faintly the colors of the spectrum arranged in order. It is a rather thick veiling, and the barrage of sun-fire meets opposition. The cliffs through it show lurid, the buttes smoulder, the mesas are ashes of roses. It is a red-and-purple mystery.

If you look now quickly to the west you will find that the Canyon, too, in some sympathy with the dust-cloud, will also show strange hues. The air down in the gorge is thick with purples, but above this a violet atmosphere lies under the Rim and around the buttes and points. The projecting promontories that, seen far down the Canyon, seem to overlap one another, now appear once more like the wings of a stage-setting illumined by dull Bengal fire. Blues and mauves and heliotropes are everywhere. It is a violet fantasy in sky and Rim and Canyon, as unreal as any vision out of the Arabian Nights. And it becomes still more fantastic, as well as exquisite, if you will lie down on your point of rock and look at it sideways, with your head on the rock. The position seems to bring into play some unusual or unfatigued portion of the retina, for the colors appear greatly enhanced and beautified. All the world now seems swimming in lilac and violet.

Turn again to the Painted Desert and you will find that the maze and mystery of it have deepened while you were looking at the Canyon. St. John at Patmos can have seen nothing more supernaturally glowing. And note that the glow is not merely in the sky but all around you. You are within it. The purple air envelops everything, and the ridges and cliffs faintly seen through it finally go out in rose colors as Point Sublime to the west disappears in gun-metal blues. The whole world now seems like some dark opal, with dull fire-spots on its surface.

Once more, from your recumbent position on the rock, look around in the growing dusk at the vast circle of the horizon. It is complete save for the small segment of forest behind you. Turn over on your back and look straight up at the sky

"Clad in the beauty of a thousand stars."

The red moon is coming up over the pines back of you, but as yet makes little impression on either the sky or the Canyon. The dusk enfolds you. By midnight the air will clear, the moon will whiten, the sky will deepen, the stars will glisten. Before dawn the morning star will look so large that, like the Arabian sun, you can fancy seventy thousand angels necessary to start it each morning on its way. But now there is nothing but a dusky world swinging in blue space and carrying with it an envelope of colored air.

How intensely impressive this purple veil of night! The Canyon is even more wonderful in color and atmosphere than in rock strata and countersunk River. It is not the eighth wonder of the world but the first.

Granite Rapid, December, 1911. The Kolbs' boat, *Edith,* is virtually indistinguishable at the head of the rapid.

Rio Colorado

IT IS FROM COCONINO that the cañon is best taken as a spectacle. But not from any one point do you immediately come into relation with it. Go back among the dark cedars and the widely spaced yellow pines until your feet find by instinct the slightly sloping ground that drops off suddenly into the abyss. Here you find yourself at the head of one of the triangular bays following the surface drainage inland to the farthest point at which it can gather erosive force. So now you perceive the structure of the Grand Cañon to be that of a true valley, kept narrow and straight-sided by the stubborn nature of its walls. Over toward Bright Angel, where the material is softer, it makes a gentler slope, or gets down from Kanab and Shinumo by broken stairs and vast amphitheaters facing the lowest land.

The thing to marvel at about the Grand Cañon, is that man should find it so in his nature to be astounded by the thousand-foot reach of a valley wall only when it happens to be arranged vertically in space. The towhee, the junco, and the piñonero flit ceaselessly over the rim and back again. The whisk-tailed squirrels are no more fearful of falling into that awful gulf than you are of dropping into interplanetary space. You wonder why we so constantly adjure childhood to be "too big to be afraid," when it is evidently a much happier state to be too small to be. The cedar and the white-fringed mountain mahogany go over, seeking down sheer walls and along the many-hued talus their familiar levels. On the Tonto plateau they give place to sage-brush, and next to the feather-foliaged greasewood. Far down on the hot zone of the lowest cañon levels, the yuccas and the agaves consort with the dust-colored cat-claw and the cacti. On the north rim, where living streams come down the rocky stairs, they bring with them all the bloom and the bird song whose succession makes the charm of long mountain slopes. Caught all at once in this vertical sweep, it fixes forever the standard of comparison for men whose constant measure is of up-and-downness.

There must be something in this way of seeing things that is native to the deepest self of man, for once it is seen, there is no way afterward of not seeing it. Any time now,—and sometimes whether I will or no,—by a mere turn of attention, over the shoulder of my mind, as it were, I see it there . . . as I loved most to see it, . . . the noiseless dance of island towers, advancing, retreating; . . . cliffs burning red from within; the magical, shifty shadows, the vast down-throw of Kaibab, grape-colored, with a bloom on it of refracted light, . . . the twin, ember-glowing towers between which in the last day all the Navajos will come riding, riding down to Sipapu; old chiefs and older, he who broke the Chaco towns, lance-armed raiders, shield on elbow from the Shiprock region, fierce renegades from El Bosque Redondo, brass-buttoned cavalry scouts, wound-striped khaki from Château-Thierry, . . . riding, riding, red fire in the west and shadows blue as morning.

But be careful whom you ask to point the place out to you, lest you be answered by one of the silly names cut out of a mythological dictionary and shaken in a hat before they were applied to the Grand Cañon for the benefit of that astonishing number of Americans who can never see anything unless it is supposed to look like something else. It is only from the north rim, however,—from Marble Cañon or from Kanab farthest west,—that you understand why the long, flat silhouette of Kaibab should be called Mountain Lying Down, as it stoops to the hidden river. There is no use trying to improve on Indian names, really!

Kaibab is manured by the snow. Sacred spruces grow there, and firs, well spaced, and plumy-yellow pines. Under them blacktail, streaking back their antlers, in the largest herds in the world; mokiách, the cougar, hunts the black-tail, and cattlemen hunt the last of the lobos. On Shinumo are ruins, mysterious, the extreme western reach of the stone-town builders. Across Kanab range dark cedars, mountain mahogany and the tree that was the younger brother of Pama-quásh. Low-lying Shivwits is gray with sage-brush and varnished creosote. All the vertical faces of the cliffs and the wide grassy flats are self-colored by the underlying formation, which is here chiefly vermilion limestone with thin beds of sea-colored shale.

Between Kanab and Uinkaret cluster the cinder-streaked cones from which lava once flowed down the river gorge until it was cooled and checked by the racing water. Between these and the mass of San Francisco Mountain, blue against the south, and east and west between the Little Colorado and the Virgin rivers, lies all the splendor of the Left Hand of God.

Is the impulse which most people confess to, on first seeing the Grand Cañon, to cast themselves into its dim violet depths, confidently as a bird launches itself from a mountain-top upon the air, a reawakened pulse of surety we once had of its being as good a thing and as joyous to go down with the Left Hand as to go up with the Right? It is at any rate, here, a magnificent thing.

The sage-brush-covered platform which you see from El Tovar, called Tonto plateau, is actually the surface of that scoured granite core on which the whole of Kaibab foundation was laid. It is a matter of three hours or less to go down to it, and so on down into the V-shaped, inner cañon which the river has cut in the most ancient rock.

There you see the frothy yellow flood making hidden bars of sand and spewing them forth in boiling fountains of fury, like a man ridding himself of nursed, secret grudges in spouts of temper. But you will do better in the way of understanding what the Left Hand is about, if you stay on the rim and study the river of clouds to which you are made privy on Kaibab and Coconino. They come up burdened and shepherdless from the delta until they strike the lift of desert-heated air above Yuma and the Salada plains. They lift great glittering sails from the Pacific, defiling between the pillars of San Jacinto and San Bernardino.

Up and up they climb the viewless stairs, growing diaphanous until at last they have hid themselves in the deeps of the middle heavens. About the intervening peaks you see them glimmer into visibility and disappear, as though mountains had the power some people claim to exercise over the passing dead, of compelling them to materialize.

Going north to find the Colorado Front, that will release them into rain again, they are caught in the eddies that play about the Grand Cañon. Here acres of naked rock give back the sun with such intensity it burns the hand to touch, and the middle depth of the gorge is blue with the quiver of heat-waves, rising. Then the cold air from Kaibab comes sliding down the russet-hued slope, and in the currents thus set in motion, whole flocks of dove-breasted clouds are netted. Sometimes they are packed close from rim to rim and in the whirl of hot and cold, struggle woundedly between the walls. Then the lightning bounds back and back from sheer rock surfaces, and the thunder loses itself in its own echo.

After such intervals, sometimes, the upper levels will be fleecy soft with snow, through which, far down, you can see the dust-colored cat-claw and the hot banks on which the gila monster sprawls; for never, never do the clouds get down to the river except they have been to the mountain and resolved themselves in rain. On that business almost any day you will see them feeling their way cautiously among the rock towers, or catch them of early mornings resting just under the Rim, behind some tall potrero.

I recall catching a flock of them there one morning, wing-folded under Yavapi Point, as I came in from watching a gibbous moon walking the Rim cautiously like a pregnant woman. I had walked too far, watching the moonlight drip down salient ledges, and the tops of the potreros swim into view out of abysmal darkness like young worlds appearing, so that moonset found me where I thought it safest to wait until the dawn came up, as it does in the Navajo country, a turquoise horse, neighing joyously.

So as I passed Yavapi, I saw the cloud flock sleeping, as I have seen seal sleep with their noses resting on a point of rock, swaying with the sea's motion. More lightly still the clouds slept, until, as if my step had startled them, they began to scatter and rise, feeling for the wind's way, taking hands when they had found it, curling up and over the rim. Almost immediately I heard, far below, the soft *hee-haw* of the little wild burros, long-eared like rabbits, rabbit-colored, coming to drink of the dew, in the pits of the rocks where the clouds had rested. It was almost at this same place that I saw on another occasion the dim face of Rainbow Boy, behind the cloud-film in the rainbow halo. I am not sure that the other tourists saw anything but the changing configuration of the cliff through the cloud-drift, but that was their misfortune. It is only as they please that Those Above show themselves in the rainbow, which when the sun is low is perfectly round here, or the moonbow, faint and fluctuating on the level floor of cloud below the cañon rim.

THROUGH
TOURIST
EYES

Kolb Brothers Studio and home at the head of Bright Angel Trail. When this photograph was taken, Ralph Cameron still controlled the trail; the sign on the left lists charges for use of his "Toll Road."

JOHN HANCE kept a visitors' book for the tourists who stayed at his tent camp in the 1890s. The inscriptions penned by those early visitors are not much different from what one hears on any rim overlook today—floods of superlatives, and allusions to the canyon as proof of God's presence. An occasional visitor is just plain terrified. On July 9, 1892, one Mrs. John Z. T. Varme wrote the following in Hance's book: "I have never witnessed anything like this. It scares me to even try to look down into it. My God, I am afraid the whole country will fall into this great hole in the ground."

However, the most common first response seems to be little reaction at all. Shortly after World War I, Marshal Foch visited the canyon accompanied by a large press contingent taking down his every utterance. Foch looked at the canyon, reflected silently for a minute, turned to his host, General Jack Greenway, and quietly said, "Let's have a cup of coffee." Such an unbecoming response would never do, and Greenway translated for the benefit of the delighted press: "Marshal Foch says that the canyon is the most beautiful manifestation of God's presence on the entire earth."

Whatever it is that one first sees, it is not easy to comprehend. Joseph Wood Krutch explains: "At first glance the spectacle seems too strange to be real . . . it is too much like a scale model or an optical illusion." To make matters worse, most visitors have had their vision impaired by too many color photographs. They tend to judge the canyon as real to the extent that it resembles the photographs. I once saw a group of tourists reacting to a splendid sunset at Yavapai Point by turning away and clustering around an amateur photographer to see the results as he developed a Polaroid snapshot.

Some visitors, of course, do succeed as both tourists and writers, in seeing clearly and writing perceptively. The pieces in this section are primarily travel writing, essays by nonspecialists seeing and doing the same things as average everyday travelers.

Two of the four essays describe that most typical of all canyon adventures: a trek down into the canyon on a Fred Harvey mule. A third essay describes a similar trek by packhorse into Havasupai Canyon, while the fourth writer hardly gets close to the canyon at all, admitting that it makes him uneasy and restless even to look at it.

Irvin Cobb was the leading humorist on the old *Saturday Evening Post.* The editor of the *Post,* George Lorimer, was a fervent propagandist for the canyon, and he frequently used the pages of his magazine to crusade for legislation establishing a national park. Lorimer once purchased a Thomas Moran painting of the canyon for his office and was said to judge the character of his visitors by their reaction to the scene.

In 1911, Lorimer sent Cobb out West to visit and write about Grand Canyon. The selection of Cobb's writing that follows appeared in *Roughing It De Luxe,* the book that resulted from that trip. Cobb's exuberant account of a mule trip down the canyon is full of exaggeration and outlandish metaphors in the best humorous style of the day. But it is also a strong and clear account of the sights, smells and sounds of the trail, a trip not much different today than it was in 1911.

Wallace Stegner, novelist and professor of creative writing at Stanford University, is best known in canyon country for his book, *Beyond the Hundredth Meridian,* a definitive assessment of Major Powell and his scientific accomplishments in the West.

Stegner here describes a horseback trip down to Havasu, a side-canyon Shangri-La inhabited by several hundred Havasupai Indians. Life at Havasu has not changed much since Father Garcés visited in the summer of 1776. Stegner's bittersweet account of these Indians and their uncertain future between two cultures applies as well today as when it was written in the 1940s. The selection is taken from his book, *The Sound of Mountain Water.*

J. B. Priestly, the British dramatist and novelist, spent the winter of 1937 at a Wickenburg dude ranch recuperating from a lung ailment. Out of that desert year, he produced *Midnight on the Desert,* a rich blend of autobiography, philosophical ruminations and insights into the Arizona desert. His chapter on Grand Canyon, one of the best and most imaginative ever written, describes two winter trips to the canyon in search of a natural "high," long before that term became synonymous with pills, chemicals and John Denver ballads.

Priestly's first high came standing on the south rim on a stormy day: "As I peered over the far edge of all familiar things, and I saw the storm clouds roll and flash in the gulf below, the rainbows tangled in the hanging woods, the sunlight turning the mist to drifting smoke and the vast shadowy walls into ruined empires, I kept muttering to myself that it had been set there as a sign. I felt wonder and awe, but at the heart of them a deep rich happiness."

Priestly's second and most intense experience came on another trip during an evening at the bottom of the canyon: "As that great half-dome of rock summit brightened to gold and then slowly faded to bronze, was stone and then fire and then stone again, some old hunger of spirit was fed at last, and I was refreshed and at peace."

Like so many other southwestern writers, Haniel Long was a transplanted easterner who put down his literary roots in Santa Fe. He arrived there in 1929, after resigning a teaching position at Carnegie Institute of Technology. He writes of the canyon's spiritual dimension in a more directly religious mode. In a short, adamantine essay entitled "When We Peer into the Colored Canyon," Long compresses God and man and earth, past and present and future into a moving statement of religious faith. The "Colored Canyon" essay was written by Long in 1941 as part of a little-known work entitled "A Letter to St. Augustine after Reading His Confessions."

Long wrote of the canyon on at least one other occasion, in a short chapter for the book *Piñon County,* a widely praised collection of interpretative essays on the Southwest. The ambivalent and uneasy tone of that piece (the canyon "gives me a kind of senselessness and sleeplessness—what I call cosmic vertigo"), also reprinted here, contrasts remarkably with the serene and beautiful prose of "Colored Canyon." More than anything, it illustrates the real difficulties in writing well of so difficult a subject.

Phantom Ranch along Bright Angel Creek at the bottom of Grand Canyon.
The guest ranch, designed by renowned southwestern architect,
Mary Jane Colter, was built by Fred Harvey in 1922.

A Pilgrim Canonized

YOU COME ON THE MORNING of the third day to the Grand Cañon in northern Arizona; you take one look—and instantly you lose all your former standards of comparison. You stand there gazing down the raw, red gullet of that great gosh-awful gorge, and you feel your self-importance shriveling up to nothing inside of you. You haven't an adjective left to your back. It makes you realize what the sensations would be of one little microbe lost inside of Barnum's fat lady.

I think my preconceived conception of the Cañon was the same conception most people have before they come to see it for themselves—a straight up-and-down slit in the earth, fabulously steep and fabulously deep; nevertheless merely a slit. It is no such thing.

Imagine, if you can, a monster of a hollow approximately some hundreds of miles long and a mile deep, and anywhere from ten to sixteen miles wide, with a mountain range—the most wonderful mountain range in the world—planted in it; so that, viewing the spectacle from above, you get the illusion of being in a stationary airship, anchored up among the clouds; imagine these mountain peaks—hundreds upon hundreds of them—rising one behind the other, stretching away in endless, serried rank until the eye swims and the mind staggers at the task of trying to count them; imagine them splashed and splattered over with all the earthly colors you ever saw and a lot of unearthly colors you never saw before; imagine them carved and fretted and scrolled into all shapes—tabernacles, pyramids, battleships, obelisks, Moorish palaces—the Moorish suggestion

From *Roughing It, Deluxe,* by Irvin S. Cobb. George H. Duran Co., 1913. Reprinted by permission of Nelson Buhler, trustee, Laura Baker Cobb Trust.

is especially pronounced both in colorings and in shapes—monuments, minarets, temples, turrets, castles, spires, domes, tents, tepees, wigwams, shafts.

Imagine other ravines opening from the main one, all nuzzling their mouths in her flanks like so many suckling pigs; for there are hundreds of these lesser cañons, and any one of them would be a marvel were they not dwarfed into relative puniness by the mother of the litter. Imagine walls that rise sheer and awful as the Wrath of God, and at their base holes where you might hide all the Seven Wonders of the Olden World and never know they were there—or miss them either. Imagine a trail that winds like a snake and climbs like a goat and soars like a bird, and finally bores like a worm and is gone.

Imagine a great cloud-shadow cruising along from point to point, growing smaller and smaller still, until it seems no more than a shifting purple bruise upon the cheek of a mountain, and then, as you watch it, losing itself in a tiny rift which at that distance looks like a wrinkle in the seamed face of an old squaw, but which is probably a huge gash gored into the solid rock for a thousand feet of depth and more than a thousand feet of width.

Imagine, way down there at the bottom, a stream visible only at certain favored points because of the mighty intervening ribs and chines of rock—a stream that appears to you as a torpidly crawling yellow worm, its wrinkling back spangled with tarnished white specks, but which is really a wide, deep, brawling, rushing river—the Colorado—full of torrents and rapids; and those white specks you see are the tops of enormous rocks in its bed.

Imagine—if it be winter—snowdrifts above, with desert flowers blooming alongside the drifts, and down below great stretches of green verdure; imagine two or three separate snowstorms visibly raging at different points, with clear, bright stretches of distance intervening between them, and nearer maybe a splendid rainbow arching downward into the great void; for these meteorological three-ring circuses are not uncommon at certain seasons.

Imagine all this spread out beneath the unflawed turquoise of the Arizona sky and washed in the liquid gold of the Arizona sunshine—and if you imagine hard enough and keep it up long enough you may begin, in the course of eight or ten years, to have a faint, a very faint and shadowy conception of this spot where the shamed scheme of creation is turned upside down and the very womb of the world is laid bare before our impious eyes. Then go to Arizona and see it all for yourself, and you will realize what an entirely inadequate and deficient thing the human imagination is.

It is customary for the newly arrived visitor to take a ride along the edge of the cañon—the rim-drive, it is called—with stops at Hopi Point and Mohave Point and Pima Point, and other points where the views are supposed to be particularly good. To do this you get into a smart coach drawn by horses and driven by a competent young man in a khaki uniform. Leaving behind you a clutter of hotel buildings and station buildings, bungalows and tents, you go winding away through a Government forest reserve containing much fine standing timber and plenty more that is not so fine, it being mainly stunted piñon and gnarly desert growths.

Presently the road, which is a fine, wide, macadamized road, skirts out of the trees and threads along the cañon until it comes to a rocky flange that juts far over. You climb out there and, instinctively treading lightly on your tiptoes and breathing in syncopated breaths, you steal across the ledge, going slowly and carefully until you pause finally upon the very eyelashes of eternity and look down into that great inverted muffin-mold of a cañon.

You are at the absolute jumping-off place. There is nothing between you and the undertaker except six thousand feet, more or less, of dazzling Arizona climate. Below you, beyond you, stretching both ways from you, lie those buried mountains, the eternal herds of the Lord's cattlefold; there are scars upon their sides, like the marks of a mighty branding iron, and in the distance, viewed through the vapor-waves of melting snow, their sides seem to heave up and down like the flanks of panting cattle. Half a mile under you, straight as a man can spit, are gardens of willows and grasses and flowers, looking like tiny green patches, and the tents of a camp looking like scattered playing cards; and there is a plateau down there that appears to be as flat as your hand and is seemingly no larger, but actually is of a size sufficient for the evolutions of a brigade of cavalry.

When you have had your fill of this the guide takes you and leads you—you still stepping lightly to avoid starting anything—to a spot from which he points out to you, riven into the face of a vast perpendicular chasm above a cave like a monstrous door, a tremendous and perfect figure seven—the house number of the Almighty Himself. By this I mean no irreverence. If ever Jehovah chose an earthly abiding-place, surely this place of awful, unutterable majesty would be it. You move a few yards farther along and instantly the seven is gone—the shift of shadow upon the rock wall has wiped it out and obliterated it—but you do not mourn the loss, because there are still upward of a million things for you to look at.

And then, if you have timed wisely the hour of your coming, the sun pretty soon goes down; and as it sinks lower and lower out of titanic crannies come the thickening shades, making new plays and tricks of painted colors upon the walls—purples and reds and golds and blues, ambers and umbers and opals and ochres, yellows and tans and tawnys and browns—and the cañon fills to its very brim with the silence of oncoming night.

You stand there, stricken dumb, your whole being dwarfed yet transfigured; and in the glory of that moment you can even forget the gabble of the lady tourist alongside of you who, after searching her soul for the right words, comes right out and gives the Grand Cañon her cordial indorsement. She pronounces it to be just perfectly lovely! But I said at the outset I was not going to undertake to describe the Grand Cañon—and I'm not. These few remarks were practically jolted out of me and should not be made to count in the total score.

Having seen the cañon—or a little bit of it—from the top, the next thing to do is to go down into it and view it from the sides and the bottom. Most of the visitors follow the Bright Angel Trail which is handily near by and has an assuring name. There are only two ways to do the inside of the Grand Cañon— afoot and on muleback. El Tovar hotel provides the necessary regalia, if you have not come prepared—divided skirts for the women and leggings for the men, a mule apiece and a guide to every party of six or eight.

At the start there is always a lot of nervous chatter—airy persiflage flies to and fro and much laughing is indulged in. But it has a forced, strained sound, that laughter has; it does not come from the heart, the heart being otherwise engaged for the moment. Down a winding footpath moves the procession, with the guide in front, and behind him in single file his string of pilgrims—all as nervous as cats and some holding to their saddle-pommels with death-grips. Just under the first terrace a halt is made while the official photographer takes a picture; and when you get back he has your finished copy ready for you, so you can see for yourself just how pale and haggard and wall-eyed and how much like a typhoid patient you looked.

The parade moves on. All at once you notice that the person immediately ahead of you has apparently ridden right over the wall of the cañon. A moment ago his arched back loomed before you; now he is utterly gone. It is at this point that some tourists tender their resignations—to take effect immediately. To the credit of the sex, be it said, the statistics show that fewer women quit here than men. But nearly always there is some man who remembers where he left his umbrella or something, and he goes back after it and forgets to return.

In our crowd there was one person who left us here. He was a circular person; about forty per cent of him, I should say, rhymed with jelly. He climbed right down off his mule. He said:

"I'm not scared myself, you understand, but I've just recalled that my wife is a nervous woman. She'd have a fit if she knew I was taking this trip! I love my wife, and for her sake I will not go down this cañon, dearly as I would love to." And with that he headed for the hotel. I wanted to go with him. I wanted to go along with him and comfort him and help him have his chill, and if necessary send a telegram for him to his wife—she was in Pittsburgh—telling her that all was well. But I did not. I kept on. I have been trying to figure out ever since whether this showed courage on my part, or cowardice.

Over the ridge and down the steep declivity beyond goes your mule, slipping a little. He is reared back until his rump almost brushes the trail; he grunts mild protests at every lurching step and grips his shoecalks into the half-frozen path. You reflect that thousands of persons have already done this thing; that thousands of others—men, women and children—are going to do it, and that no serious accident has yet occurred—which is some comfort, but not much. The thought comes to you that, after all, it is a very bright and beautiful world you are leaving behind. You turn your head to give it a long, lingering farewell, and you try to put your mind on something cheerful—such as your life insurance. Then something happens.

The trail, that has been slanting at a downward angle which is a trifle steeper than a ship's ladder, but not quite so steep perhaps as a board fence, takes an abrupt turn to the right. You duck your head and go through a little tunnel in the rock, patterned on the same general design of the needle's eye that is going to give so many of our prominent captains of industry trouble in the hereafter. And as you emerge on the lower side you forget all about your life-insurance papers and freeze to your pommel with both hands, and cram your poor cold feet into the stirrups—even in warm weather they'll be good and cold —and all your vital organs come up in your throat, where you can taste them. If anybody had shot me through the middle just about then he would have inflicted only a flesh wound.

You have come out on a place where the trail clings to the sheer side of the dizziest, deepest chasm in the known world. One of your legs is scraping against the everlasting granite; the other is dangling over half a mile of fresh mountain air. The mule's off hind foot grates and grinds on the flinty trail, dislodging a fair-sized stone that flops over the verge. You try to look down and see where it is going and find you haven't the nerve to do it—but you can hear it falling from one narrow ledge to another, picking up other boulders as it goes until there must be a fair-sized little avalanche of them cascading down. The sound of their roaring, racketing passage grows fainter and fainter, then dies almost two o'clock the following morning; and then she came against her will in a litter borne by two tired guides, while two others walked beside her and held her hands; and she was protesting at every step that she positively could not and out, and then there rises up to you from those unutterable depths a dull, thuddy little sound—those stones have reached the cellar! Then to you there comes the pleasing reflection that if your mule slipped and you fell off and were dashed to fragments, they would not be large, mussy, irregular fragments, but little teeny-weeny fragments, such as would not bring the blush of modesty to the cheek of the most fastidious.

Only your mule never slips off! It is contrary to a mule's religion and politics, and all his traditions and precedents, to slip off. He may slide a little and stumble once in a while, and he may, with malice aforethought, try to scrape you off against the outjutting shoulders of the trail; but he positively will not slip off. It is not because he is interested in you. A tourist on the cañon's rim a simple tourist is to him and nothing more; but he has no intention of getting himself hurt. Instinct has taught that mule it would be to him a highly painful experience to fall a couple of thousand feet or so and light on a pile of rocks; and therefore, through motives that are purely selfish, he studiously refrains from so doing. When the Prophet of old wrote, "How beautiful upon the mountains are the feet of him," and so on, I judge he had reference to a mule on a narrow trail.

My mule had one very disconcerting way about him—or, rather, about her, for she was of the gentler sex. When she came to a particularly scary spot, which was every minute or so, she would stop dead still. I concurred in that part of it heartily. But then she would face outward and crane her neck over the fathomless void of that bottomless pit, and for a space of moments would gaze steadily downward, with a despondent droop of her fiddle-shaped head and a suicidal gleam in her mournful eyes. It worried me no little; and if I had known, at the time, that she had a German name it would have worried me even more, I guess. But either the time was not ripe for the rash act or else she abhorred the thought of being found dead in the company of a mere tourist, so she did not leap off into space, but restrained herself; and I was very grateful to her for it. It made a bond of sympathy between us.

On you go, winding on down past the red limestone and the yellow limestone and the blue sandstone, which is green generally; past huge bat caves and the big nests of pack-rats, tucked under shelves of Nature's making; past stratified millions of crumbling seashells that tell to geologists the tale of the salt-water ocean that once upon a time, when the world was young and callow, filled this hole brim full; and presently, when you have begun to piece together the tattered fringes of your nerves, you realize that the cañon is even more wonderful when viewed from within than it is when viewed from without. Also, you begin to notice now that it is most extensively autographed.

Apparently about every other person who came this way remarked to himself that this cañon was practically completed and only needed his signature as collaborator to round it out—so he signed it and after that it was a finished job. Some of them brought down colored chalk and stencils, and marking pots, and paints and brushes, and cold chisels to work with, which must have been a lot of trouble, but was worth it—it does add so greatly to the beauty of the Grand Cañon to find it spangled over with such names as you could hear paged in almost any dollar-a-day American-plan hotel. The guide pointed out a spot where one of these inspired authors climbed high up the face of a white cliff and, clinging there, carved out in letters a foot long his name; and it was one of those names that, inscribed upon a register, would instinctively cause any room clerk to reach for the key to an inside one, without bath. I regret to state that nothing happened to this person. He got down safe and sound; it was a great pity, too.

By the Bright Angel Trail it is three hours on a mule to the plateau, where there are green summery things growing even in midwinter, and where the temperature is almost sultry; and it is an hour or so more to the riverbed, down at the very bottom. When you finally arrive there and look up you do not see how you ever got down, for the trail has magically disappeared; and you feel morally sure you are never going to get back. If your mule were not under you pensively craning his head rearward in an effort to bite your leg off, you would almost be ready to swear the whole thing was an optical illusion, a wondrous dream. Under these circumstances it is not so strange that some travelers who have been game enough until now suddenly weaken. Their nerves capsize and the grit runs out of them like sand out of an overturned pail.

All over this part of Arizona they tell you the story of the lady from the southern part of the state—she was a school teacher and the story has become an epic—who went down Bright Angel one morning and did not get back until two o'clock the following morning; and she was as hysterical as a treeful of chickadees; her hat was lost, and her glasses were gone, and her hair hung down her back, and altogether she was a mournful sight to see.

Likewise the natives will tell you the tale of a man who made the trip by crawling round the more sensational corners upon his hands and knees; and when he got down he took one look up to where, a sheer mile above him, the rim of the cañon showed, with the tall pine trees along its edge looking like the hairs upon a caterpillar's back, and he announced firmly that he wished he might choke if he stirred another step. Through the miraculous indulgence of a merciful providence he was down, and that was sufficient for him; he wasn't going to trifle with his luck. He would stay down until he felt good and rested, and then he would return to his home in dear old Altoona by some other route. He was very positive about it. There were two guides along, both of them patient and forbearing cowpunchers, and they argued with him. They pointed that there was only one suitable way for him to get out of the cañon, and that was the way by which he had got into it.

"The trouble with you fellows," said the man, "is that you are too dad-blamed technical. The point is that I'm here, and here I'm going to stay."

"But," they told him, "you can't stay here. You'd starve to death like that poor devil that some prospectors found in that gulch yonder—turned to dusty bones, with a pack rat's nest in his chest and a rock under his head. You'd just naturally starve to death."

"There you go again," he said, "importing those trivial foreign matters into the discussion. Let us confine ourselves to the main issue, which is that I am not going back. This rock shall fly from its firm base as soon as I," he said, or words to that effect.

So insisting, he sat down, putting his own firm base against the said rock, and prepared to become a permanent resident. He was a grown man and the guides were less gentle with him than they had been with the lady school teacher. They roped his arms at the elbows and hoisted him upon a mule and tied his legs together under the mule's belly, and they brought him out of there like a sack of bran—only he made more noise than any sack of bran has ever been known to make.

Coming back up out of the Grand Cañon is an even more inspiring and amazing performance than going down. But by now—anyhow this was my experience, and they tell me it is the common experience—you are beginning to get used to the sensation of skirting along the raw and ragged verge of nothing. Narrow turns where, going down, your hair pushed your hat off, no longer affright you; you take them jauntily—almost debonairly. You feel that you are now an old mountain-scaler . . .

CHAPTER
TEN

Midnight on the Desert

AT HEART YOU ARE ONE with all those fools who see life as so many mountaineers must see Switzerland, that is, unendurable, not to be borne for an hour, if it were not for its shining peaks. You do not seem to be close to any summit at present. Your mind is sober and it's wishing it could be drunk again. When will be the next time, and what high moment is on its way? I couldn't answer this. But now both question and answer came together. When and where was the last high moment? It was during our recent trip to the Grand Canyon and while we were on the floor of the Canyon. Both selves agreed, became one again, and remembered.

This was not our first visit to the Grand Canyon. I plunged farther into recollection, and arrived at that first visit. We had planned "a stop-over" of a few hours. Your coach leaves the main west-bound train at Williams, Arizona, wanders up the sixty-four miles to the station at the Southern Rim of the Canyon, doing this during the night when you are fast asleep, and when you wake in the morning—there you are. That is the theory of this "side trip." It did not work well for me in practice. The night that had seemed very convenient and comfortable in the railway time-table was actually most unpleasant. First there were giant shuntings and bangings that made sleep impossible. By the time I had adapted myself to these shuntings and bangings, they stopped, and the train was left paralyzed in an uneasy silence and stillness, a doomed train that whispered, "Sleep no more." In the end I must have slept a little, for I remember

From *Midnight on the Desert,* by J. B. Priestley. William Heinemann, Ltd., 1937. Reprinted by permission of the publisher.

[101]

waking to find that we were somewhere very high and it was snowing. Heavy and hot about the eyes, I put on some clothes, then went blinking and shuffling out into the cold blue morning, a peevish passenger.

The little station looked dreary. The young man waiting with the hotel bus did not look dreary, but he looked all wrong, for he wore a ten-gallon hat and an embroidered cowboy coat with English riding-breeches and long boots, like a cowboy in a musical comedy. The bus turned two corners and landed us at the front door of an hotel that was so tremendously Western that it might have been created by a German scene-designer who had never been farther west than Hamburg. I felt grumpy about all this. A lot of nonsense. The interior of the hotel took my breath away, not because it was very beautiful, but because it was overheated and seven thousand feet above sea-level. I continued to disapprove of everything, but condescended to eat a large breakfast. After breakfast it was still snowing a little and there was nothing to be seen through the hotel windows but snowflakes and mist. I went panting up and downstairs several times, a man in a temper with a large breakfast getting at him, and then very soon it stopped snowing, so I went out. A few paces in front of the hotel there were some seats, a low wall, and then nothing. The world did not extend beyond that wall. Apparently it was a flat world, after all, and here was the edge. I stared over these battlements and saw a few last snowflakes fall into misty space. I walked a few paces through the slush, moving parallel with the wall, and it was wet and raw and there was nothing more to see. I might have been standing on the Thames Embankment on a foggy morning, except that the misty nothing over the edge here had a vaguely illimitable look about it. I decided that I had had enough of this. I threw a last glance over the wall, and then, down there somewhere, there was a swirling, a lifting, a hint of some early creative effort in the mist of Time. The next moment what breath I had left was clean gone. I was looking into the Grand Canyon.

Once I had made sure it really was like that, I hurried back to the hotel, shouted the good news, arranged to stay on, and canceled the seats we had booked in the next train. There was to be no thought of trains. Even this one misty glimpse told me that a miracle had happened. At last, in all my travels, I had arrived and there had been no anticlimax, and my imagination, after weeks or months of expectant dreaming, had not cried, "Is that all?" Reality, stung by my many peers at its poverty, had gone to work to show me a thing or two. I thought I could imagine a better Grand Canyon, did I? Well, cried Reality, take a look at this—and—oh boy!—you ain't seen nothing yet.

It juggled with all kinds of weather for us during that first short stay. We saw snow falling into that vast gulf, saw clouds stream below us, looked down on thunderstorms, stared at Nineveh and Thebes, rusty in the sunlight, coming through the mists, and watched rainbows arch and brighten and fade over the Painted Desert. We seemed to be witnessing, within a few hours, all the mad prodigality of Nature. One stupendous effect was piled on another; veils of mist and broken rainbows were caught in forests hanging in midair; the sunlight far below fell on ruined red cities; and to one hand, across the gulf, was a vertical Egypt, and to the other a perpendicular Assyria. There was in this immensity, although the weathers of four seasons and several climates seemed to chase one another down there, a silence so profound that soon all the noises from the life about us on the Rim were lost in it, as if our ears had been captured forever, drowned in these deeps of quiet. We had only to walk a few hundred yards to find ourselves staring at new gigantic vistas, more forests hanging in the mists, more temples crumbling in the sunlight, more rosy peaks, green chasms, and cloud shadows like wandering stains. But it is useless to try to describe the Grand Canyon. Those who have not seen it will not believe any possible description; and those who have seen it know that it cannot be painted in either pigments or words.

I have heard rumors of visitors who were disappointed. The same people will be disappointed at the Day of Judgment. In fact, the Grand Canyon is a sort of landscape Day of Judgment. It is not a show place, a beauty spot, but a revelation. The Colorado River, which is powerful, turbulent, and so thick with silt that it is like a saw, made it with the help of the erosive forces of rain, frost, and wind, and some strange geological accidents; and all these together have been hard at work on it for the last seven or eight million years. It is the largest of the eighteen canyons of the Colorado River, is over two hundred miles long, has an average width of twelve miles, and is a good mile deep. It is the world's supreme example of erosion. But this is not what it really it. It is, I repeat, a revelation. The Colorado River made it, but you feel when you are there that God gave the Colorado River its instructions. It is all Beethoven's nine symphonies in stone and magic light. Even to remember that it is still there lifts up the heart. If I were an American, I should make my remembrance of it the final test of men, art, and policies. I should ask myself: Is this good enough to exist in the same country as the Canyon? How would I feel about this man, this kind of art, these political measures, if I were near that Rim? Every member or officer of the Federal Government ought to remind himself, with triumphant pride, that he is on the staff of the Grand Canyon.

This incredible pageantry of sunlight and chasm, I thought, is our nearest approach to fourth-dimensional scenery. The three dimensions are on such a scale that some of the fourth has been added. You do not see, hung before you, the seven million years that went to the making of these walls and their twisted strata, but you feel that some elements of Time have been conjured into these immensities of Space. Perhaps it is not size nor the huge witchery of changing shapes and shades that fill us with awe, but the obscure feeling that here we have an instantaneous vision of innumerable eons. There must be the profoundest of silences there because all the noises made through these years have no existence in this instantaneous vision of the ages, in which the longest time that any individual sound could take would be represented by the tiniest fraction of an inch on these mile-high walls.

Strangely enough—and now I am not being fanciful—the only certain example I have of that fourth-dimensional element in dreams, which I described in my account of Dunne's theory, is concerned with this Grand Canyon. After I had spent several hours, staring at it from various viewpoints, I had a growing feeling that I had seen it before. Those exquisitely shadowed reddish pinnacles and domes and towers were vaguely familiar to me. True, I had seen photographs and possibly a picture or two; but as every fellow visitor will agree, the Canyon landscape has a unique and indescribable quality. It was significant, too, that I had not expected to see what I did see, and it was only after I had spent some time looking at it that I began to ask myself why I should feel that somehow once before I had stared at this scene and more or less as I was doing it now, across and down from some high place. Then at last I remembered. Some years before I had had a dream that, unlike nearly all my dreams, had remained in my memory. In this dream I had found my way into an empty theater, one of those colossal and monstrous dream buildings, like the nightmare prisons that Piranesi drew. This theater was so high I could not see the roof, and its tiers of balconies were so broad that they came out of darkness and ran into darkness again. I had climbed up to one of the highest of these balconies, and now looked across the great dark gulf of the building towards the stage. But there was no stage in the ordinary sense, no proscenium, no platform, no curtains. What I saw there was real landscape, and I seem to remember feeling that this was not strange, considering the fabulous wealth and influence of this theater. But the scene itself was quite strange to me, had some of the bright rock-coloring of Egypt and yet was not Egyptian. Now, looking at the Grand Canyon, I knew what I had seen, years before, in that dream. I had—and have—no doubt about it. You may say that my dreaming gaze made a prodigious leap through space, catching a glimpse of the Canyon, half the world away. But I prefer to believe, with Dunne, that the self who stood on that theater balcony had an eye that moved along a Time dimension, not a spatial one, and went forward years, in a second, to share with my future waking self one of the moments I would spend staring down at the Canyon from the South Rim. Possibly there was something in the quality of this experience that lay along my Time One scale in the direction of the Future, that attracted the attention of my dreaming self, my Observer Two, and made him telescope into this dream, as a fitting spectacle for this greatest of all theaters, a glimpse of the most awe-inspiring landscape in the world. Certainly, nothing I had seen or experienced before in America matched this first sight of the Grand Canyon. I felt that God had set it there as a sign. Of what, I didn't know: I made no intellectual response to this challenge. But as I peered over the far edge of all familiar things, and I saw the storm clouds roll and flash in the gulf below, the rainbows tangled in the hanging woods, the sunlight turning the mist to drifting smoke and the vast shadowy walls into ruined empires, I kept muttering to myself that it had been set there as a sign. I felt wonder and awe, but at the heart of them a deep rich happiness. I had seen His handiwork, and I rejoiced.

Now this winter we had gone up there again, all of us this time, by road from the ranch. We filled two motor-cars, with a cowboy at each wheel. After leaving Prescott, we turned away from the main road, zigzagged fearfully among the mountains, and then dropped down into Oak Creek Canyon, where the storekeeper at Sedona was astonished to find his grocery counter suddenly besieged by six English children (all in tattered blue jeans, their parents and their nurse, and two grinning cowboys, demanding bread, butter, meat, cheese, fruit, chocolate, beer, and lemonade. He would have been even more astonished if I had told him that, in my opinion, he and his son and the old-timer smoking his pipe in the far corner were all living in Turner's vision of the Garden of the Hesperides. Oak Creek is Arizona turned idyllic. Here the mountains have married the desert, and their union has been most fruitful. At one moment you are among the firs and the ice-cold waterfalls, and the next moment you are looking down again on sand and cactus. It is said that on one forty-acre lot in Oak Creek you may find firs and figs, trout and cactus, mountain pines and tobacco plants, desert sand and roses. If you filmed the extravagant place, you would be accused of impudent and careless faking. When we ate our lunch there, outside that astonished store, the valley was filled with an exquisitely soft gold sunshine. The hillsides were fresh and green. There was the happy noise of running water everywhere. Around the floor of the canyon, very sharp and bright in the sunlight, were great twisted shapes of red sandstone, looking like ruined fairy-tale castles and mysterious monuments. It was all strangely beautiful, very remote but very friendly, like some place not quite in this world, a lost lonely valley in some antique tale. I felt like saying that at last we had arrived in Avalon and must stay here forever, vanishing from the world that had known us. Why go on? Why make plans and consult time-tables and go on and on when we could sit in the shade of these great oaks and "fleet the time carelessly as they did in the golden world"? Here within a morning's walk were all the climates worth having, with the Highlands of Scotland and Canada within waving distance of Africa and Australia, and the children who were tired of the warm sand and the prickly cactus could go and find fir cones in the snow. And yet this place was not a little bit of everything neatly assembled, but was itself and unique. These giant red sculptured rocks, like the last ruins and monuments of the oldest city in the world, gave the green valley a charm as deeply romantic as that of any South Sea islands I had seen, and it had none of their failings, their clammy messiness, their monotonous sighing palms, their eternal flavorless afternoons. Here was the perfect haven. Why go on?

But after lunch, off we went, corkscrewing over more mountains, plunging into winter again, and in the early dark of that night we arrived at the new Lodge on the South Rim. Its welcome was warm and liberally laced with the smell of pine logs and varnish. The waitresses and the few other guests in the dining-room were entertained by the sight of our rosy English cheeks and tattered jeans and by the splendor of our appetites. The next morning, after arranging to take the older children with us and our two cowboy guides down into the Canyon, we discovered Bernard Shaw and Mrs. Shaw, who had just arrived from San Francisco with a party from a cruise ship. That miraculous elder had just spent two nights in a train, and there he was, at eighty, as pink and bright-eyed as ever, ready to look at anything, go anywhere, contradict anybody. We had known him in England, but the children hadn't, and I found a special pleasure in presenting them to the great and indestructible G.B.S. To meet the Grand Canyon and Bernard Shaw on the same morning—what an adventure! Then the children went rambling along the Rim, and were constantly being photographed by the people of the cruise party, who all thought they had found some genuine young raggle-taggle Westerners and were drolly surprised when they learned, after a question or two, that these picturesque youngsters came from London, too. There was a bookstall in the hotel and I wanted something to take with me into the Canyon, so I had a look at it. Once again the little miracle happened. The very first row of books I saw were novels that had been reduced in price because nobody wanted them. There under my hand was a translation of Franz Kafka's *The Castle,* a novel I had been wanting to read for some time. I knew then that everything was all right, that for a little while the stars were on my side. Into the kit-bag, with my pajamas and tooth-brush and slippers, went *The Castle.* Off we went, four excited children, two vaguely apprehensive parents, and the two cowboy guides, fine young fellows, several miles along the Rim, past snowy pine woods and peeping deer, to the head of the Kaibab Trail.

Here it was that I was first introduced to a creature that is now a character in our family epic. If ever since that day I have been called upon to draw some gigantic bus, airplane, ship, or castle for the younger children, and to show us all enjoying ourselves in the fantastic vehicle or dwelling, then I have had to include this creature. He is part of the domestic legend. He was—and I hope still is—a very large white mule, the largest of the trail mules, specially created by an all-wise Nature to carry my formidable bulk and weight up and down seven thousand feet. His name was Marble. He had two tricks that distinguished him from the other mules and brought him immortality. When he came to a sharp turning in the horribly narrow trail he did not sidle and shuffle around it at once, as the others did, but leaned forward so that his head and neck and shoulders were in midair and his unhappy rider was wondering how soon he would be pitched into the precipice. Sometimes, with shocking malice, he would slowly lower his head over the dreadful edge, so that I would find myself clinging to the saddle-horn and looking down several thousand feet. His second trick was that he would suddenly stop on the trail and try to eat something. Anything would do, vegetable or mineral; he was the coarsest and craziest of feeders; and we began to invent gluttonous feats for him, until in the end we decided that it was Marble who had eaten out most of the Grand Canyon. I spent three days in the company of this strange monster, and came to have a kind of exasperated affection for him, like that of a wife for an incorrigible husband.

Perched gigantically, then, on Marble, I followed the others and found myself descending the south wall of the Canyon. The Kaibab is a new trail that appears to have been blasted and scraped out of the vast rock faces, and there has never been a serious accident on it. After the first half-hour, I began to enjoy it, but during that first half-hour I kept wondering which of us would be hurled first into the rocky gulf. We descended through one geological age after another, and as the afternoon wore on, the very climate changed. The Canyon itself lost nothing of its awful immensity. New chasms and precipices, with richly stained walls, came into view, and behind us the rock face, with great trees that now looked like tiny bushes, climbed to the sky. The trail would go forward to a spur, beyond which was a huge space and a simmering reddish vision of a vertical desert. Into that space the malevolent Marble would push his idiot head while the others, having safely turned the corner, would look back and up and laugh. The cowboys, who had mounted themselves on young fresh mules, would cavort on the edge of nothing, and shout bad jokes to one another and to the children, who were in a slithery, dusty paradise. There was a great deal of dust now and we were in full summer, apparently a thousand miles away from the snowy Rim. The Colorado River, which had looked like a length of string from the top, now seemed a fair-sized stream. The Canyon went up and up, but it also still went down and down. Whole tracts of it invisible from above suddenly arrived, to be zigzagged down for the next half-hour or so. Nothing in this descent diminished the size of the Canyon by so much as an inch. It lost no impressiveness. On every hand it opened out into new marvels of form and color; there was no end to it; what had seemed like dim ruined temples from above now towered as separate sunset-colored peaks, as if a whole mountain range had been tumbled into the vast chasm. But now we had left the sculptured red rocks above and behind us and were sliding dustily down rough tracks of limestone. The Colorado had turned into a menacing broad flood, thick and heavy, like dirty cream. It carries so much silt in it that if a man falls in, his clothes are so heavily saturated that he sinks at once. We could see a suspension bridge over to our right, and immediately below us was the entrance to a tunnel in the rock. This tunnel brought us straight on to the bridge and we went swinging high above the sinister Colorado.

Once across the river, fairly at the bottom of the Canyon, I felt not only that expansion which follows accomplishment, but also a sense of deep satisfaction and peace. It was warm down here—and by this time we were all very dusty, hot, and rather tired—but it was beginning to look green and fresh. We went along the bank of the great river a little way, turned a corner, and passed a camp occupied by the fortunate young men of the C.C.C. who worked in the Canyon, chiefly at keeping the trails in good order. I call them fortunate because winter was six thousand feet above them, they could sit in the sun, they had some decent work to do for the good of their own community, and they were being reasonably well sheltered and fed and paid in one of the most enchanting places on earth. And when I remembered that these brown, husky lads who waved at us were the new American equivalent of the unemployed English youths who stand outside our labor exchanges and at slushy street corners, just miserably kept alive by the dole, I could not see that we could teach the Americans much about social services. It seemed to me, however, that unemployment in this southwest could never be the drab tragedy it is with us, because here there is the sun, and it can never be so hopeless doing nothing and eating little in this sunlight as it is in the rain and sleet. If ever I have to endure neglect and poverty, I thought, I hope I am given sufficient warning so that I can at least crawl into the sunshine, where I shall need less shelter, fuel, food, and clothes, and can at least be warm when I sit and remember past happiness. So, as I jogged rather wearily by the camp on Marble, who seemed as indifferent about ending the journey as he had been about starting it, I felt a sudden deep compassion for my own people, six thousand miles away in the cold rain and fog, and was disturbed by a vague uneasiness, as if my conscience whispered that I should not be here, happy in the sun, when they were still there, in an England that had long ceased to be merry for most of them.

I saw something then, however, that whisked away that uneasiness, and made me want to cry aloud my happiness. This was our lodging for these next two days, Phantom Ranch. It had an orchard bright with blossom. To come at the end of this fantastic journey, hours of rock and dust and giant stone shapes, to this little green place and to find it snowing blossoms there, like May in Hereford, was an enchanting experience. We went to our cabins, washed off the dust and quenched our thirst, then separated, to go birding, to explore, to splash in the stream, in the last hour of full daylight left us. Phantom Ranch is at the entrance to Bright Angel Creek, its bright angel being the clear stream of good drinking water that refreshed the early explorers. It is a beautiful side-canyon, with high narrow twisting walls, exquisitely green along the banks of the stream. There I went strolling, up the Creek, feeling a little sore and stiff after those hours with Marble, but expanded, at ease, and for once in a restless life, at peace. Before I had gone very far, moving slowly, almost luxuriously, and lighting my pipe, the sunlight had crept away from the green depths of the creek and was now high on the walls, lighting up their russet and bronze faces. As I went forward, there came into my view up to the right a magnificent great half-dome of rock, full in the sunlight, and deep gold against the sky. The long descent, the sudden vision of the blossom, the clear running stream, the blue-birds and goldfinches flashing in the green dusk, and now this tremendous sun-crowned rock! Yet it was not the beauty of the place or the hour, though they were beautiful, that I remembered best, but the peace of mind, the peace of heart, I felt as I walked there. Something was due to the mere sense of accomplishment, even though I had done no more than any elderly woman with good nerves and the dollars to spend might accomplish. Something was due to the sense of physical well-being after the exercise I had taken. Perhaps, too, a certain release and expansion after having left Marble and finding myself still whole, for I may have been more apprehensive deep down than I thought I was. And if I am at heart a Romantic, then this tiny green valley, a mile deep and almost in another world, possibly satisfied some hunger of my spirit. So much must be allowed, and to it must be added the sunset loveliness of the scene.

Yet there was something more, some deeper satisfaction still, came then to bring that peace. Remembering our time down there at Phantom Ranch, there returned a series of little pictures: the vast happy-family meals we had in the ranch dining-room; the noisy round games we played with the cowboys after-wards in the recreation room ("Best and liveliest bunch we ever had down here," they said, and we knew that the family had been awarded its highest decoration); the ride up through the narrowing Creek to Ribbon Falls and the picnic there; the deep indigo nights with so many stars hidden by the vast dark-ness of the Canyon walls; my midnight hours in my cabin with Kafka's book, a journey from this strangeness of the Canyon floor to the further strangeness of Kafka's allegorical world, with its tormented land-surveyor hurrying through the dark snowy village streets, trying to find somebody who will admit him into the mysterious Castle, with its vision of bewildered and blundering humanity looking for divine grace, in a tale entrancingly shaped and as haunting as a clear dream, yet with something in it alien and vaguely repellent to me.

All this and more came back to me now, yet the little walk I had up the creek that first evening remained the dominant memory and I found myself constantly returning to it. I remembered very little of what I must have seen, which is one more proof that I am not naturally very observant. I could not re-call what I had been thinking about during the walk, and I suspected, on that account, that for once that busy upper level of my mind, the professional department with its themes and topics and smart debating points, had given itself a holiday. No, all that remained was the quality of that hour, the deep satisfaction, the peace. My memory clung to it as if every step I had taken along that path had been set to exquisite music. The time value was queer, perhaps significant. It lasted hardly any ordinary time at all, at most an hour, yet though I cannot fill its space in my memory with any details of what I saw and thought and felt, it seems to have had more real time in it than some whole years of hurrying and scurrying I have had. Or you can say, with equal truth, that it had a timeless quality; there were no ticking clocks gnawing it away. It is almost like a remembered little life, and a perfect one. As that great half-dome of rock summit brightened to gold and then slowly faded to bronze, was stone and then fire and then stone again, some old hunger of the spirit was fed at last, and I was refreshed and at peace. That I was alone was a mere physical accident, for I do not think the experience came out of solitude and that the soul of it was solitary. It would have been just the same, I believe, if I had gone looking for birds or had idly splashed in the stream with the others. Though I happened to be alone, the others were in this with me, and had they not been there, had they not traveled and arrived as I had traveled and arrived, the experience would not have had this quality. Just as we had shared the trip, so too, I believe, on some mysterious rich deep level of feeling, we were still sharing. Thus the hour was immensely enriched.

Tourists follow switchbacks on the Bright Angel Trail to
go through the steep cliffs of the Red Wall formation

CHAPTER
ELEVEN

Packhorse Paradise

ONE OF THE SPECIAL PLEASURES about a back road in the West is that it sometimes ends dead against a wonderful and relatively unvisited wilderness. The road from Grand Canyon to Topacoba Hilltop ends dead against a ramshackle shed and a gate that closes the bottom of the gulch. The whole place looks less like a hilltop than anything we can imagine, but our Indian guide is there, along with a half-dozen other Indians, cooking beans over an open fire. He waves his hands, white with flour, and says we shall be ready to go in thirty minutes.

Eating a lunch of oranges and cookies and a thermos of milk, we look out from the end of the gulch to the outer rim of a larger and much deeper canyon —possibly the Grand Canyon itself, possibly some tributary or bay. The heat is intense, and light glares from the rock faces and talus slopes. Ahead of us is a fourteen-mile ride into Havasu Canyon, the deep-sunk, cliff-walled sanctuary of the Havasupai Indians.

At twelve-thirty the white-handed Indian, a boy of about eighteen, leads up a skinny packhorse and loads on our sleeping bags, tarps, cooking gear, and the small amount of food we are taking for a three-day trip. He is handy at his diamond hitch, but uncommunicative; his hair grows down over his forehead and he wears big blunt spurs. The horses he brings up look to us like dwarfs, unable to carry our weight, but they do not sag when we climb on. My saddle is too small, and the stirrups won't lengthen to within six inches of where I want

From *The Sound of Mountain Water,* by Wallace Stegner. Copyright 1969 by Wallace Stegner. Reprinted by permission of Doubleday & Co., Inc.

[113]

them; I console myself with the reflection that if I did put them down where they belong they would drag on the ground, the horse is so small.

For a quarter mile we circle the shoulder of a hill, and then, turning the corner, Mary looks back at me as if she can't believe what she has seen. Below us the trail drops in an endless series of switchbacks down an all but vertical cliff. And this is no cleared path, no neat ledge trail built by the Park Service. This trail is specially created for breaking necks. It is full of loose, rolling rocks, boulders as big as water buckets, steep pitches of bare stone, broken corners where the edge has fallen away.

Our guide, whose name turns out to be Hardy Jones, starts down casually, leading the packhorse, and we follow with our seats uneasy in the saddle, ready to leap to safety when the horse slips. We have ridden trail horses and mules before, but never on a trail like this. But it take us less than a half hour to relax, and to realize that our horses have neither stumbled nor slipped nor hesitated. They know all the time where all their feet are. At bad places, with a thousand-foot drop under them, they calmly gather themselves and jump from foothold to foothold like goats.

As we descend, we learn too how these stunted horses got this way. Far up on the canyon walls, among house-sized boulders and broken rockslides, we see wild horses grazing as contentedly as if they were up to their knees in bluegrass in a level pasture. A half dozen of them are in absolutely impossible places, places where no horse could get. But there they are. And there are signs too that surefootedness is not innate: two thirds of the way down we pass a week-old colt dead by the side of the trail at the bottom of a fifty-foot drop. I ask Hardy what happened. "He fall down," Hardy says.

Ahead of us, in the bottom of a wide sandy wash, a wriggly canyon head begins to sink into the red rock. As soon as we enter this deepening ditch, Hardy turns the packhorse loose up ahead to set the pace. He himself dismounts and lies down in the shade with his hat over his eyes. After a half hour he catches and passes us, and after another fifteen minutes we pass him again, snoozing in the shade. I suspect him of all sorts of things, including nursing a bottle on the sly, but I finally conclude I am wronging him. He is simply sleepy. On occasion his yawns can be heard a half mile.

Once or twice he rides up close and starts a conversation. We discover that he is a good roper, and later in the month will ride to Flagstaff to compete in a rodeo. He has three good horses of his own, and he has finished the sixth grade in the Havasupai school. I ask him what he'll take for the pony he is riding, a sightly, tiny-footed, lady-like little mare, and he tells me, I am sure inaccurately, fifteen dollars. Then he asks me what I had to pay for the camera slung around my neck, and when I tell him, he looks incredulous and rides on ahead to take another sleep.

The canyon cuts deeper into rock the color of chocolate ice cream. At times the channel is scoured clean, and we ride over the bare cross-bedded stone. The *Grand Canyon Suite* inevitably suggests itself, and we are struck by the quality of the sound produced by hoofs on sandstone. It is in no sense a clashing or clicking sound, but is light, clear, musical, rather brittle, as if the rock were hollow.

The packhorse leads us deeper into the rock, going at a long careful stride down hewn rock stairs, snaking along a strip of ledge, squeezing under an overhang. It is an interminable, hot, baking canyon, but there are aromatic smells from weeds and shrubs. None of the varieties of trees we meet are known to us. One is a small tree like a willow, with trumpet-shaped lavender flowers, another a variety of locust covered with fuzzy yellow catkins. Still another, a formidable one to brush against, is gray-leafed, with dark-blue berries and thorns three inches long. I pick a berry and ask Hardy what it is. "No eat," he says.

For three hours we see nothing living except lizards and the occasional wild horses grazing like impossible Sidehill Gazinks on the walls. Then around a turn comes a wild whoop, and a young horse bursts into view, galloping up the bouldery creek bed past us. After him comes an Indian boy swinging a rope, and they vanish with a rush and a clatter up a slope that we have just picked our way down as a careful walk. In ten minutes the new Indian and Hardy come up behind us leading the colt, which has a foot-long cut across its chest as if from barbed wire, and which leaves bloody spots on the trail every time it puts its feet down.

Hardy is pleased at the neatness with which he roped the colt as it tried to burst past him. He breaks into a wild little humming chant, accented by grunts and "hah's," a jerky and exclamatory song like the chant of a Navajo squaw dance. As we ride he practices roping the hind feet of the horse ahead of him. After a while we are somewhat astonished to hear him singing with considerable feeling, "Oh, why did I give her that diamond?"

Now on a high rock we see a painted sign, "Supai." A handful of Indian kids whose horses are tied below sit on the top of the rock and wave and yell. We shift our sore haunches in the saddle and wonder how fourteen miles can

be so long. At every turn the tight, enclosed canyon stirs with a breath of fresh-
ness, and we look ahead hopefully, but each time the walls close in around a
new turn. A canyon comes in from the left, and a little brackish water with it,
and there are cottonwoods of a cool and tender green, and willows head-high to
a man on a stunted horse. There is a smell, too, sharp and tantalizing, like witch
hazel, that comes with the cooler air as we make a right-hand turn between
vertical walls.

Then suddenly, swift and quiet and almost stealthy, running a strange
milky blue over pebbles like gray jade, Havasu Creek comes out of nowhere
across the trail, a stream thirty feet wide and knee-deep. After more than four
hours in the baking canyon, it is the most beautiful water we have ever seen;
even without the drouthy preparation it would be beautiful. The horses, which
have traveled twenty-eight miles today over the worst kind of going, wade into
the stream and stand blowing and drinking, pushing the swift water with their
noses. The roped colt tries to break away, and for a moment there is a marvelous
picture at the ford, the white-toothed laughter of the Indian boys, the horses
plunging, the sun coming like a spotlight across the rim and through the trees
to light the momentary action in the gray stream between the banks of damp
red earth.

That wonderful creek, colored with lime, the pebbles of its bed and even
the weeds at its margins coated with gray travertine, is our introduction to
Supai. After five minutes we come out above the village and look down upon
the green oasis sunk among its cliffs. There are little houses scattered along a
mile or so of bottom land, and at the lower end a schoolhouse under big cottonwoods. Men are irrigating fields of corn and squash as we pass, and fig trees are
dark and rich at the trailside. At the edge of the village a bunch of men are
gambling under a bower of cottonwood branches, and two kids, fooling away
the afternoon, gallop their horses in a race down the trail ahead of us.

Both of us have from the beginning had the feeling that we shall probably
be disappointed in Havasupai when we reach it. We have been deceived by the
superlatives of travelers before, and we have seen how photographs can be made
to lie. But this is sure enough the Shangri-la everyone has said it is, this is the
valley of Kubla Khan, here is Alph the sacred river, and here are the gardens
bright with sinuous rills where blossoms many an incense-bearing tree.

When we mount stiffly again and ride on after registering with Mrs. Guthrie, the wife of the Indian subagent, we pass little cabins of stone and logs,
orchards of fig and cherry and peach, hurrying little runnels of bright water, a

swinging panorama of red-chocolate walls with the tan rimrock sharp and high beyond them. Havasu Canyon is flat-floored, and descends by a series of terraces. We camp below the first of these, within fifty feet of where Havasu Creek pours over a fifty-foot ledge into a pool fringed with cress and ferns.

The terrace above our campsite is full of what I take at first to be the twisted roots of dead fig trees, but what turn out to be rootlike lime deposits left by the stream, which used to fall over the ledge here. Probably they were originally grasses and water plants on which the mineral deposit formed a sheath; now they writhe through the terrace, fantastically interwound, some of them six inches in diameter. In the center of each is a round hole, as if a worm had lived there. In these holes and in the rooty crevices is lizard heaven. Geckos and long-tailed Uta lizards flash and dart underfoot by hundreds, as harmless as butterflies.

The same kinds of deposits are being formed under the pouring water of the falls; the whole cliff drips with them. And all down the creek the water has formed semicircular terraces like those at Mammoth Hot Springs in Yellowstone. Each terrace forms a natural weir, and behind each weir the water backs up deep and blue, making clear swimming pools eight to ten feet deep and many yards across. No creek was ever so perfectly formed for the pleasure of tourists. We swim twice before we even eat.

When we crawl into our sleeping bags at dusk, the bats and swallows fill the air above us, flying higher than I have ever seen bats and swallows fly before. It is a moment before I realize that they are flying at the level of the inner canyon walls, catching insects at what seem from the valley floor to be substratospheric heights. For a while we wonder how bats fly so efficiently and dart and shift so sharply without any adequate rudder, but that speculation dwindles off into sleep. Above us the sky is clouded, and in the night, when my face is peppered by a spatter of rain, I awake to see the moon blurry above the rim. For a moment I think a real storm is coming on, until I realize that the noise I hear is Havasu Creek pouring over Navajo Falls and rushing on down through its curving terraces. It is for some reason a wonderful thought that here in paradise the water even after dark is blue—not a reflection of anything but really blue, blue in the cupped hands.

Below our camp a quarter of a mile, past a field half overgrown with apparently wild squash vines and the dark green datura, the Western Jimson weed, with its great white trumpet-flowers, Havasu Creek takes a second fall. Apart from its name, Bridal Veil, it is more than satisfactory, for it spreads wide along the

ledge and falls in four or five streamers down a hundred-foot cliff clothed in
exotic hanging plants and curtains of travertine. The cliff is green and gray and
orange, the pool below pure cobalt, and below the pool the creek gathers itself
in terraces bordered with green cress.

A little below the fall a teetery suspension footbridge hangs over a deep green
pool, dammed by a terrace so smooth that the water pours over it in a shining
sheet like milky blue glass. And down another half mile, after a succession of
pools each of which leaves us more incredulous, the stream leaps in an arching
curve over Mooney Falls, the highest of the three. At its foot are the same tall
cottonwoods with dusty red bark, the same emerald basin, the same terraced
pools flowing away, and below the pools is another suspension footbridge on
which we sit to eat lunch and converse with a friendly tree toad.

It is a long way to the mouth of the canyon, where Havasu Creek falls into
the Colorado in the lower end of Grand Canyon. We stop at the abandoned
lead and copper mine below Mooney Falls, where we ponder the strength of the
compulsion that would drive men to bring heavy machinery piecemeal down
into this pocket on the backs of horses, set it up under incredible difficulties, construct an elaborate water system and a cluster of houses and sheds, bore into the
solid cliffs for ore, and then tote the ore back out miles to some road where
trucks could get it. The very thought gives us packhorse feet, and we make our
way back to camp, yielding to temptation at every pool on the creek until we
have a feeling that our skins are beginning to harden with a thin sheath of lime.
After a day, we are beginning to realize how truly paradisiac the home of the
Havasupai is.

There are in the West canyons as colorful and as beautiful as Havasu, with
walls as steep and as high, with floors as verdantly fertile. There are canyons
more spectacularly narrow and more spectacularly carved. But I know of none,
except possibly Oak Creek Canyon south of Flagstaff, which has such bewitch-
ing water. In this country the mere presence of water, even water impregnated
with red mud, is much. But water in such lavish shining streams, water so
extravagantly colorful, water which forms such terraces and pools, water which
all along its course nourishes plants that give off that mysterious wonderful
smell like witch hazel, water which obliges by forming three falls, each more
beautiful than the last, is more than one has a right to expect.

Yet even Shangri-la has its imperfections, the snake lives even in Eden. As we
are working back from the canyon walls, where we have been inspecting a

small cliff dwelling, we hear the barking of dogs. Below us is a field surrounded by fruit trees, and in the middle of the field, staked out in a line, we find four miserable starving mongrels. Each is tied by a length of chain to a post; at the top of each post is a bundle of branches loosely tied on to give a little shade. Around the neck of each dog is a collar of baling wire wrapped with rags, and near each a canful of muddied water is sunk in the sand. Yelps and whines grow frantic as we cross the field, and out of the bushes at the far end comes a staggering skeleton with a drooping tail. In the brush from which she emerged we find four squirming puppies.

The job of these dogs is obviously to serve as scarecrows, and they are obviously completely expendable. Clearly they have not been fed for days, and none of them can live beyond a day or two more.

The usual Indian callousness toward animals is not unknown to us, and we are willing in theory to accept that cultural difference without blaming the Indians. Perhaps this Indian thought is a good idea to get rid of some of his excess dogs, and at the same time protect his fruit. But our passing through the field has stirred the miserable animals into hopefulness. The tottering skeleton of a mother dog, dragging her dry teats, tries to follow us to camp; the others howl and whine and bark until we feel like running.

Our own food is meager, since we underestimated our appetites when we packed the grub bag, and there is nothing to be bought in the canyon. All we have left to serve us for our last two meals is a can of grapefruit juice, two oranges, a can of lamb stew, four slices of bacon, six slices of bread, and a handful of chocolate bars. The oranges and the grapefruit juice will be of no use to the dogs. Chocolate might make their starving stomachs sicker. The bread and bacon and lamb stew are slim pickings for ourselves.

After a half hour of trying not to hear the howling, I go back and clean out all the water cans, refilling them from the irrigation ditch. None of the dogs is interested in the nice clean water. They are all howling louder than ever when Mary and I start a fire and heat the lamb stew, butter half the bread, lay out the oranges and the chocolate bars for dessert. They howl so loud we can't eat; the stew is gravel in our mouths. We end by spreading two slices of bread with all our remaining butter and taking those and half the stew over to the field. What we bring is a pitiful mouthful apiece, gone so quickly that we wince. Hope has leaped so high in the starving mongrels now that Mary gets three chocolate bars and distributes them. Aware that we are absurd, that our humanitarianism is stupid and perhaps immoral, granting that the dogs have to starve to death day after tomorrow anyway, we carefully divide the meal according to size of dog, and give the skeleton mother a double dose of chocolate.

Then we go home and swim and crawl into our bags, but the dismal howling goes on after dark. It has dwindled off to an occasional sick whimpering by the time we get to sleep, and we have wondered seriously if we should not rather have knocked all nine dogs on the head and paid their owner a suitable fee for the loss of his scarecrows. James Russell Lowell to the contrary notwithstanding, it is a wretched thing either to give or to share when you haven't enough to do any good.

To heighten our disenchantment, we are both bitten during the night by the bloodsucking beetles known locally as Hualpai Tigers, which leave an oozing inflammation about twenty times as irritating as a flea or chigger bite. Next time we come down here we will come with a supply of roach powder.

Not an absolutely idyllic paradise, despite its seclusion and peace and its shining blue water. We see other things when we mount Hardy's horses the next morning and start on our way out. Looking with less eager and more critical eyes, we see girls and women and old men lying on couches in the sun outside the little stone and log cabins. Tuberculosis. We notice among the Supai what Dickens noticed among all Americans a hundred years ago—the habit of spitting all the time and everywhere, even into the creek—and we are glad we dipped our drinking water from a spring. We learn from Mrs. Guthrie that the tribe is less numerous than it used to be, and that it barely holds its own now at about two hundred. A year ago a dysentery epidemic carried off more than half the young children in the village, and measles has been deadly among them.

We learn too that some of the young men, especially those few who served in the armed forces, are restless in the static life of the canyon, and want to get out. We see signs of change in the tractor that the Guthries have had packed in, a piece at a time, and which the Indians can rent for a small fee. We hear speculation about the possibilities of an automobile road into Havasu, and of a guest lodge to be owned by the Indians and run by them and for them, with Indian Service assistance. We hear of the need of increasing the income of the tribe, and of the benefit that increased tourist travel might bring. Out at the fence we hear Hardy Jones, sitting and swinging his big spurs far under the belly of his little mare, singing "Oh, why did I give her that diamond?" which he has laboriously and inaccurately transcribed from the radio onto a piece of cardboard.

The problem of what is best for Havasu—the place and the people—is curiously complex and difficult. If one looks at it purely from the standpoint of conserving natural scenery, the conclusion is inevitable that an automobile road and a guest lodge would spoil a spot that is almost unbelievably beautiful, clutter it with too many people, bring the regulation and regimentation that are necessary when crowds come to any scenic area. Fifty people at one time in Havasu would be all the canyon could stand. The present two hundred visitors a year leave no real mark, but five times that many would. If the conservation of the canyon's charm is the principal end—and this is the view of the National Park Service, which does have a voice in the matter since the Havasu reservation lies within the Grand Canyon National Park—the canyon should be left primitive, a packhorse paradise.

What of the people, the two hundred Havasupai? Those who work with them and see the need for medical care and education and guidance know how difficult it is to bring the tribe even these minimal things under present conditions. Communication is by packhorse and telephone; the mail comes in twice a week, and supplies the same way, on the backs of horses. Though there is a school, Mrs. Guthrie is teaching everyone in it, both primary and advanced pupils, because it is impossible to get another teacher. It is equally impossible to find and keep a doctor and a nurse; when dysentery swept the canyon there was little anyone could do but bury the dead; when the Guthries' own son fell ill last winter he had to be taken out to a doctor by horse litter.

Though at the bare subsistence level the canyon can be nearly self-sufficient, there are considerable and growing needs induced by contact with civilization. There are clothes—because the Havasupai no longer wear the garments of beautifully dressed white deerskin that they used to wear. They wear boots and Levis and shirts and Stetson hats. They like sugar, candy, coffee, radios, dozens of things that take cash; and cash they can now obtain only from two sources: sale of horses or cattle to the outside, or charges at ten dollars a head for packing in tourists. The Guthries are inclined to feel that if the flow of tourists could be increased, and if accommodations could be created for them, the standard of living and health and education of the whole tiny tribe could be raised considerably.

There is no doubt about the truth of that opinion. The canyon could be made a commercial "good thing" with a little promotion, and if the enterprise were carefully watched, the Indians could get the whole benefit. But there is something to be said against this proposal, too. We are morally troubled as we talk about it, for how sure can we be that the loose and indefinable thing called "well-being" will necessarily be promoted by greater prosperity, better education, even better health, when these things may bring with them the dilution or destruction of the safe traditional cultural pattern? Is it better to be well fed, well housed, well educated, and spiritually (which is to say culturally) lost; or is it better to be secure in a pattern of life where decisions and actions are guided by many generations of tradition?

There is a threat that one feels in this paradise. The little tribe with its static life may be at the edge of stagnation, of fatalistic apathy, as some villages of the Hopi are reported to be; it barely holds its own, the dynamics of its life reduced to the simple repetition of a simple routine, its needs few and its speculations uncomplicated. It is easy for that kind of equilibrium to be broken, for that kind of society to be utterly confounded and destroyed by contact with the civilization of white America. It takes intelligence, and patience, and great strength of character, and a long period of time, for any people safely to cross a cultural boundary as these Indians must. Perhaps doubling or trebling the number of tourists in Havasu Canyon each year would not materially increase the danger to the Havasupai. But build a road in, let the gates down on the curious and careless thousands, and the whole tribe would be swept away as the last big flood washed away the orchards of peach trees, introduced by John Doyle Lee when he was hiding from the Federal officers after the Mountain Meadows Massacre.

Yesterday I wanted to take a snapshot of an old Supai packer with bushy hair and prickly thin whiskers. His asking price was a dollar and a half. We finally settled for a half dollar, but even at that price that packer was getting dangerously close to the commercialized status of the Indians who with Sioux feathers in their Mojave or Paiute or Yuman hair wander around in populous tourist spots being picturesque for a fee. There is something to be said for the policy that urges keeping the barrier canyons around this tribe unbridged, for according to the ethnologist Leslie Spier, the Havasupai retain their native culture in purer form than any other American Indians. Other Indians, losing their hold on their native culture, have ceased to exist.

I doubt if there is a clear-cut answer to the problems the Havasupai face. Inevitably there will be more and more intrusion on their isolation, and inevitably they must proceed through the phase of falling between two cultures, of being neither Indian nor white American. If they are lucky, they can make that transition slowly enough so that eventually they can patch up a new order of cultural acceptances taking good things from both the warring cultures of their inheritance. I should say they might learn something from the white man about how to treat animals; they would do ill to lose their own native gentleness in dealing with children. They can borrow the white man's medicine and keep their own simple unspeculative friendliness with the earth. If they are lucky they can do this. If they are not lucky, their paradise might in fifty or a hundred years be like the retreat of old Yosemite, beaten dusty by the feet of tourists, and no trace of the Havasupai except squash vines gone wild in the red earth by a spring, or an occasional goat-wild horse on the talus slopes.

I should not like to be God in this paradise, and make the decisions that will decide its future. But I can hope, looking at Hardy Jones lolling in the saddle, singing, "Oh, why did I give her that diamond?" that on the difficult cultural trail he is traveling no one will crowd him too hard. The trail between his simple civilization and the inconceivably complex world beyond the rims is difficult even for those who can go at their own pace. Hardy has gone part way without apparent demoralization; he listens to his radio and will go to Flagstaff and perhaps win a roping prize. But the smoke-colored colt lying with his neck broken below Topacoba Hilltop is warning what can happen to the too young and the too inexperienced on that path.

In 1903, at the present site of Grand Canyon Village, U.S. Senator
Ralph H. Cameron built this hotel on mining claim land.

When We Peer
into the Colored Canyon

WHEN WE PEER into the colored canyon for light upon the inward mystery of ourselves, we are told what our Lord himself told us, that human life must center its faith in love and in children, or it will leave no trace. It is a good deal for the history of earth to tell us. Yet I am not sure that it is all.

If a person does not fear to look into the canyon and see distance such as he has never seen elsewhere, depth such as he has never dreamt of, and if he becomes lost in shades of gentian and cherry and trout-like silver, watches the unceasing change of hue and form in depth, distance, color, he will have feelings that do not well go into words and are perhaps more real on that account. Through the beautiful obscurities of color he may feel inexpressible realities shining. Or an evanescent thought may come to him, fragile, far away, and yet destined more than great events to shape his own life and sometimes the lives of people near him.

The body of man, the body of earth, they may be part of the same reality. And so, lying beside the Grand Canyon of the Colorado this sunny morning, looking into deeps filled with the quiet and the color of the Ancient of Days, let us in our fancy place the very greatest historical figures, Alexander, Akbar, on the rim of the gulf across from us; they disappear, only a telescope can find them and their irrelevancies. But Francis of Assisi keeps his stature; he collects beautiful stones yonder to mingle with the stones of the Umbrian countryside in the walls of the church eternal. And you, my Bishop? At least, nothing can ever

From *A Letter to St. Augustine* by Haniel Long. Duell, Sloane & Pearce, 1950. Reprinted by permission of Anton V. Long.

dwarf you when you say, "You have made us for Yourself and our hearts are restless until they find rest in You," or when you speak of ". . . our most sweet and dear habit of living together." I wish, almost, that you might have said these words in a million ways, and said nothing else! There is so much to say and too little time to say it in. And so much to listen to, in the stillness of our eternity. And there is never time to listen, really listen, unless one sacrifices the transient and the unimportant to hear it.

We are mammals. We bear children. We beget and conceive the future. We have eluded blind alley after alley where the other mammals lost their way and their secret hope. We are part of the great mystery we call earth, are bound from the past to the future, have learned a few things about cherishing and nourishing that future we bear within us, in the eternity we live in. Now, after earth has said the quiet overwhelming thing it has to say about your school days and all school days, and what should be taught all school children, we see the figure of our Lord standing before us still, only more wonderful, because more honestly ours. They were right, the medieval artists and decorators of books, who pictured him walking among the creatures and the flowers. He is here in the Canyon too, among the clouds and crevices and flowerlike colors. He told us to hold our children in common love in the world of the kingdom in which we can *right now* take care of one another. The teaching of earth blossoms in what he said.

CHAPTER THIRTEEN

The Canyon

After three days Captain Melgosa and one Juan Galeras and another companion, the three lightest and most agile men, made an attempt to go down. They returned about four o'clock in the afternoon, not having succeeded in reaching the bottom. They said they had been down about a third of the way, and that the river seemed very large. Those who stayed above had guessed some huge rocks on the sides of the cliffs might be about as tall as a man, but those who went down swore that when they reached those rocks they were bigger than the great tower of Seville in Spain.

—Castañeda's *Narrative of the Coronado Expedition*

BIGGER THAN THE GREAT TOWER of Seville; the first response by white men to the Grand Canyon of the Colorado. The Spaniard could be vivid when he was startled. Take another phrase from Castañeda, "The country was so flat you could see the sky under the belly of a horse."

The Canyon is beyond a human being's range of response. We can say vivid things, even poetic things, but they make a curious collection when you see a group of them (a little book of things people have said has been printed). I visited the Canyon first by rail, and the porter told me of his first sight of it.

"I took my head in my hands and walked back and forth, moaning, 'How come that big hole thar?'"

From *Piñon Country,* by Haniel Long. Duell, Sloane & Pearce, 1941. Reprinted by permission of Anton V. Long.

Witter Bynner once told me that at his first sight of it he thanked heaven for the relief of an indifferent blue jay wheeling over the depths. Count Hermann Keyserling in *The Travel Diary of a Philosopher* was reminded of something Kant had said, and a few pages later is not sure that he agrees with whatever it was Kant said, for after all Kant had never seen the Canyon. A Chicago business executive took a single look from his hotel window, then pulled down the shade, and never lifted it again while he was there.

The extent to which erosion will go is terrifying. This colored panorama of destruction was caused by a not very big stream carrying silt and pebbles. There is a tiny petrified crab in a case in the museum at Yavapai Point. It was disturbed thousands of feet down, uncovered thousands of years later, by the river. But it is perfect. Lucky crab, to be in evidence at all; we shan't be—that reflection is bound to come to everyone who sees it, I suppose. And as one is sure to have a number of such reflections, bearing on man against the cosmos, I think of the Canyon as first of all an exercise for the intelligence.

Most sensitive persons wherever you meet them are still deep in *Weltschmerz*. The way the Southwest helps is not in its remoteness from the crowded places of our age, as Easterners seem to think. Nothing is remote any longer. You can leave New York at dusk and have breakfast at your dude ranch in New Mexico or Arizona the next morning. What the Southwest does is to remind you constantly of the great age of the earth and the brief span, so far, of the human race.

Once I was talking to Erna Fergusson about the Canyon. She knows it gives me a kind of seasickness and sleeplessness—what I call cosmic vertigo. But she also knows that I go to see it whenever I can. I asked her how she herself handled such a spectacle. She gave me the exact answer I was after. She told me about hearing James Harvey Robinson give the lectures that went into that fine book *The Mind in the Making:*

"Here was a man who thought history should include all human experience, so we could understand the present and deal with it better.

"He did something I've never forgotten. He showed us a clock dial to illustrate human culture on this planet. He allowed twelve hours for the whole show, with today as high noon. That meant our civilization began in Egypt only twenty minutes ago. The Greeks precede us by only seven minutes. Scarcely half a minute has passed since the invention of the steam engine showed that starvation and slavery could be brought to an end.

"It makes it seem foolish to shed tears over the ineptitudes of us babies not yet out of human kindergarten. Maybe not yet even admitted to our kindergarten."

The Canyon, I think, lectures you to much the same effect as Dr. Robinson. You are forever hearing people say that Congress and the President should be made to visit it once a year. Hitler would have been a vastly different man, too, if he had only seen the Canyon. All Americans should be required by law to see it while they are still young and impressionable. Their way should be paid if necessary. Americans need to experience the feeling of time the Canyon gives. We are too much in a hurry. We have funny ambitions. This is the way people talk about the Canyon; they feel it as educational, and able to improve you. If they don't come away obviously improved themselves, and go home and start being better citizens, still they have registered a moral shock of some kind.

Probably we need hope more than the Vitamin B or Haliver oil pills nearly everybody who can afford them takes today. This hope really lives in a lot of little things we are feeling even if we are still in our prekindergarten stage—for example, that we don't like pleasures other people are debarred from because they are sick, or poor, or handicapped. A feeling like that, which comes out in Whitman and Emerson and other American writers, is working inside us in its molecular way, to help build the new world of man. Many things can cause it in us, and among them is certainly the sight of the Canyon. It debunks the ego like nothing else.

Many people make a pilgrimage to the Canyon every year. Once I went there with Gustave Baumann, stopping along the way at the near-by Painted Desert country and the Blue Forest. Those devastated areas are like a million butterflies fluttering in the luminous air, over debris of tortoise-shell. They are like a million leopards leaping on a million zebras in a world of opal. And they are an exceedingly cold world of geometry in which for millions of years the rhomboid has pertained to the parallelogram, and neither to anything else. Utterly irrelevant, and utterly beautiful.

I said to Baumann, "It isn't a million painted butterflies, it's a million gray-blue rhinoceroses of the Heroic-Romantic-Ego ages, perished in a bunch here."

"Looks to me like a New England barnyard turned to stone," he answered.

We got out of the car and took a long saunter down below in the great basin. Red trunks were severed from red thighs, and the heads also lay apart. Gray seaweed or hair comes down from the tops of the mounds. Those shapes—"elephant's guts," Baumann called them, those kidney and liver shapes.

The rhomboid keeps on addressing the parallelogram in ambiguous color.

Miles away on the horizon the high blue heads of mesas rest on sloping shoulders till the mirage guillotines them. Convoluting clouds trail like spray or hair. Where there is only sand very little can grow. Even the sagebrush quits at last, leaving it to the clouds to do something.

Near Lee's Ferry we saw the first signs of the Canyon. We came to a place where everything was parallel and long shadows from the clouds streaked the buttes and brought out unsuspected forms. Baumann began to talk about the Canyon, the nightmare of it from a painter's point of view.

"You see a wonderful composition and when you look back again, it's gone. See how fast those clouds are moving.

"This is the reason nobody can paint the Canyon. There was a fellow came out from Chicago some years ago. He had an eight-foot canvas-stretcher in his car. He said he *knew* he could paint the Canyon.

" 'Have you ever seen it?' I asked him.

" 'No,' he said.

" 'Then take your stretcher and start right back to Chicago.'

"He thought I was trying to keep the Canyon to myself. But four months later he came back. He had his picture, of course, but it was no good, just like everybody else's. He said he kept seeing swell compositions and losing them. He was tired and a little frightened.

"Then there was a woman about ten years ago. At first she did some very nice things, seized little parts of the living country; but she soon grew tired battling with the shadows, and used to sit quietly by a tree and paint the tree."

Last year my wife and I stayed at the Canyon several days. We walked the rim at night, saw the moon come up and drop long streaks of silver and jet into the depths. I could feel no feeling, for I was all chronology, zoology, geology, geometry, algebra, and astronomy. Those outer worlds where I am not at ease captured me. But I broke free the moment we took the road homeward.

THE
SCIENTISTS

The Colorado River near the mouth of Havasu Creek, December, 1911. A tinted version of this photograph appears as the frontispiece on the many editions of the Kolb book *Through the Grand Canyon from Wyoming to Mexico.*

THE GRAND CANYON fairly bristles with questions of how and when. The answers to such questions are by no means obvious. When Joseph Wood Krutch called it "the most revealing single page of earth's history anywhere open on the face of the globe," he might have added that the page can be read only with the aid of geological and biological translators.

One of Powell's early followers, G. K. Gilbert, described the canyon's scientific allure in more precise if less poetic language: "The simplicity of its structure, the thoroughness of its drainage which rarely permits detritus to accumulate in its valleys, its barrenness and the wonderful natural sections exposed in its canyons, conspire to render it indeed the paradise of the geologist."

John Strong Newberry, the Columbia professor who accompanied the Ives expedition, was the first geologist to study the canyon walls and publish a cross section of the strata. Newberry did his studies in extremely trying circumstances, but his work was carefully done and his conclusions remain essentially valid to this day.

John Wesley Powell was the second scientist to study the canyon. As a result of his river trips, Powell made major contributions to understanding the processes of erosion that created the canyon. But Powell's most lasting contribution lay in recruiting and inspiring a group of talented young scientists, including Clarence Dutton, G. K. Gilbert and Charles Walcott, who ignited an explosion of knowledge about the canyon country.

Dutton spent several years mapping the plateau region and formulating the erosional theories set forth in his *Tertiary History*. In 1890, Walcott blazed a trail from the north rim down Nankoweap Canyon and spent the winter contentedly studying the Precambrian strata, totally cut off from the outside world by heavy snows on the rim. By 1891 the canyon was so well known as a geological showcase that Powell and his men hosted a convocation of the International Geological Congress at the south rim.

In the first selection, Edwin D. McKee tells the geological story of the canyon as it has been patiently pieced together by many geologists over the last century. McKee starts his tale two billion years ago, deep in the granites of the inner gorge, and works his way upward, layer by layer, to the rim. From the evidence in rocks and fossils, McKee infers an incredibly long sequence of the rise and slow destruction of immense mountain ranges, ancient seas advancing and retreating across the land, deserts and river deltas and the slow beginning and accelerating evolution of life from primitive one-celled organisms in the ancient Precambrian rocks at the bottom of the canyon.

McKee began his career at park naturalist at the canyon in 1929 where his studies included such diverse topics as the Grand Canyon rattlesnake, the "dwarf" horses of Havasupai Canyon, and the distribution of bird species. But geology was and is his prime interest, and his detailed monograph studies of the rock layers of the canyon have become classics of sedimentary geology. His popular pamphlet, *Ancient Landscapes of the Grand Canyon Region,* from which this selection is taken, has been selling steadily since it was written in 1931.

Many people think of Grand Canyon as an eternal, unchanging part of the land. Not so, says Bill Breed, curator of geology at the Museum of Northern Arizona. In a short essay written for *Arizona Highways,* Breed provides several striking examples of the geological truth—mountains and canyons, just like men, must eventually return to dust.

Breed also explains how a great dam built upstream in Glen Canyon has permanently changed the downstream environment in Grand Canyon, eroding away beaches and clogging the river channel with massive boulders. His message is clear: "The human spirit needs places where nature has not been rearranged by the hand of Man."

For all their efforts, geologists still do not agree on how the canyon was actually formed. The basic problem is that the Colorado River and its canyon were cut directly across a gently upwarped mountain (the Kaibab Plateau) in apparent defiance of the simple law of gravity which dictates that streams must run downhill. Earlier geologists favored the theory that the river came before the mountain and held its course as the country was uplifted, much like a log being pushed through a stationary saw. More recent radioactive dating studies cast serious doubt on that theory, and some geologists now favor a different concept called "stream capture." The controversy remains intense, awaiting a new generation of geologists with new insights.

The biologists, overshadowed by the more obvious geological wonders, got off to a slower start. The first study of lasting importance began in 1890 when C. Hart Merriam, a scientist in the Department of Agriculture, studied and elaborated the "life zone" concept, demonstrating how plant and animal communities vary with differences in elevation. Merriam's studies ranged from the desert environments of the inner canyon up to the 12,000-foot slopes of the nearby San Francisco Peaks.

In the selection printed here, Joseph Wood Krutch discusses the implications of Merriam's pioneering work. Krutch also describes the famous case of the tassle-eared squirrel, showing how the canyon serves as a barrier to migration, causing squirrels on opposite rims to evolve somewhat differently. Krutch was a well-known professor of dramatic literature at Columbia University when he retired to the desert outside Tucson in 1950 to begin a new career as a naturalist. Krutch's southwest books, *The Desert Year* and *Grand Canyon, Today and All Its Yesterdays,* are more than mere science tracts; they are literature and natural philosophy in the tradition of Henry Thoreau. Krutch's unforgettable description, in *The Desert Year,* of the symbiotic relationship between the Yucca and the moth which pollinates it, raises issues that go far beyond mechanistic science. Krutch also worried in print over man's thoughtless destruction of the fragile desert environment. He once summed up that concern: "When a man despoils a work of art, we call him a vandal; when he despoils a work of nature, we call him a developer."

In the third selection, Edwin McKee describes in detail the varied biological communities in each of the Merriam life zones, the trees, shrubs, birds, mammals and reptiles characteristic of each life zone from the cool spruce forests of the North Kaibab down to the hot, dessicated slopes of Granite Gorge. The selection "By the Trailside" is taken from the book *The Inverted Mountains.*

The study of human history and prehistory has lagged behind the other sciences. Early explorers quickly located the two Indian tribes residing in the canyon. Padre Garcés discovered the Havasupai Indians in Cataract Canyon in 1776 and Lieutenant Ives located the Hualapais along Diamond Creek in 1858.

Powell speculated in his journal about the origin of the extensive ruins scattered throughout the canyon. He conjectured that no one would willingly live in such harsh surroundings, thus the canyon must have been populated by

Indians fleeing from Spanish domination. His theories were incorrect. However, his hungry explorers were delighted to discover and raid a Paiute Indian squash garden growing beside the river.

In recent years, archaeologists have begun a systematic study of the hundreds of pueblo sites scattered through the inner canyon with many interesting results. In a chapter reprinted from the book *The Grand Colorado,* Robert Euler first tells the fascinating story of the mysterious split-willow figurines found in caves throughout the canyon country and only recently discovered to be of very great antiquity. Euler himself added to scientific knowledge of figurine culture while excavating Stanton's Cave, the very cavern in Marble Canyon where Stanton had stashed his supplies before retreating to the north rim in 1889.

Euler also sketches the emerging outlines of the Great Pueblo occupation of the inner canyon from about A.D. 700 to A.D. 1200, speculating about the ways in which the Indians adapted to this harsh environment, their routes of travel, methods of agriculture and seasonal migrations. As we learn more of these ancient canyon dwellers, the words of Paul Horgan seem especially apt: "They solved with restraint and beauty the problem of modest physical union with their mighty surroundings."

Ancient History
of the Grand Canyon

THE ARCHEAN ERA

LOOKING INTO THE DEPTHS of Grand Canyon from any point within the Bright Angel section, one is immediately impressed by the narrow V-shaped gorge cut in the black rocks at the bottom. This is popularly termed the Granite or Inner Gorge. Within its walls one is in another world, both scenically and geologically. Their steep, bare sides, whose surfaces are chaotic in the extreme, have a history—long and complex. The rocks of which they are formed—some of the oldest known today on the surface of the earth—partially tell the story of the first great era in geologic history.

Other rocks of this, the Archean age, are found in the Rockies, in the Adirondacks of New York, and to a very great extent in eastern Canada. In the last named place they contain valuable deposits of iron, nickel, cobalt, and copper. Rocks which probably also correspond in age occur in Scandinavia, Brazil, China, India, and Central Africa.

At the Grand Canyon, although we are impressed by the depth of the dark Archean rocks, beneath the plateau surface approximately a mile, yet we marvel even more when we contemplate their great age and the important series of events whose history they partially record. Built up originally as great horizontal deposits of sand and mud, they were bent by mighty crustal movements until high mountains, probably comparable to the present Alps, were formed. Pres-

From *Ancient Landscapes of the Grand Canyon Region,* by Edwin D. McKee, 1931. Reprinted by permission of the author.

sures from the northwest and southeast apparently folded them. The rocks themselves were greatly compressed and heated, with the result that complete recrystallization and the development of a banded structure were brought about. The present vertical altitude of these ancient beds, together with their dense crystalline character, is evidence of the great depth at which they were formed and of the extreme pressures to which they were subjected. In brief, the rocks that we see today in the Canyon bottom represent merely the roots of once lofty mountains, and the flat surface cut on these rocks is an old plain that resulted from the wearing down of high country in this region.

As yet no definite traces of either plant or animal life have been found in rocks of the Archean age in Grand Canyon. Though various forms of life may have existed then, and may have been preserved in the original rocks, their record has since been entirely removed by those extreme pressures which altered even the composition and structure of the rocks themselves.

Within the black, crystalline rocks of the Inner Gorge may be seen many large streaks, bands or irregular masses of a lighter color. From the Canyon rim these appear white, but from nearby they are usually pink. These light colored rocks are granites with a coarse crystalline texture.

Granites derive their name from their granular texture. They are formed by the slow cooling of molten masses that have been forced into older rocks from the earth's interior. From a similar source are formed lavas and volcanic ash, but these flow out or are ejected on the surface of the earth where they cool so rapidly that no crystals form. Exceptionally fast cooling or chilling of molten masses, moreover, forms volcanic glass or obsidian. It is by the application of this same principle that crystal forming is prevented in the manufacture of common glass.

The large size of the crystals forming the granite that fills cracks and fissures of the Inner Gorge at Grand Canyon indicates the considerable depth at which it was formed and is further evidence of the great mountains that existed in this region during the first era in geologic history.

THE ALGONKIAN ERA

Rocks formed during the second great era of the earth's history are distinctive in several respects. They are not highly altered or completely changed in form and structure as are those of the oldest era, but are largely free from such changes and, for the most part, similar to rocks which are seen in the process of formation today. Furthermore, they are known to contain definite traces of plant life, though no certain forms of animal life have yet been found in them. They represent a period probably as great as all of subsequent time.

Along Bright Angel Canyon and in several other places in the Grand Canyon, rocks of Algonkian age, representing accumulations of sediments several thousand feet in thickness, are found. Below and to the north of Desert View (southeast of Cape Royal on the North Rim) they form the open floor of the Canyon. Everywhere the most conspicuous stratum of this series is a mud rock of brilliant vermilion color. However, the rocks also include a conglomerate or pebble layer, a dark limestone formed principally by plants, and a purple quartzite made by the consolidation of the grains of a sandstone.

FORMATION OF MOUNTAINS
(THE ALGONKIAN ERA)

The Algonkian rocks of the Grand Canyon region were bent and broken into mountains at an early date. In many places sloping layers showing the steep angle at which they were tilted are easily visible, even from the Canyon rim. Folded areas and strata which have been shattered are also conspicuous features here and there. The mountains which they formed, however, are now missing for they were worn away in large measure by slow erosion. Today only remnants—small hills on a general level surface—remain in the lower parts of Grand Canyon to tell the story.

EARLY CLIMATES
(THE ALGONKIAN ERA)

The rocks of Algonkian age are roughly estimated to be at least six or seven hundred million years old, yet from all indications they were formed under conditions of climate not unlike those of far later periods of history. In several parts of the world traces of great ice sheets—glaciers which scratched and eroded the surface—are found preserved in Algonkian rocks. In other places, including the Grand Canyon, ancient flows of lava are found where they gushed out upon the surface of an old land mass. Among the rocks below Desert View (Navajo) Point and bordering on the Colorado River may readily be seen several black cliffs formed by the volcanic activity of this early age.

The brilliant red shades of Algonkian age found in the lower parts of the Grand Canyon were formed as muds, accumulated probably by large rivers. In these muds are found preserved great quantities of ripple marks, indications of changing currents, also the moulds of salt crystals, and large shrinkage cracks resulting from a very hot sun. In brief, these criteria point toward a hot and probably arid climate in this region during that chapter of history.

OLDEST KNOWN LIFE
(THE ALGONKIAN ERA)

The oldest forms of life represented in rocks of Grand Canyon are found in strata of the Second, or Algonkian, Era. Certain layers of limestone showing peculiar structural patterns on their surfaces are interpreted as being the reefs built up through the activities of primitive one-celled plants known as algae. Similar structures are being formed today by plants of this type. Near Harper's Ferry, West Virginia, for example, algae are building up limestone layers almost identical to the fossil ones found in the Algonkian rocks of Grand Canyon. In this connection, it is interesting to note that because of this similarity of the present to the past, the reality of the ancient plant structures was recognized a few years ago. They were discovered at a place in the Grand Canyon just west of the mouth of Bright Angel Creek.

THE PALEOZOIC ERA

It was during the third or middle chapter in the earth's history that all of the apparently horizontal, upper layers in the Grand Canyon walls were formed. As will be seen in the succeeding pages, some of these rocks are sandstones formed from the sands of early beaches or sand dune areas, other are shales—the hardened muds of ancient river deltas—and still others are limestones built up by accumulations of plant and animal remains on sea bottoms. All are rocks formed by the deposition of sediments by wind and water during vast intervals of time. In them have been hidden and preserved many forms of life. Seashells, footprints, fern impressions, and various other traces of early plants and animals remain to tell the story of these ancient times. It is of special interest to note that in rocks formed during the earliest part of this chapter are found the first definite traces of animal life, that in other rocks of this chapter have been found evidences of primitive fish, and that in the most recent rocks of this group occur the traces of early reptiles, insects, ferns, and cone-bearing plants. In the walls of Grand Canyon examples of all of these fossils have been found, and these will be described in detail in the succeeding pages.

FIRST ANIMAL LIFE—THE TONTO ROCKS
(CAMBRIAN PERIOD)

Great highlands which were formed in the Grand Canyon region during the Second Era of history were afterwards gradually worn away by erosion until near the start of the next era a flat, almost featureless plain existed. Here and there, however, isolated hills of dark, crystalline rocks of the First Era stood above the general surface, as seen opposite Yaki point. In other places, such as to the west of where Bright Angel Creek now flows, small mountains of red Algonkian rocks (Second Era) remained. Around and against these, sediments were then deposited. Pebbles and sands accumulated, forming a thick layer which today appears as the brown sandstone rim of the Inner Gorge. These represent the first deposits of the Third Era. But the sea was encroaching upon the land during this period, and gradually the sand deposited near shore was covered by mud and this in turn by lime far out from the beach. Today this series of sand, mud and lime is found represented in the rocks of the Tonto Platform in Grand Canyon.

Along the Tonto Trail a few hundred yards east of Indian Gardens numerous primitive sea animals have been found buried and preserved in layers of thin shale. Many of these are creatures with rounded shells smaller than the nail of a person's little finger, others are animals related to the snail, and still others are crab-like creatures known as trilobites. The trilobites undoubtedly were the rulers of that age for they excelled not only in numbers but in size. Some specimens from Grand Canyon have measured over three inches in length. Despite this size, however, the trilobites and their associates from the Tonto Platform represent some of the earliest known forms of animal life.

THE MISSING PERIODS OF THE THIRD ERA
(ORDOVICIAN AND SILURIAN PERIODS)

The geologist has found that two long periods of history are lacking in the great succession of ages represented by the strata in the Grand Canyon walls. These missing periods which belong to the Third Era are known as the Ordovician, the time when fish first appeared in the seas, and the Silurian, the time when millipedes and scorpions became our first air breathers. These ages immediately followed the Cambrian and involved millions of years. The absence of the first of them is explained by some geologists as the result of its rocks having been completely worn away at a later time. It seems more probable, however, that the Grand Canyon region was above sea level during these two ages so that no sediments were accumulated and consequently no rocks formed.

THE AGE OF FISH
(DEVONIAN PERIOD)

During that period of geologic time commonly known as the "age of fish," sands and limes were accumulated on the surface of the Grand Canyon region filling in old river channels and burying the bodies of fish and other animals. The deposits formed at this time were later eroded to a large extent. The surface of the land was worn and washed away, until finally only isolated patches or pockets of limestone and standstone remained. These we find today exposed in the walls of the Grand Canyon occurring just at the base of the great Redwall cliff in about fifteen different localities.

Although fish were rulers of the age during Devonian times, they were of primitive types and apparently depended for defense upon bony skin armour rather than upon speed. The plates and scales of fresh-water fish have been found preserved in the lavender rocks of this age in the Grand Canyon.

One of the most prominent and conspicuous features of the Grand Canyon is the great red cliff of limestone about midway in its walls. This cliff is the highest in the Canyon—averaging about 550 feet in the area of Bright Angel Canyon. In most places it is almost vertical, and in some it even overhangs to such an extent that a visitor once aptly said, "The Washington Monument might be placed beneath it and kept out of the rain."

To the prospector this formation is known as the Blue Lime; to the geologist it is the Redwall Limestone. Both are correct. Actually the rock is a rather pure limestone of a grey or bluish color, but in most places where seen, its surface has been stained a bright red by iron oxides from above. It appears throughout the Grand Canyon as a wide band or ribbon of red.

Large amphitheaters, many curving alcoves, caves, and solution tunnels are all characteristic features of the great Redwall. It is composed of relatively pure lime so rain and other waters have a chemical action upon it—they leach and dissolve it. Waters all tend to drain toward curving centers, and so increase this curving. Everywhere the rounding off of corners takes place. Thus has the graceful form of the Redwall been brought about.

The origin of the Redwall Limestone is as interesting as its form. The purity of the lime indicates that it was built up in a relatively wide and quiet sea. Its composition represents a vast accumulation of the skeletons of ancient plants and animals. Seashells are found in great numbers, some of them preserved in delicate detail. These and other forms of ocean life clearly indicate that a great sea connection then existed between this region and that of western Canada to the north.

TRACKS IN THE SUPAI SANDSTONE
(PERMIAN PERIOD)

During that period in geological history known as the Permian, when some of the beds of soft coal in eastern America were being formed, a large area in northern Arizona was receiving red sediments from the east, probably carried by rivers from the granitic highlands of that region. Today these sediments appear in the Grand Canyon walls as alternating layers of red sandstone and shale immediately above the great Redwall. They are almost a thousand feet in thickness.

When the red beds were accumulating in this region, the climate probably was more or less arid; the vegetation consisted principally of ferns and other lowly plants; and the animal life included a group of large but primitive four-footed creatures. Numerous tracks of the latter, preserved in the walls of Grand Canyon, have provided one of the most interesting discoveries of recent years. Some of these footprints are several inches in length, and the number of toes varies between three and five. They show no close relationship to the tracks of other localities, and apparently represent a fauna new to North America.

Concerning the conditions under which the topmost red stratum of the Grand Canyon (the Hermit Shale) was formed, and the means of its formation, we have today a rather definite and interesting picture. A wealth of fossil plants and a number of tracks of animals have been found excellently preserved in its muddy layers, and by means of these and other indications the following conclusions have been drawn.

The Hermit Shale represents accumulations of mud and fine sandy material deposited probably by streams flowing from the northeast. Here and there are found evidences of pools and arroyos with wavy ripple marks on their borders and a thin film of shiny slime covering the surface. The trails of worms, the footprints of small salamander-like animals, and the fronds of ferns, mostly mascerated or wilted, are found delicately preserved in this slime. Raindrop impressions, the molds of salt crystals and numerous sun-cracks also add to the picture. This region has been described by Dr. David White as "the scene of showers, burning sun, hailstorms, occasional torrents and periods of drought and drying up of pools" during Hermit times.

Thirty-five species of plants are at present known from the Hermit Shale of Grand Canyon. Many of these have not been found elsewhere in the world, though some were representatives of European plants, and others had their closest relations in Central Asia, India, Australia, Africa, and South America. This fossil flora consists principally of ferns and small cone-bearing plants, all of which were relatively dwarfed in size and appear less dense than those of corresponding age found in eastern America. They apparently indicate a semi-arid climate with long dry seasons, for the absence of moist-climate and swamp-loving types is noticeable.

Several insect wings have been found in the Hermit Shale, one of which was four inches in length. Numerous footprints of vertebrate animals have also been found, and undoubtedly represent an interesting fauna.

WIND-BLOWN SAND—THE COCONINO
(PERMIAN PERIOD)

The light-colored formulation which appears as a conspicuous ribbon-like band around the upper part of the Grand Canyon has long presented a puzzle concerning its origin. The grains of white sand of which it is composed apparently were deposited at steep angles, for the many and varied slopes which were formed may be readily seen today on the surface of the rock. These slopes were probably once the lee sides of sand dunes deposited by winds in an area bordering the sea. We find the only traces of life in this formation represented by the trails of ancient worms and insects, and by the foot-prints of early lizard- or salamander-like creatures. Already the tracks of some 27 species of animals have been discovered in this sandstone within the Grand Canyon, though strangely enough no bones have yet been located.

WARM SEAS FROM THE WEST—THE TOROWEAP
AND KAIBAB FORMATIONS
(PERMIAN PERIOD)

Along both sides of Grand Canyon at the top, two buff and gray layers of limestone stand out as massive cliffs separated by a tree-covered slope. The upper of these limestones forms the plateau surface and may be seen for a great distance in every direction. Both layers were formed as the result of vast accumulations of organic and sandy materials on sea bottoms, and in places are composed largely of the remains of marine life—shells, corals and sponges. The teeth of sharks have also been found in the upper limestone.

During the early stages of the period when these marine animals lived and multiplied in the region, a great body of salt water extended over its surface from far to the west, remained briefly, then retreated from the area. Soon, however, marine waters advanced once more and another sea was formed with its shoreline extending eastward even beyond the region in which we now find Grand Canyon. Evidences of the second and larger sea are found beyond Flagstaff to the south, in the Painted Desert to the east, and almost to Zion Canyon to the north.

The presence of corals and sharks' teeth not only indicate that this region was covered on more than one occasion by marine waters, but also suggests that these seas were warm and shallow. This is estimated to have been some 200 million years ago.

Upper Phantom Creek and Canyon

CHAPTER
FIFTEEN

Our "Unchanging" Canyon

IN A WORLD OF RAPID CHANGE, stability is an elusive shadow that is more and more difficult to find. Who of us has not gone back to a warmly remembered place of our youth to find a favorite climbing-tree chopped down, a childhood home remodeled or demolished, a familiar woods replaced by tract housing, shopping or industrial center, or parking lot? Change seems inevitable, yet we seem to *need* places to which we can return and find familiar even after 10 years, or 15 years, or 50 years.

Perhaps our desire for unchanging places explains why America's national parks are so popular, why so many of us return again and again to the same park. For parks supposedly are, after all, preserves officially set aside from change, places that we can always come back to—and they will always look pretty much unchanged.

Among our parks, the Grand Canyon National Park in northern Arizona seems to be as unchanging as any of them. However, even a place like the Grand Canyon itself, which to the casual eye appears unchanging even over a long lifetime, is actually undergoing constant change—change caused by nature and change caused by Man himself. Let's look at some of the past changes and those now underway in our "unchanging" Grand Canyon of the Colorado River.

The horizontal layering of rocks in the Grand Canyon vicinity reveal the area was a flat plain for several hundred million years before the beginnings of

"Our 'Unchanging' Canyon," by William J. Breed. *Arizona Highways,* May, 1976. Reprinted by permission of the author and *Arizona Highways.*

the Grand Canyon itself. At various times the area was below sea level, a fact recorded today by the presence of fossilized marine organisms in the sedimentary rock. Much of the time the land was above sea level and received deposits of mud and sand from ancient rivers; a great thickness of sediments of varying color and composition was accumulated over those millions of years. The deposited layers were transformed by heat and pressure into rock. Tracks of reptiles and amphibians are preserved in the layered rocks, along with impressions of the primitive plants that also flourished in long-past times. As the land was slowly raised by great forces within the earth, the Colorado River, in its passage to the sea, began to carve into the layered rocks. Slowly—ever so slowly over millions upon millions of years—the land rose and the great river scoured its ever-deepening channel. The rims of the great chasm are now approximately a mile and a half above the level of the sea; today, the upper walls of the Grand Canyon tower a mile or so over the river whose unceasing energy has carved it and changed it—indeed, which it continues to do to this day.

Almost-imperceptible natural changes are made in the Canyon's surface soil and rock each time water freezes or rain falls in the Grand Canyon. Water, by chemically dissolving part of the rock and by transporting particles of rock downhill toward the Colorado River, causes side canyons to grow slowly in width and depth. (Keep in mind that all the major side canyons, where they join with the River, are just as deep as the Canyon itself!) That same rainwater results in the erosion which can be seen in the tributary canyons of the Colorado River in the Grand Canyon, for the boulders and pebbles at the bottom of such canyons were once part of the towering walls of the Grand Canyon.

A particularly dramatic example of natural change occurred in 1966 when more than sixteen inches of rain fell within 36 hours on a limited area of the North Rim. The resulting flash flood which roared down the canyons of Bright Angel and Crystal Creeks caused major changes in the Grand Canyon. A new pipeline under construction in Bright Angel canyon (to furnish water to the South Rim facilities from Roaring Springs via Phantom Ranch and Indian Gardens) was severely damaged and nearly swept away. So much material was tumbled down Crystal Creek and spewed into the Colorado River that a major and particularly violent rapids was created in the River itself.

Man, too, has changed the Canyon. The swarming of people to the Rim areas, onto the trails and adjacent wilderness, the river-running and attendant camping upon the River's banks and beaches, all directly contribute to changes of the Canyon by exposing previously-inaccessible areas to heavy human traffic.

Some of our man-made changes are obvious, while others are more subtle; how many times can a trailside or riverside plant be stepped upon, before it dies?

Some of these changes are not so direct. Perhaps the single most drastic man-made change that has affected the Canyon, and particularly the River, was the completion in 1963 of Glen Canyon Dam just below the Utah line upstream of the Grand Canyon. Even before the waters started to collect behind the new dam to form Lake Powell, it was realized—too late—that the new dam and lake would drastically alter the Colorado River downstream of the dam. Although considerable time and money was spent studying the geology, animal and plant life, and Indian ruins which would be affected by the rising waters *upstream* of the dam, apparently little consideration was given potential changes which might occur *downstream* of the dam.

Before it was dammed upstream, the Colorado River used to roar, untamed, through the Grand Canyon in periodic spring floods with snowmelt from the Rockies, and in late summer floods due to overabundance of rainfall upstream. It was a turbulent, muddy river, "too thick to drink, too thin to plow." Tremendous quantities of mud, silt, sand, and rock were moved through the Canyon; these were the cutting tools, the scouring agent which enabled the River to wear down the land and rasp a mighty gash in the earth to create the Grand Canyon.

Since 1963, however, all this has changed. The River is tamed. It is no longer muddy, for the rocks and boulders which formerly would have tumbled along the river channel are now buried in the sediment of Lake Powell. There are no more swirling floods raging through the Canyon—only the man-made "tides," created by distant Bureau of Reclamation engineers in satisfying the daily electric power demands of Phoenix and Los Angeles. Even the temperature of the River has been controlled; it's neither tepid in summer anymore, nor cold enough to freeze in winter. For the clean, tamed water now comes from deep in the new lake behind the dam, its temperature almost constant year-round.

What effect have these changes in the River had on the Canyon? Were he alive today, Major John Wesley Powell (leader of the first organized passage through the Canyon, in 1869) would be startled by the changes. The periodic floods which used to race through the Canyon have been stopped by the dam. Because of the absence of the sweeping floods, permanent vegetation can grow along the river for the first time. The banks of the River are now crowded with willow, an occasional cottonwood, and particularly with tamarisk, a foreign plant introduced into the Southwest around the turn of this century. This vegetation, in turn, has allowed species of birds and animals which formerly could not survive there to live in the Canyon. Such changes in the plant and animal life of the Canyon are being noted and studied by the Museum of Northern Arizona; it's unfortunate that a complete scientific study of Canyon life was not made prior to construction of the dam. The Museum can determine what is there *now,* but it's difficult to determine and scientifically reconstruct what was there *before.*

Other changes in the Canyon are perhaps not so noticeable. The statistics about how much material the Colorado River used to move through the Canyon are astounding: an average of 500,000 tons per day, enough material to fill 2,000,000 quarter-ton-capacity pick-ups! It's also interesting to contemplate that the River has been moving that amount of material through the Canyon each year for the past 8 to 10 million years (since 1963, though, the River's dissolved load has averaged but 80,000 tons daily). Now, however, there's a different River flowing through the Canyon; a River no longer forceful enough to move large boulders, but still hungry for silt, mud, and sand. The River thus tends to remove the sand from the old beaches that line its ancient course, but is incapable of occasionally moving the large rocks and boulders which compose the rapids which ruffle its smooth course within the Canyon. Thus the rapids tend to grow larger from deposits brought to the emasculated River from its still-virile tributaries, while sand beaches built up along the riverbank by countless past floods tend to be swept away downstream and disappear.

Man has been responsible also for some other subtle but significant ecological changes, particularly in the western portion of the Grand Canyon. Early-day prospectors and miners searching for precious metals brought in burros to carry their gear and supplies. The miners left, but the burros stayed on, and multiplied; in fact, the burros' adaptation to the Canyon has been so successful that they have diminished the diversity of other animals and plantlife within their range, thereby making survival much more difficult for other wildlife such as the bighorn sheep.

An "unchanging" Grand Canyon? Certainly not! It should be apparent that the Grand Canyon is a product of natural change and that even the seemingly momentous changes that we see in the Canyon and River today are trifles in the total long-term geologic picture. However, we should be careful to keep Man's changes to the Canyon at a minimum. Animals from trilobites to dinosaurs to sharks have lived in this area, but Man is privileged to be here when the events of the past have culminated in the scenic masterpiece that we know as the

Grand Canyon. We are now entrusted with the preservation of the Canyon for a moment in its long history. There are some among us who feel that the Canyon would be made more "useful" by building more dams, turning part of the Canyon into a lake supplying even more electric power to the Southwest. Others would like to build tramways into the Canyon, or cut additional roads to make the Canyon more "accessible."

Sometimes, though, in making more areas of the Grand Canyon accessible, we destroy what we went there to experience in the first place. The human spirit needs places where nature has not been re-arranged by the hand of Man. These places, with which the Grand Canyon area is still uniquely blessed, certainly should be preserved. Preserved to refresh, preserved to educate, preserved to inspire and fulfill the future inhabitants of this fragile planet.

In Granite Gorge below Sockdologer Rapid, December, 1911

Thus Far Shalt Thou Go

CARDENAS, THE FIRST WHITE MAN ever to approach the Canyon, spent five or six days trying to find his way down into it and then turned back in despair. Unknowingly, he was doing only what many different animals—and for that matter, many plants—had been doing before him during thousands of years. Thus the Canyon is, among many other things, one of the most effective of the barriers which shut off one habitable area of the earth's surface from another.

Few mountain ranges are as effective, because they seldom stretch for so long a distance without a pass through which the persistent can make their way. And though even the Canyon once had (toward the shallower east end, where climbing is possible) a ford known as Horse Thief Ford because of the stolen horses led to safety from Utah to Arizona or vice versa, this was the only crossing known. And only a horse thief would risk it.

Even today, when good roads lead the long way around both ends, the Canyon still functions as a physical as well as a psychological barrier between human as well as natural communities. The region to the north, commonly known as "the Strip," is cut off from the rest of Arizona and is nearly empty. The few scattered inhabitants came mostly, like the flora and fauna, from Utah to the north, and they are so isolated that a little band of heretic Mormons could establish at Short Creek an independent community where they practiced exuberant polygamy and in general defied the authority of the national govern-

From *Grand Canyon, Today and All Its Yesterdays,* by Joseph Wood Krutch. Columbia Unisity Press, 0900. Reprinted by permission of the publisher.

ment for years until in 1953 a raiding party (dubiously justifiable, as many thought) broke it up.

Man, being the most mobile of animals and also the only one to have developed a science of logistics, has by now flowed around the ends of the Canyon and so, though he still rarely crosses the barrier, he has mingled with his fellows on the opposite side. On the other hand, some plants and animals have never crossed the barrier at all, and the Canyon marks the limit of their distribution, northward or southward as the case may be. They cannot make their way, not even slowly in the course of generations, down one side and up the other, because the journey would carry them through regions where for one reason or another—unsuitable climate, lack of the accustomed food or what not—they cannot survive. They must turn back even as Cárdenas did.

The most striking and best known example of two closely related animals which, for many thousands of years, have been kept separate by the Canyon is that of the Kaibab and the Abert squirrels which happen to be the handsomest representatives of their family in the United States and likely to win admiring attention from any traveler who sees either the one or the other, even though he knows nothing of their story.

Both are large, noticeably larger than the eastern gray squirrel. Both also have rich, reddish-brown backs, handsome ear tufts or tassels which appear only in winter and huge fluffy tails providing a panache extravagant even for a squirrel. But they are also strikingly different. The Abert has a white belly and a grayish tail; the Kaibab a black belly and an astonishing pure white plume behind. The first is the commoner, occurring in isolated but favorable mountain areas south of the Canyon and scattered over both the Southwestern United States and northern Mexico. The Kaibab is restricted to an island plateau some twenty by forty miles in extent, which is the northern half of the dome through which the Canyon is cut and which is isolated, not only by the Canyon to the south, but by deserts to the east, and west and the north. In that restricted area he is by no means uncommon. Sometimes he is seen around the north rim camp grounds, though in my experience the surest place to see him for either aesthetic or scientific reasons, is in the great forest of pines at Jacob Lake, through which all visitors headed for the north rim must pass.

The habits of the Abert and the Kaibab are essentially identical, and both are restricted vertically as well as horizontally. All live in the region of high pines at six to eight thousand feet, making only rare forays a short distance down to the live-oak region or a short distance up to the firs. Sometimes they inhabit tree holes but mostly they build bushel-sized homes of leaves lined with grass or bark and put high in the trees where, in bad weather, the inhabitants may stay for a week or ten days at a time. They have the engaging habit of transporting their young under their bellies, tail between their forelegs and with the baby holding on for dear life. They store little food, and though they some-times rummage around the ground for seeds and tubers, they are wholly de-pendent for their main food supply on the living inner bark of the pine tree —principally the ponderosa. In winter they climb out to the ends of small branches, cut them off, and then, on the ground, gnaw through to the nourish-ing layer where life is still going on.

More or less omnivorous animals can range widely. Those confined to a special diet are naturally confined to the regions where it can be found and they are always to some extent in danger. If something cuts off their essential food, they are doomed and at best they are closely restricted to regions where it is obtainable. The Australian koala, which eats only the leaves of the eucalyptus, is a notable example, and some believe that the disappearance of the passenger pigeon was less the result of wholesale slaughter by man than of the fact that he was so largely dependent upon the fruit of the beech tree. Certainly the odd his-tory of the two tassel-eared squirrels has been wholly determined by the fact that they are "obligated," as the ecologists say, to the tall pines. They cannot leave the regions where they happen to have been born, because such regions are separated by the to them impassable deserts and by canyon bottoms. Hence, the northerners and the southerners have been prevented from intermarriage for so long that they have evolved into different races.

Probably—though fossil evidence is lacking—a single race once occupied pretty much the whole area from northern Mexico up into Utah. Then the Rockies were lifted and, slightly later, about the beginning of the Pleistocene, the ranges in southern Arizona. This means that something like a million years ago the lowlands began to be transformed into deserts. During the succeeding ice ages the region was cold, but as it warmed up about 35,000 years ago, aridity and heat drove the pines higher and higher into the mountains, and the squir-rels were compelled to follow them. Hence, neither the pine nor the squirrel is now commonly found at less than eight thousand feet elevation. Thus little communities of squirrels were cut off, one from another, with no avenue of communication open, and interbreeding, which cancels out the heritable varia-tions plants and animals alike tend to develop, became impossible.

Much more ancient history furnishes, of course, more spectacular examples of what happens when certain plants or animals are isolated for long periods. When the white man first came to Australia, there were no mammals other than primitive marsupials except for bats, rats and a wild dog, all of which could have crossed the water either on their own wings, on floating logs, or in the boats with the aboriginal human colonizers. Still more striking is the fact that when white men first came to New Zealand, there were not even marsupials. And the explanation of both phenomena seems clear. Australia was cut off from the other main continental masses by a salt estranging sea before any mammals other than the marsupial had been developed; New Zealand at a still earlier period. But the less striking case of the tassel-eared squirrel is especially interesting, both because the isolation by mountain and canyon and desert is so much less immediately obvious than isolation by sea, and even more, just because the fact that it is so recent delights evolutionists by giving them an example of a very first step in, to use Darwin's famous phrase, "the origin of species."

Are the Kaibab and Abert squirrels different species or still merely "varieties"? C. Hart Merriam, who first described the Kaibab squirrel, called it a different species. Some of the present-day classifiers disagree. But there is not really much point in the dispute. The term "different species" had a very definite meaning before the doctrine of evolution was generally accepted. It meant a kind of plant or animal which had always been different from every other from the day of its "special creation." But since we have come to assume that all animals have evolved from common ancestors, and since every degree of differentiation exists between certain kinds, there is no objective criterion for determining what distinguishes a "species" from a "variety" and it is largely a matter of opinion. Either the two squirrels are well-marked varieties or they are just barely distinct species. You may take your choice. Edwin McKee puts the situation thus: "We appear to have here . . . a fine example of evolution in its first stages, not yet well defined in its trends and not yet in operation for a very long period, but having definite opportunities to develop well isolated forms along independent lines."

Of course, students of evolution would be even happier if they could point to some unmistakable way in which the difference between the two squirrels conferred upon each a positive "survival value" in his special environment. Did "natural selection" tend to favor a northern race with white tails? The best guess that anyone has been able to come up with is this: There is much snow where the Kaibab squirrel lives, much less in most of the Abert's range. And since both habitually carry their tails over their backs, a white tail would help camouflage its owner on snow-covered ground.

Farfetched? Perhaps. Variations do exist even when they have no obvious survival value. Perhaps the differences between the coloration of the two squirrels helps them to survive in their different environments no more than the difference between an Alabama accent and that of a down-Easterner constitutes adaptation to their environments. But on the other side it may be pointed out that various northern animals—the snowshoe rabbit, for example—do turn white in the season of snow and that the advantage seems clear. Or, going back to the other side again, we may ask why didn't both squirrels adapt to a less restricted diet which would probably have been a good deal more advantageous to the race than white tails are?

Here, in other words, is another example of the fact that evolution is not as simple, as clear, and as perfectly understood as is sometimes assumed. It does take place, and the natural selection of useful variations does also take place. But there are fundamental questions as well as questions of detail which still have to be asked. Nearly everybody will agree that organisms have not always tended to provide just those variations which are potentially most useful. The Kaibab squirrel did not vary his diet, though he did change the color of his tail, and possibly natural selection did enable him to take advantage of that variation even though it may have originated merely by chance. Some—perhaps an increasing number but still a minority—would also agree that though the mechanical selection from among chance variations may account for the different tails on the two kinds of tassel-eared squirrels, it is not so certainly by itself sufficient to account for, say, the cooperation of the yucca moth with the yucca, the complicated techniques of the agricultural ant, or the seeming wisdom of those Australian birds who so carefully regulate the temperature in the incubators they build in lieu of brooding nests.

Nature seems to love variety—perhaps, as the mechanists would say, because the more different kinds of creatures there are, the more niches can be inhabited; perhaps because, like Thoreau, she would just like to have as many different kinds of men (and animals and plants and bugs) as possible. Perhaps she is still experimenting to see just how different she can make the two squirrels; and unless she, or man himself, breaks down the barrier before the experiment is complete, they may be even more interesting to some future evolutionist than they are now. As usual, however, she will take her time while even the most interested of us find it impossible to wait.

The great barrier of the Canyon itself is only one of the many things which make the whole region one of the most astonishingly varied in America or, for that matter, anywhere else. Within a rectangle some two hundred miles long and a hundred miles broad there are differences of altitude totaling more than ten thousand feet and climates varying from the subtropical to the arctic. There are low, flat, burning deserts; there is a mighty river, and there are dark, volcanic peaks reaching nearly thirteen thousand feet above sea level. Scenically, one may pass in less than an hour from one world to another which seems totally unrelated and pass at the same time from shirt sleeves to overcoat.

The geological "when" and "why" of this is another story and one that reaches down to a time, not very long before the first white man came, when some of the newest rock in the world was spewed out over an area next door to some of the most ancient anywhere exposed. But the biological consequences of this variety are obvious to any traveler who passes.

What he notices will depend upon the nature and extent of his interests, but unless he has accustomed himself so completely to an artificial environment that he has no awareness whatever of the natural world, he will notice something: perhaps only the difference between the arid desert and the pine-clad summits; perhaps, if he is interested in plants, the transition from alpine meadows to temperate oak, to cactus and creosote bush; perhaps, if he notices birds, the huge crested jays of the high woods which give place so soon to the desert sparrows and the sage thrashers of the hot flatlands. And whatever aspect of the changing scene he may take note of, it is part of a larger picture in which geology, climate, vegetation and animal life are all linked together. The forests are there because of the mountains and the jays because of the pines.

Merriam's contemporary, Ernst Haeckel, invented the term "ecology" (literally "housekeeping") to describe that new science which was to the plant and animal communities what "economics" is to human societies. Of course, naturalists had long known that Siberia was too cold for lions and that marsh plants couldn't live in the desert, but while they were busy for a century or two classifying and naming the inhabitants of the earth and then a little later busy with anatomy and physiology, they had made relatively little attempt to understand the complicated web of interrelations which controls the flora and fauna of any region and establishes a balance which is often so delicate that either a slight change in physical condition or the failure or success of some one element contributing to the balance can set off a series of changes which may have enormous consequences for man himself—especially when he is the one who interferes with the balance.

Merriam himself was one of the earliest American ecologists to make important contributions to the new science, and it is no wonder that it was his survey of the Canyon region, made originally for the United States Government, which suggested to him one of ecology's most important concepts, namely that of life zones. Because so many of these zones—as many as there are at sea level from Mexico to beyond the Arctic Circle—are so dramatically crowded together within the Canyon rectangle, they forced themselves upon his attention.

This concept of life zones is based upon the fact that climate is one of the most obvious of the things which determine the range, not merely of this or that particular plant or animal, but of an association or community of plants and animals dependent upon one another as well as upon the climate. These plants and animals often compete; but they are also often necessary to one another—sometimes reciprocally, sometimes, as in the striking case of the tassel-eared squirrel and the pine, merely in a one-sided dependence. Thus a stable community is established in which even sworn enemies sometimes cannot prosper without one another as when, say, foxes depend upon mice as an essential part of their diet while, if there were no foxes, the unchecked growth of the mouse population would drive them to exhaust their food supply, perhaps to exterminate their food plants, and finally themselves succumb to disease or starvation. But once a balance is established, the community tends to remain in stable equilibrium until something upsets it—sometimes man's intervention, sometimes a catastrophic event like the rearing of the mountains which destroyed the pine squirrel community over a large part of what had once been its territory and thus prepared the way for other communities, including those in the hot desert.

If the earth were flat, then the climatic zones would correspond more or less with the geographical. We would have a Tropical belt, a Subtropical, and so on to the Arctic. But since altitude bears a relation to climate just as definite as that of latitude, there is no such correspondence, and you may even have, as you do in Arizona, an Arctic life zone near the top of the San Francisco Mountains and a Subtropical at the bottom of the Canyon or at Cameron, barely fifty miles from the mountain's Arctic.

Of course, some factors besides altitude and latitude affect climate. For instance, the slopes of the two sides of a valley may lie in different life zones just because the sun shines longer on the one side than on the other. Moreover, identical temperature zones in widely separated regions of the earth do not always have identical plant-animal communities because, for one thing, moisture and the character of the soil favor or inhibit the organisms which might otherwise be at home there. Thus, there is a community appropriate to, say, an arid Subtropical and another to a moist Subtropical. Then, too, certain plants and animals have never colonized some suitable areas, because barriers formed by seas or mountains or deserts prevented their migration. Thus, there are neither koalas nor native eucalyptus trees upon which they could feed in the Northern Hemisphere, but the eucalyptus flourishes wonderfully when introduced into southern California, and so might the koala if animals with which it cannot compete (including man!) were not already established.

Such facts are of immense importance to man who introduced plants and animals into zones suited to them, as for instance when he took sheep to Australia—where there had been no large native mammals except the marsupials—or to South America. Even more important, perhaps, is the history of food plants, many of which were once local forms, sometimes perhaps local accidents, later intentionally transplanted to other suitable zones. And it is a curious fact that in almost every instance—as in the case of wheat, Indian corn, tobacco, bananas, sweet potatoes, etc., etc.—the present centers of most flourishing production are rather far removed from the place of origin, though they are in a corresponding life zone. Bananas, for example, came to Central America from Asia via Africa and the Canary Islands.

Because so many factors besides temperature influence a plant-animal community, present-day ecologists usually substitute a more complicated system than Merriam's for the classification of environments. But within a relatively limited area like the western half of the American continent his concept is very workable and enlightening.

Merriam recognized seven sharply distinguishable zones on the American continent ranging from the Tropical to the Arctic. On the eastern seaboard where there are no great variations in altitude you have to travel from Key West (just barely within the Tropical) all the way to northern Maine to pass through five of them. But in the West, where such tremendous differences in altitude occur within a few miles, the traveler is constantly passing from one zone to another and then back again.

Go up any steep slope, and you pass in a matter of hours through worlds which in the East are days apart; and the steeper the slope, the narrower the bands which fall within each zone. The most famous case of such narrow banding is the eastern slope of Mount San Jacinto just above Palm Springs, California, where the nearly ten-thousand-foot peak rises in just three airline miles eight thousand feet above the desert and so compresses within those three miles six of the seven life zones. Mounting, the traveler passes in a matter of minutes from one plant-animal community to another, and many organisms are confined sharply to their narrow band or layer. To get an equal variety on the eastern seaboard, you would have to go from central Florida to northern Canada.

Many trees, like the oak and the large pines, are found in their appropriate zones on each side of the continent. Other plants and also animals are characteristic of the East or West only, so that there is, for example, no sage brush in the East. Because of these differences caused by variations in the amount of moisture and other differences, special local names are now given to some of the western zones to distinguish them from the corresponding eastern zones. What, for instance, is called Austral in the East is called Sonoran in the West to indicate that though they correspond in temperature, they differ sharply in that the Sonoran is extremely arid. The communities flourishing within any of the western zones are, on the other hand, remarkably like those in a corresponding zone far away and equally unlike those of another zone which may be geographically next door. This is so generally true that Merriam recognized various "indicator" plants and animals—organisms, that is, which by themselves would serve to identify the zone and to all but guarantee the presence of others normally part of the same community.

Each of the six zones within the Canyon rectangle is thus sharply distinguished. In the Lower Sonoran (or Subtropical) the characteristic plants include the greasewood (Atriplex), Mormon tea (Ephedra), one of the yuccas and various cacti. There are also many lizards, pocket mice, and kangaroo rats but only a few birds—especially desert sparrows and sage thrashers. Just a little higher into the Upper Sonoran, evergreen oaks become the dominant tree, often mixed as they are on the south rim of the Canyon with the small piñon pine. Here the piñon jay and the rock squirrel abound. But at about seven thousand feet the Transition zone begins, the ponderosa pine flourishes and the tassel-eared squirrel is an indicator animal. At about nine thousand the Canadian zone begins, and the Douglas fir tends to replace the pine. Here the chickaree or spruce squirrel also appears. Another thousand feet up, in the Hudsonian zone the fir persists but spruce appears; and under the trees more northerly herbaceous plants like the columbine and the pyrola grow profusely. Clark's crow is a dominant bird, and the porcupine a prevalent animal. Finally, at twelve thousand feet or so, as at the summit of San Francisco Peak, one is definitely within the Arctic zone and, while standing in a meadow sprinkled with flowers which also grow within the Arctic Circle, one may look down upon a Subtropical desert.

This Arctic meadow is nearly two thousand miles from the Arctic Circle. It is also more than 250 miles from the nearest peak reaching into its zone. The golden eagle raises its young there, and Merriam was delighted to discover a number of plants which Greely had brought back from Lady Franklin Bay north of the northernmost part of Greenland and not many degrees from the pole.

Here, they are growing within a very small area from which they cannot possibly escape and at least 250 miles from other members of their species. How did they get there in the first place? Only one explanation seems possible and it is that the Arctic flora advanced southward in front of the glaciers during the great ice age. Then, as the glaciers retreated and the climate warmed, they took refuge higher and higher into the cool mountains until only the tips of the highest peaks were to them habitable. Should the world grow much warmer (and there is some evidence that it is warming up), they may disappear from even the San Francisco Peaks. If it should grow colder first, they will probably descend down the sides of the mountain, replacing the plants which now occupy these lower slopes but which could not stand the temperature the Arctic plants flourish in.

After I had made in one day the billion-year journey from the Archean rocks to the rim, the fancy struck me to make in another the journey in latitude from Subtropical to Arctic. Visually it is even more striking, because one *sees* rather than merely *knows about* what one is doing, and thanks to that dubious boon, the automobile, it can be made in a mere matter of hours. From the Canyon rim the Arctic peak is plainly visible, but to reach it one must first descend to the Subtropics from the Upper Sonoran zone in which the rim lies.

Strike eastward, and the road, which keeps close to the rim for many miles, carries you down the slope of a dome-shaped Kaibab Plateau and consequently past a canyon growing steadily shallower. At one point you may see in the distance the small canyon of the Little Colorado near where it joins the big canyon of the Colorado itself. Presently one is following the Little Colorado, cutting through country now definitely desert, and before long one reaches the cross-roads at Cameron, an Indian post and gas station, all but lost in a flat sandy desert some three thousand feet lower than the south rim and so desperately arid that it is almost bare of vegetation.

To the south and now a little nearer at hand the dark mountains reach up, and if one takes the road running toward them, the ground surface changes from red-sandy to dead-black because its surface is a porous lava spewed out from these same mountains, all of which are volcanic cones and quite recent—in fact, the most recent large-scale phenomena of the whole region. One, called Sunset Crater, can be definitely dated as having been cast up less than a thousand years ago into a region then inhabited by man of a fairly advanced culture. The highest peak is somewhat earlier but of an age measured in thousands of years. It was once perhaps three thousand feet higher than now but it still rises 12,611 feet above sea level or five thousand above the plateau through which it burst, and it is the highest elevation in Arizona.

The road going south from Cameron presently begins to mount the steady slope of the thickening lava bed. The air grows somewhat cooler, the vegetation is more profuse and represents a different community. For the moment we are retracing in an opposite direction the stages we passed through when we descended from the rim to the desert around Cameron. Cactus now gives way to the piñon pine characteristic of the rim and then, as we mount higher, to the ponderosa which dominates the high north rim. A few miles north of Flagstaff one must turn west onto an unsurfaced mountain road leading toward a pass over which it mounts steeply, up and up. Presently it ends at a ski bowl above which the ultimate summit towers darkly. We are in a forest of pines and firs which "indicate" the Hudsonian zone and we have thus passed through five of the life zones of the Northern Hemisphere. The air is chilly, but in very early October there is no snow yet, though there might have been and soon will be. Obviously there has been hard frost just above, since the great patches of aspen which break the mantle of evergreen are dazzlingly colored in the clear sunshine. Looking almost vertically upward one can see the tree line and above it the Arctic meadows.

It would be a long hard climb to reach them from this side, but one may at least look into the Arctic zone and realize that one has seen, within a few hours, the whole range of vegetational communities of North America except for the truly Tropical. Nowhere in the East and only at a few places in the West can one journey so far in so short a time. When Thoreau said that he had traveled extensively in Concord, that was a paradox. To say it of Coconino County is to make a simple statement of fact.

That evening my mind went back to the brilliant patches of aspen which here and there, for no apparent reason, seemed to be successfully disputing the mountain slopes with the more prevalent evergreens, and I wondered why. Some people think it is better to leave such questions alone and to take the beauty of nature for granted. If sufficiently phlegmatic they may take the attitude of the legendary English visitor who refused to see anything wonderful about all the water which tumbles over Niagara because, as he asked, "What's to prevent it?" Some of the more philosophically inclined may, like Wordsworth, object to what he called "peeping and botanizing." But there are others —and I am among them—who find themselves seeing it more vividly when nature is not merely a spectacle but a phenomenon interpretable in terms of the infinitely complex and subtle processes of which the spectacle is an outward and visible sign. And I have never found either the beauty or the wonder diminished.

Why then the colorful aspens? In this region the evergreens represent the climax vegetation. They are in stable equilibrium with themselves and their environment. They may tolerate a few aspens here and there but they would never, if left undisturbed, permit them to take over as they so obviously have done in the large brilliant patches. It is not, be it understood, that evergreens are always in other parts of the world a climax. Throughout many places in the East the situation is reversed. Pines are the first trees to take over a cleared spot and then, three-quarters of a century later, they are being ousted by the deciduous trees whose seedlings grew up in the shade they provided, and these deciduous trees establish the stable equilibrium which will last until something violent disturbs it. But here it is the evergreens that are ultimately dominant.

The first part of the answer to the question, "Why large patches of aspen in a climax forest of pines?" is "fire." A bolt of lightning or perhaps a camper's match burns a patch an acre or many acres in size. Then the wind or some animal agency brings in the aspen seeds which have been produced in vast numbers just waiting for such an opportunity and are light enough to blow. Not only do they seize their chance quickly, but they have several advantages over the pine. For one thing, the seedlings can stand the heat of an unbroken flood of sunlight; for another, they can take root in the ash to which the humus covering of the lava has been reduced; for a third, they grow very quickly. And for all these reasons they can take over before the pines can reoccupy the land.

But they are not, for all that, a permanent or climax growth. They are quite short-lived. Within a century or even less they are growing old. They are also killing one another off by their own shade. Meanwhile, however, they have added new humus to the soil and they have provided shade fatal to them but not to pine seedlings. By the time they die or are crowded out, the evergreens are already occupying their former plot of ground. Thus in Arizona aspen stands are nearly always mere stopgaps, and within a few generations the climax has been reached again, though meanwhile fire has probably prepared elsewhere the way for another patch of aspen to gladden the traveler's eye. Nor is the human traveler the only creature who profits from them. Many animals from rabbits to porcupines, beavers, deer and, northward, even the moose are to some extent dependent upon the aspen's buds or bark. In many places the animal community would not be what it is, were it not for the accidents which permit the stability of the climax condition to be, from time to time, broken.

To know this does not diminish my purely aesthetic pleasure in the splashes of gold against the dark green of the mountain side. They are perhaps no more beautiful; but they are more interesting. And they are also something more than an occasion for an isolated piece of information. As another evidence of the intricate wholeness of the natural world, they are what I would call "an aid to contemplation."

Photo by Kolb Bros.

Hauling lumber on the Bright Angel Trail to build Emery Kolb's Indian Gardens darkroom

Natural History of the Trailside

THERE ARE IN THIS WORLD many who would "improve" on nature at every turn. I once knew a rancher who, while among the wonders and beauty of Kanab Canyon, could talk of little but how that region might be blocked off into a magnificent pasture for Brahma steers. I have met engineers who practically dreamed of the great "contribution" they could make to civilization by building a road into Grand Canyon. I have seen the forester who scorned the desert because good forests would not grow there. An amazingly widespread notion is entertained by civilized man that it is his duty to remodel and rearrange all things in nature and to tame all that which is wild.

One of the real pleasures of traveling through most of the canyons in the Southwest is that so little evidence of man's endeavors is found within them. Much of their charm is due to the fact that rocks and plants and animals are still where nature placed them. Each form of life seems perfectly adapted to its environment—the result of ages of trial-and-error experiment in the game of life. On every side are demonstrated ingenious stratagems, contrived in the never-ending struggle for existence. There are reptiles that match the rocks, plants that survive drought because of small leaf surface or large water-storage space, mammals developed to walk easily on loose sand, others that can eke out a livelihood from plants despite spines and thorns. These and many other forms of life meet the special requirements of their local communities and therefore add interest and appeal to the trailside.

From *The Inverted Mountains,* by Edwin D. McKee, edited by Roger Peattie. Vanguard Press, 1948. Reprinted by permission of the publisher.

With knowledge comes appreciation. A visitor to the Grand Canyon once told me that he found it easier and more entertaining as he climbed the trail to count his steps in terms of geologic formations rather than of miles. He realized that he was literally passing through the ages as he progressed and that his trip took him through strata representing many millions of years in the earth's history. Such thoughts doubtless would have been even more intriguing had he been aware of the many ancient plants and animals buried in the rocks about him and of the stories they had to tell concerning climates and landscapes of the past.

In similar manner the botanist or ecologist obtains a certain feeling of satisfaction as he recognizes his approximate elevation through the appearance of certain plants or groups of plants along the way. He knows, for instance, that the catclaw or Acacia greggii seldom grows above four thousand feet in this latitude, that the lower level of the ponderosa or yellow pine is at about seven thousand feet, and that each of a host of other species will furnish him with information. Likewise, the bird enthusiast, the mammalogist, the student of reptiles will all find satisfaction in the knowledge that enables them to understand and appreciate various features along the trail. But one does not need to be a specialist to derive such pleasures. The amateur natural-history student who observes with care and enthusiasm will find an abundance of drama being enacted all about him on any of the canyon trails.

Glance about that portion of trail located at high elevation—say eight thousand or nine thousand feet—as found at Bryce Canyon or in the Kaibab on the north side of Grand Canyon. Here a person familiar with trails in the mountains of New England or in the lake region of Minnesota will recognize many familiar friends among the plants and animals, but with them will be some new and strange associates. Here one may enjoy the game of trying to recognize the many types of evergreens by their shapes or of testing cross-sections of needles to see whether they are round as in the pine, square as in the spruce, or flat as in the fir. One also may become interested in the groves of quaking aspen, whose white bark suggests from a distance the birch and whose leaves quiver with the slightest breeze, thus justifying the species name of *tremuloides*. If it is early summer these aspens may be causing a local "snow storm" by filling the air and covering the ground with their white, fluffy, cotton-like seeds. If it is autumn, the brilliant golden-yellow leaves may be bringing joy to some color photographer or artist.

In among these trees of higher altitudes are birds and mammals that also bring memories of the northland or of mountain peaks in other regions. The bright red or yellow crossbill, whose name is derived from its peculiar scissor-like beak, adapted to cutting seeds from the spruce cone, is apt to fly past. The noisy Clark's nutcrackers of the jay clan may call attention to their presence by raucous sounds. Red-breasted nuthatches, three-toed woodpeckers, solitaires, and many feathered associates of cool climates bring to mind the fact that these are trails due to be covered deep with snow during a long winter ahead. Here and there a tree trunk chewed by porcupine or the scattered remains of a chipmunk's feast of pine cones are reminders that four-legged forest dwellers also are about, and, if one is lucky, a deer or a spruce squirrel may be seen.

Canyon trails at lower levels in this region traverse what are commonly known as the "pygmy forests." These forests are composed of the small nut pines or piñons and the junipers, together with various shrubs such as the cliff rose, serviceberry, and wild currant. Trees grow well apart, and in most places there is little underbrush. Readily apparent is the interesting fact that in this region one goes down, instead of up, to approach timber line, for the lower limit of the pygmy forest is the beginning of the open desert. Of course, there is an upper timber line, too, but at this latitude it is attained only on the highest mountain peaks—above eleven thousand feet.

A majority of the canyons in the Southwest are at least partly within the belt of piñons and junipers. Many of these canyons have a pygmy forest along their rims and upper slopes but extend downward into the desert zone. The trails passing through such forests contain many features of natural history that are unique to the region and for that reason of especial interest to the visitor from afar. It is here that one finds large flocks of garrulous piñon jays, wearing Prussian blue but no crest, and making a terrific noise as they come picnicking through the woods. Here also one normally encounters groups of plump, short-tailed pygmy nuthatches, hanging upside down or in other acrobatic poses, talking continuously in friendly fashion. The more reserved Rocky Mountain nuthatches, the cheery mountain chickadees, and others that call to mind similar forms throughout the United States are also present among the trees.

Where the canyon walls become rocky and rugged, other types of birds appear abundantly. The canyon wren is especially conspicuous because of its weird song that starts high and comes tripping down the chromatic scale with a great display of exuberance. Frequently, even when the wren itself is too far away to be clearly seen with the unaided eye, its rich, vibrant song carries back and forth among the rocks. Another equally typical sound of the deep, narrow canyons is the coarse croak of the raven. This call echoes between canyon walls where the large, black birds, looking like overgrown crows, fly about singly or in pairs from cliff to cliff. Then there is the startling sound, like a bullet passing near, made by white-throated swifts as they circle and wheel and dart about with terrific speed among the cliffs. It seems almost unbelievable that any living creature can go so fast and yet keep such perfect control as is demonstrated by these long curving wings that sometimes move, first one and then the other, like a man swimming the crawl. It is a thrilling experience of the Canyon Country to watch and hear these birds zip past one's head and "power dive" into the depths below.

Back among the piñons and junipers again, along the ground, many other creatures of strange habit but of more silent ways come to the attention of the observant hiker. On relatively level stretches, especially along canyon rims, a horny lizard with circular body plan and flattened profile, commonly known as the horned toad, makes his abode. The color scheme of his body blends well with the ground about. Disturb him, and he will puff up as though suddenly inflated and may even emit a hissing sound. He would look as ferocious as any reptile of the ancient Mesozoic were he enlarged a few dozen times, yet for the most part he is a mild-mannered, gentle creature.

Not far away the peculiar home of another catcher-of-insects may attract attention. It is a conical-shaped hole in the sand about an inch deep and half again as wide at the top. Actually it is more than a house—it is a trap used by the wily and cunning flesh-eating larva of an innocent adult insect. Down at the bottom of the cone, hidden under loose sand, stays this insect larva—clumsy, covered with spiny hairs, and having mousetrap jaws with which it grabs any hapless ant or similar creature that falls into the pit. Many a fascinating half-hour may be spent in watching the movements of this creature commonly known as the ant lion or doodlebug.

Everywhere along the trail are other fascinating features typical of the pygmy forest area. Usually in spring and summer there are brilliant flowers here and there, varying in type and color with the season. There may be clumps of trumpet-shaped scarlet buglers, and, if there are, hummingbirds are likely to be near by, "treading" the air and whistling shrilly. There may be patches of bluebonnets, the state flower of Texas, or deep blue larkspur, orange mallow, and red or yellow paintbrush scattered about. Later in the season these flowers are largely replaced by others such as the snakeweed and rabbitbrush, and the blues and reds give place to yellows. As in all regions of semiarid climate, the display of trailside flowers varies tremendously with the local rainfall, but under optimum conditions it is almost unbelievably brilliant and beautiful.

So far nothing has been said concerning the main varieties of shrubs that are characteristic of the piñon-juniper belt. There is the cliff rose, which is very common and very beautiful when covered with yellow-centered, cream-colored blossoms, and which, despite a bitter taste that gives it the name of quinine bush, is a favorite food of the deer. It is an evergreen with waxy leaves and, like many other members of the rose family, develops lovely little plumes for transporting its seeds when the wind blows. Even more striking are the larger seed-plumes of a close relative called the Apache plume. Then there is the mountain mahogany of the same family—interesting because the Navajo Indians formerly made a lovely red dye from its roots. Representing the apple family is the serviceberry, very common along many trails and, when in bloom, a mass of white. Its berries are edible. Most beautiful and fragrant of all the wayside shrubs in the area, however, is the syringa or mock orange.

Descending any canyon trail toward the lower limit of the evergreens, one encounters many changes in the plant and animal life. Lizards are found in greater abundance, especially the small-scaled Utas, while some of the larger types, such as the brilliant orange or green collared lizards, make an appearance. The birds are semidesert types, including the rock wren, the black-throated desert sparrow, and the sage thrasher. Mammals are seen less frequently here than in the wooded areas above because most forms are nocturnal, but abundant evidence of their presence usually can be found. Under rock ledges or beneath large cactus plants huge piles of sticks, branches, and various kinds of rubbish testify to the industry of the so-called "pack rat," while on sandy surfaces the tracks of silky-haired, jumping pocket mice or of trim little white-footed mice are common. The mammal most likely to be seen and almost sure to be heard any time any day is the rock squirrel, which rushes about among the crags whistling lustily.

In the zone of dwarfed piñons and junipers and of increased desert conditions, various types of plants peculiarly adapted to the dry environment appear in great abundance. Among these is the century plant or mescal, which forms veritable "forests" in places. This interesting plant grows for many years with only a clump of sharp, saw-toothed leaves above the ground, and then some spring will send up a slender flower-bearing stalk, twelve or fifteen feet high, in a matter of days. After the flowers come the seeds, and then the entire plant dies, leaving only a brown hollow spear to wave and rattle like a ghost for months afterward. The tender shoots of these mescals have long been considered a deli-cacy by various Indians of the region, and circular rock pits in which the plants have been roasted are visible near many trails.

The yucca—swordlike but friendly—is another conspicuous plant common near the "lower timber line." Its leaves form queer-looking clusters about the base of a stalk as do those of the century plant, but they are narrower and with-out teeth on the sides, while the stalk normally extends upward but a few feet. Its larger blossoms are creamy-white and at once suggest relationship to the lily family. Of all the many plants in this semidesert region, the yucca has been one of the most useful to aboriginal man. Its pods form a food, its leaves are used for basketry, its fibers for thread, and its roots for soap.

If variety is the spice of life, these canyon trails must have an abundance of spice. A number of them, especially those in Zion and Grand Canyon, extend their lower reaches well down into a true desert environment, and there the fea-tures of natural history along the way make a remarkable contrast with those seen at higher elevation. Down where spring comes early and plants grow far apart, the vegetation is of a typical desert type. The little spotted skunk and raccoon-like ring-tailed cat leave tracks in the sand and often examine camp sites at night. Now and then a large scorpion with brown body and yellow legs is found beneath a rock, or a centipede crawls by—reason enough why the camper should shake out his shoe before putting it on in the morning. But by and large there is little to worry about and nothing to fear among the queer denizens of this lower realm, and there is much of beauty and of interest to be found. Large bluish pipe-vine swallowtail butterflies, friendly but noisy ash-throated flycatchers, harmless king snakes with black and white stripes, and a host of other creatures soon convince the observant hiker that this desert is far from desolate and lifeless.

Wherever water comes to the surface, or even near it, in this land of drought, an oasis is formed. Like most oases these are regular paradises for all forms of life, and their beauty is enhanced many times by contrast with sur-rounding dry areas. The largest of the oases in the canyons of the Southwest are those formed along permanent stream courses. The deep-rooted mesquite and the grabbing catclaw of the desert thrive in these places, but they are secondary in prominence to the large, shade-giving cottonwood, to the box elder, and to thickets of willows and arrowweeds. Down below the trees and larger shrubs, in many places, are clumps of that peculiar jointed plant known as horsetail, whose ancient lineage goes back to the great Coal Age; also there are pretty red or yellow monkey flowers and, in especially sheltered localities, the columbine and maidenhair fern. Trails that follow such water bodies offer many a thrill and surprise for the nature lover, and seldom a dull minute is experienced.

Down among the boulders, wherever permanent streams rush by with white foam and swift current, one is almost sure to encounter the little gray dipper or water ouzel. Continually bobbing up and down on a rock ledge, diving under water and coming into full flight as it reaches the surface, or singing beautifully within narrow canyon confines, this little bird seems strangely out of place to those who have always associated him with high mountain regions. But the dipper appears to be just as much at home and to enjoy life as fully in the depths of hot desert canyons, wherever he has rushing water, as in the highest and boldest mountains. One group of geologists working in the depths of Grand Canyon and climbing about with great effort among granite walls noted the ease with which a little water ouzel flew from cliff to cliff and thereupon adopted as a theme song for their expedition, "If I Had the Wings of an Ouzel . . ."

Equally surprising to most people schooled in less arid regions is the discovery that beaver are perfectly at home in many desert canyons of the Southwest. As a matter of fact, the first Americans to visit Grand Canyon—the Patties, father and son—came up the Colorado River in 1826 trapping beaver. Along the permanent streams, wherever the encroachments of man have not forced a retreat, are found trees and logs cut by these busy animals. Occasionally a dam across some stream or a burrow in a mud bank is discovered, though most of these are temporary and difficult to find.

A multitude of other creatures add distinctive flavor to the setting of a desert canyon oasis. There are the ever present red-spotted toads, with low voices, and the canyon tree toads, with shrill, piping calls. The tree toads continually appear in unexpected places, for suction disks on their toes enable them to climb smooth, vertical surfaces. Down in the water are polliwogs, striders, whirligig beetles, and many of the other interesting animals typical of most bodies of fresh water throughout the country, while in the air may be dragonflies, caddis insects, and damsel flies. The trail through the oasis is a source of unending surprises.

Supai Mary (a Havasupai Indian), c. 1910

The Canyon Dwellers

4000 Years of Human History in the Grand Canyon

FOUR THOUSAND YEARS before Major Powell's men tumbled through the Grand Canyon in their wooden boats, before geologists and archaeologists investigated its lessons and records, before photographers adjusted their focus and tourists stood on the south rim in awe—four thousands years before all this, human beings had wandered the Canyon's depths.

These men were prehistoric American Indians, primitive hunters and gatherers who used isolated caves in the Canyon's bottom. as religious shrines. In several limestone-solution caverns they deposited caches of ingenious split-willow figurines of animals. Many of these effigies were pierced, probably in ritualistic fashion, with tiny wooden sticks seemingly meant to represent spears, and archaeologists believe that this was some type of imitative hunting magic. If a miniature figure of the animal to be hunted were ritually killed, success would be more certain in the actual quest.

When such split-willow figurines were first discovered in the Canyon in 1933, their great antiquity was not realized. In the late 1950's some of the figurines were radiocarbon-dated at the University of Michigan and the University of Arizona. These analyses indicated an age of 1580 B.C. $\pm$ 300 years and 1150 B.C. $\pm$ 110 years, and led to the suggestion that the tiny figures may have been associated with the Desert Culture which was widespread over western North America from about 7000 to 2000 B.C. Recent archaeoolgical investigations support the figurine dates and hypotheses. In 1963 additional split-twig figurines,

From *The Grand Colorado,* by Robert C. Euler. American West Publishing, 1969. Reprinted by permission of Crown Publishers.

recovered from a huge limestone cavern in Marble Canyon and examined at the University of California, revealed a radiocarbon date of 2145 B.C. ± 100 years, the earliest date yet recorded for such specimens. Other archaeologists have discovered similar figurines in portions of the Mojave Desert in eastern California and Nevada, and south of Grand Canyon near Flagstaff and the Verde Valley.

In the early spring of 1964, what may be an important clue to the identity of the makers of the figurines was discovered on the summit and slopes of Red Butte, a prominent sandstone- and lava-capped pinnacle a few miles south of Grand Canyon. Here archaeologists found projectile points and other chipped-stone tools affiliated with the Pinto Complex, a Desert Culture people first recognized in the Pinto Basin of the Mojave Desert. While the Pinto Complex is not yet fully understood or dated with incontrovertible accuracy, most archaeologists feel that an age of three to four thousand years would not be out of order. Thus, although split-twig figurines have not been found in absolutely certain association with Pinto Complex artifacts, the discovery of a Pinto site near caves containing the figurines in Grand Canyon supports the probability of some association.

The split-twig animal figurines, then, give mute evidence for the beginnings of human history in Grand Canyon. It is not known how long these hunters and magicians continued to use its limestone caves, but they had probably disappeared long before the opening of the Christian era. Archaeologists have found no record of further human occupation of the Grand Canyon until about 700 A.D., when Indians who were culturally much different began tentative exploration of its depths. These were Pueblo peoples, most probably direct ancestors of the Hopi. For almost one hundred years, prehistorians have been studying the history of the Pueblo Indians, and we now have a relatively complete picture of how their culture developed.

It is quite probable that they, too, began as a Desert Culture people in the Great Basin. Some time around the year 1 A.D., or slightly earlier, they moved into the northern portions of the Southwest, near the Four Corners (where Arizona, Utah, Colorado, and New Mexico meet). Archaeologists refer to this period in their culture as that of the "Basketmaker," a name derived from their most common material attribute. These hunters and gatherers had added corn and squash to their economy by using rudimentary agricultural techniques acquired from Indians farther south. In fertile valleys they raised their crops, and in surrounding uplands they hunted deer, mountain sheep, and rabbits. They cultivated the soil with digging sticks and hunted game with spears, spear-throwers, and curved throwing sticks; rabbits were driven into nets stretched across defiles.

The early Basketmakers wove beautiful baskets, fine sandals, loincloths, and twined bags. Blankets woven of cords covered with rabbit fur kept them warm in winter. Fired pottery was not made at this time, but they produced crude clay vessels.

Caves or rock-shelters seem to have been preferred for dwellings, and into their floors the Indians dug storage chambers that later became burial cists. Occasionally they constructed saucer-shaped wooden houses in the protection of cliffs.

Around 500 A.D. (the exact date varying with the section of the Southwest) the Basketmaker style of life changed in several ways. New varieties of corn were developed, and beans introduced. Caves became less popular than circular, open-pit houses, often grouped in a manner suggestive of the beginnings of village life. The weaving of sandals reached its highest development, and baskets were still widely made. Fired pottery was introduced—usually gray with simple designs painted in black—and the bow and arrow came into use to supplement the spear-thrower. This was an important era in the lives of these people. They enlarged their geographic range westerly to the lower Little Colorado River, almost to Grand Canyon, and laid a foundation for the later flowering of their culture.

With a stable economic base that combined hunting and gathering with corn, bean, and squash agriculture, the Pueblos turned to other matters. They refined their ceramic art, producing corrugated cooking ware, vessels with broad- and fine-lined black-on-white decoration, and some red pottery decorated with black paint. They added cotton to their agriculture, spinning and loom-weaving it into fabrics for clothing, and made good stone axes and hoes. Surface storage rooms, made first of mud and poles and later of masonry, became common. These ultimately developed into above-ground dwellings, the pit houses being reserved for religious and ceremonial functions.

By the middle of the eleventh century A.D., this development flowered into the classic traditions of Pueblo culture, apparently reaching a zenith first in the east, in the Chaco district of northwestern New Mexico, and later in northern Arizona. This period, continuing into historic times, saw the rise of great communal pueblos, up to five stories high and housing several hundreds of people.

Subterranean religious structures (kivas) became specialized, with local variations in details. Exquisite pottery, black-on-white, black-on-red, and polychrome, abounded. Objects of personal adornment appeared—turquoise mosaics, beads, pendants, and shell bracelets. Communal living must have been highly organized, and if we can judge by the social, religious, and political structures of modern pueblos, authority probably centered in a theocratic hierarchy of priests.

During these centuries other great changes were taking place. Precipitation patterns that may have affected the maturation of crops began to vary in certain parts of the Southwest by the middle of the twelfth century; more intensive drought conditions came a century later. About this time, too, seminomadic non-Pueblo peoples made their appearance from the northwestern horizon.

These ancestors of the Southern Paiute may have been responsible for what appears to have been an intercultural relationship similar to a "cold war." Apparently, the strangers soon reached the northern rim of Grand Canyon. About this time the Pueblos consolidated their numbers along the more reliable water courses—the Little Colorado and the Rio Grande, and the usually infallible springs of the Hopi country. Here they were when the Spaniards found them in the summer of 1540.

Yet, even as the Pueblos were flourishing and, later, reconsolidating, other indigenous peoples of the Southwest were following different patterns of culture. In west central Arizona were the Cohonina people, whose presence on the plateau of northern Arizona has been recorded from about 700 to 1150 over a range that included the south rim of Grand Canyon.

The Cohonina adopted a veneer of Pueblo culture. They attempted to build pit houses and masonry pueblos. Their pottery, although of a different technique, was gray and decorated with black painted designs in imitation of that made by their eastern neighbors. Apparently unable to produce the red pottery of the Pueblos, they slipped some of it after firing with a fugitive red paint to give it the superficial appearance of true red ware. They farmed essentially the same crops but hunted to a lesser extent. Their social and religious life probably differed considerably from that of the Pueblos.

About 1150, or perhaps slightly later, the Cohonina disappear from the archaeological record. By then, and continuing until about 1300, the Cerbat, probably direct ancestors of the Walapai and Havasupai, moved from the deserts near the lower Colorado River Valley to the plateaus that had been the

Cohonina homeland. These Indians were but incipient farmers, planting near permanent springs. Hunting and gathering was their economic mainstay. They lived in rock-shelters or impermanent brush wikiups. Their material culture was simple and their interest in ceramics confined to the production of brown, undecorated vessels. Yet they established a very stable way of life on the plateau, for it was here that the Spanish Franciscan, Father Garcés, first described them in 1776; and it was here they remained until forcibly removed to their present restricted reserves in the early 1880's.

It was these native peoples—the Pueblos and to a lesser extent the Cohonina, the Havasupai and Walapai, and the Southern Paiute—who made the indigenous history of the Grand Canyon.

There is no evidence that Pueblo Indians entered the Canyon before the opening of their Developmental Period (about 700 A.D.). Then, and for the next three centuries, there was halting exploration and limited seasonal occupation. The few Developmental sites that have been discovered are marked on the surface only by fine-lined black-on-white pottery fragments. These are mostly in the eastern reaches of the Canyon, but at least one such site has been recorded near Deer Creek, 136 miles down the Colorado River from Lees Ferry. In all probability, these and later Pueblo Indians approached the great gorge from the heartland of their territory to the east.

At about the same time, but probably coming from the opposite direction, small groups of Cohonina Indians made their appearance. One excavated site of this period, located on the south rim near the Tusayán Pueblo ruin in the eastern portion of Grand Canyon National Park, consists of a circular house, two storage rooms, and several storage pits, all dug into the shallow, limestone-studded soil of the area. Wtihin the next three centuries, the Cohonina occupied many more sites along the south rim, but not in the Canyon itself. Their buildings were mostly surface masonry structures, a style evidently acquired from contact with the Pueblos.

By 1150 A.D., for reasons not yet fully understood, the Cohonina disappeared as a cultural group. Some archaeologists believe that they became the Havasupai, while others have presented evidence that both the Havasupai and the Walapai were descendants of the prehistoric Cerbat people.

Meanwhile, about 1000 A.D., there began a much larger influx of Pueblo peoples into the Canyon, culminating a century later in a major occupation of hundreds of sites in its myriad recesses and on both rims. The overwhelming majority of prehistoric ruins in Grand Canyon consists of small, surface masonry pueblos with associated storage rooms, mescal pits, and occasional kivas. Frequently these were built on open, relatively flat terraces. Many Indians did take advantage of the towering cliffs and built against them at the tops of steep talus slopes, but true cliff dwellings are not often encountered.

The ruins are now visible as low remnants of masonry walls that mark room outlines. The ground around them usually is littered with broken pottery and stone tools, such as arrow points, scrapers, and milling stones. Storage rooms and the talus-top pueblos are usually found in a better state of preservation, and in a few instances the original wooden roofs are still intact. At one site in Shinumo Canyon, for example, the masonry walls of a room are spanned by cottonwood timbers, crossed at right angles with smaller poles, slabs of rock, and finally a layer of earth, as is typical of Pueblo architecture elsewhere. The storerooms, placed in protected niches or overhangs, ordinarily are well preserved, but except for an occasional corncob, their contents have long since been consumed by rodents. Mescal pits, where the roots and tender young shoots of the Agave plant were roasted, are marked by large circular depressions, some with diameters of 20 to 25 feet, ringed with masses of small, charred rocks.

Today, visitors viewing Grand Canyon only from the comfortable vantage of the rim may wonder how Indians could have survived down in the Canyon and, indeed, why they entered it in the first place. The answers to these questions can be found in the cultural adaptations the Pueblos made to their natural environment. One must remember that these Indians had a well-balanced economy based upon hunting, gathering of many wild edible plants, and agriculture. While deer-hunting undoubtedly was excellent on both north and south rims, such other game animals as mountain sheep and rabbits were to be found below the rims. Wild food plants grew in abundance on the rims, but only those ecologically adjusted to the high plateau elevations (7,000 to 8,000 feet). In the Canyon below, many other staples could be gathered: the tasty fruits of certain varieties of cactus, the edible beans of the mesquite, the catclaw, and the Agave. Furthermore, successful farming of beans, squash, corn, and cotton depends upon a rather long, frost-free growing season and sufficient water. Both were obtainable at Canyon elevations below 3,000 feet. While both rims are relatively devoid of dependable water sources, the recesses of the Canyon contain many springs and, particularly in the side canyons near the north rim, permanently flowing streams. While there undoubtedly have been some climatic changes in the several centuries since the Pueblo occupation was at its height, particularly changes in rainfall pattern, it is worthwhile to note that in some side canyons where there are permanent streams or springs today, there are ruins; where there is no water now, prehistoric sites are lacking.

Environmentally, then, the Canyon provided excellent resources to sustain Pueblo life, though in all probability occupation was in large part seasonal. While archaeologists will not be more certain until excavations are undertaken at selected ruins in the inner canyons, the lack of an extensive fuel supply for winter warmth would seem to suggest habitation of the lower reaches in the summer growing season and of the well-wooded plateau back from the rims, particularly the south rim, in the winter. Indeed, this was the pattern of the Havasupai until they were restricted to their present village in the Canyon bottom around 1895.

But this is not to say that every spring saw mass migrations of Indians into the Canyon. Hundreds of ruins on both north and south rims indicate that many families remained on the plateau and farmed there during the summer months.

One of the most significant of the twelfth-century Pueblo agricultural communities was on the plateau near the Canyon's rim. (Its precise location is withheld to prevent vandalism.) Here, along a relatively shallow drainage for a distance of some two and one-half miles, archaeologists recorded 44 small masonry pueblo ruins and, in the drainage itself, 77 agricultural check dams. Here, for perhaps a hundred years, a number of family groups, possibly interrelated, planted crops, hunted, and gathered wild plants in the Canyon below. On the Canyon walls nearby are remnants of precipitous trails, marked in one instance by a small masonry storeroom tucked into a recess in the cliff some two thousand feet below the rim; below that, only a few hundred feet above the Colorado River, is a prehistoric wooden bridge that spanned a crevice on a narrow ledge. From this trail it was possible to cross the river and climb out the other side.

Throughout many tributary canyons, especially in the eastern portions of Grand Canyon, are similar Pueblo masonry ruins in association with low check dams. At one site there is a long stone wall that was apparently built to divert sheet drainage from the hills above to agricultural fields. There is abundant evidence that these Indians practiced erosional control and other conservation measures.

Studies have been made that indicate a strong correlation between the locations of prehistoric sites and routes of access into the Canyon where its sheer walls are broken down. In one such area there exists additional evidence that the Indians moved from plateau to Canyon and from rim to rim with relative ease. On a ledge, seemingly inaccessible from ruins in the Canyon below or from the rim above, is a small limestone cave that contained corncobs and two pottery vessels. Presumably, this was a way station along a prehistoric trail to the rim, where travelers could find a cache of food and water. The ledge marks the only place within many miles where it is possible to climb out of the Canyon.

At another locale, in the eastern portion of the Canyon below Lipan Point, a one-room masonry structure with what appear to be loopholes in its walls may have been some type of look-out on a cross-Canyon trail. The structure commands an excellent view up the river and across to a large concentration of Pueblo ruins on the north side. And from this site it is possible to climb to the south rim near Desert View.

It should be noted that along the south rim from Desert View west to the Great Thumb peninsula, several masonry structures stand on small, and sometimes quite isolated, sections of cliff that project out from the main rim. Often massive limestone walls rim the edges of these "islands." To many observers, these Pueblo buildings seem to have been fort-like in character, but absolutely no evidence of actual hostility has ever been discovered in Grand Canyon. In fact, these south rim "forts" would have been virtually indefensible against attack from the "mainland," for they are *cul-de-sacs,* cut off from all food and water save that which might have been stockpiled before a siege.

Grand Canyon and its immediate environs to the north and south were almost completely abandoned by 1150 or 1200 A.D., not only by the Pueblos but by the Cohonina population on the south rim. Why did they leave? Present evidence would seem to point to climatic changes rather than the presence of hostile peoples. It is true that about 1150 A.D. the Cerbat Indians made their appearance on the plateaus along the south rim and the forerunners of the Southern Paiute penetrated the high, forested lands near the north rim, but there is nothing to indicate that either the Pai (as the combined Walapai and Havasupai once termed themselves) or the Southern Paiute forced the Pueblo abandonment.

In adjacent regions of the northern Southwest, however, studies of fossil pollen rains and annual tree-ring growth point to a shift from winter to summer precipitation at about this time. Since successful maize agriculture depends in large part upon soil storage of water from winter snows and rains, such a change could well have made farming impossible, or extremely marginal except near a few choice springs or streams.

The mystery of the exodus from the Canyon indicates a need for more detailed archaeological excavation (only two ruins on the south rim and none in the Canyon or on the north rim have been dug scientifically) and for more paleo-climatological studies based upon detailed examination of soil stratigraphy, pollen, and tree-ring growth.

Soon after 1150 A.D. the Pai spread over the southern plateau and penetrated much of the western and central part of the Canyon. By 1300 they had reached their maximum range and occupied all of the south portion of Grand Canyon and its plateau east to the Little Colorado River. Throughout this region they hunted, gathered, and carried on some farming near permanent springs and streams. The habitation sites discovered within the Canyon consist of rock-shelters, on the floors of which lie trash and cultural debris, including reddish-brown potsherds, flat-slab milling stones, and small, triangular, side-notched arrow points, all differing from those of the Cohonina or the Pueblos.

On the north rim uplands and in their tributary canyons, the Southern Paiute maintained a similar existence after the twelfth century. Their fingernail-incised brown pottery, milling stones, and arrow points were somewhat different from those of the Pai, but they also occupied rock-shelters and roasted Agave in stone-ringed pits. Now and then they camped in abandoned Pueblo ruins, for their pottery sometimes has been found mixed with that of the Pueblos around the masonry structures.

Both the Pai and the Paiute occupations were stable and long lived. From about 1150 until the latter part of the nineteenth century, they continued to use the natural resources of Grand Canyon.

There is some evidence that both groups maintained amicable trade relations with the Pueblos in the present Hopi country. By 1300 the Pueblos had ceased to make black-on-white and polychrome pottery, and had developed a yellow ware, exquisitely decorated with designs in brownish-black paint, similar to the Hopi ceramics of today. Fragments of this black-on-yellow pottery are found on many Havasupai, Walapai, and Southern Paitue ruins in Grand Canyon, probably the remains of vessels traded from the Hopi Pueblos in exchange for deer skins, red paint, and mescal.

Occasionally, too, from 1300 until relatively recently, the Hopi periodically returned to Grand Canyon to collect salt from a natural deposit near the confluence of the Little Colorado and Colorado rivers. They approached these salt mines either by way of the Little Colorado gorge or down what is now known as the Tanner Trail below Desert View. On both these routes are former camp sites of the Hopi, marked by the bright yellow potsherds.

The discovery, or rather rediscovery, of one such Hopi site near the mouth of the Little Colorado River involved some elementary archaeological detective work. In August of 1869, when Major Powell camped there on his first exploration down the Colorado, his men reported finding traces of an ancient Indian habitation. Eighty years later, when professional archaeologists first surveyed the river banks through Grand Canyon, they could not find this ruin. The only sign of human habitation by the blue lagoon at the mouth of the Little Colorado was a one-room stone cabin built by a prospector named Beamer about 1889. After two later visits, archaeologists noted some erosion in the bank at the front of the cabin. Protruding from this bank were fragments of Beamer's trash— broken bottles and rusted tins. Beneath them were aboriginal potsherds, first the post-1300 Hopi yellow wares and then, lower down, the earlier Pueblo black-on-white and gray types. Between the time of Major Powell's observations and that of modern archaeologists, Beamer apparently had modernized a prehistoric Pueblo structure!

Beamer was not the only Anglo-American to explore Grand Canyon in those decades after Major Powell's trips. Mormons investigated the north rim and visited the Southern Paiute. On the south side, after the United States had forcibly established peaceful relations with the Pai and placed them on separate reservations in the early 1880's, other Anglo prospectors tramped over former Indian trails and discovered copper, asbestos, lead, and other mineral deposits. They dug shafts, transported heavy mining equipment on the backs of mules, and even constructed cable crossings of the river. Intrepid boatmen left the wreckage of their craft and the graves of some of their men by the river. Early tourist accommodations, forerunners of modern hotels and motels, were built on the south rim. Today, even these structures are in ruins—if not obliterated. History and prehistory are absorbed by the contemporary scene, and hundreds of thousands of tourists who come to gaze in awe at the Canyon are unaware that this great natural wonder has formed the stage and the backdrop for four thousand years of human endeavor.

A SENSE
OF PERSONAL
ADVENTURE

Emery Kolb crossing Havasu Canyon on a ladder

To a very few of the three million who visit each year, Grand Canyon is a stage for personal adventure, physical challenge and self-discovery. Way out there, beyond ten or twelve thin ribbons of improved trail, the adventurer steps into two thousand square miles of chromatic rock wilderness, sealed off from mechanical vehicles by a thousand miles of vertical limestone cliffs.

Big game hunters were the first sportsmen to utilize the canyon. They began coming around 1900, not to the canyon proper, but to the luxuriant blue forests of the north rim, primarily to hunt lions and trophy deer. The north rim was so isolated that many hunters reached it from the south, descending into the canyon and climbing up to the north rim on the Bass or Kaibab trails.

Most of the lion hunters hired "Uncle Jim" Owens as their guide. Owens was an old-time Texas trail cowboy who retired to the canyon as a lion bounty hunter and to experiment with raising a small herd of buffalo that he brought from Yellowstone.

Teddy Roosevelt was the most famous of the canyon cougar hunters. But his interest in the canyon went a lot deeper than hunting big game. As president, he established the North Kaibab Game Preserve and proclaimed the Grand Canyon a national monument. In May, 1903, he stopped over at the south rim to deliver a brief speech to a small crowd of cowboys, Indians and tourists. He urged Americans to preserve the canyon for future generations, stating:

> In the Grand Canyon, Arizona has a natural wonder which, so far as I know, is in kind absolutely unparalleled throughout the rest of the

world. . . . Leave it as it is. You cannot improve on it. The ages have been at work on it, and man can only mar it. What you can do is to keep it for your children, your children's children, and for all who come after you, as the one great sight which every American . . . should see.

Roosevelt returned to the canyon in the summer of 1913 with two of his sons for a week of lion hunting with "Uncle Jim." The hunting party assembled at El Tovar, camped overnight at the bottom, and took the Kaibab Trail up to the north rim. Roosevelt wrote a vigorous account of their experiences trailing and shooting lions along and under the canyon rim. "A Cougar Hunt on the Rim of the Grand Canyon," reprinted here, was originally published with other Arizona essays in a book entitled *A Book-Lover's Holidays in the Open*.

Roosevelt's enthusiasm for killing off lions and other predators may have been progressive thinking for its day. However, without the lions to check their numbers, the deer herds proliferated far beyond the available food supply, resulting in massive starvation and decline of the herd in the 1920s. The situation became so desperate that local residents attempted to round up several thousand deer and drive them across the canyon to populate the south rim forests. The great "deer drive" broke up in confusion and stormy weather before the first deer set foot on a canyon trail. Today the role of natural predators in preserving ecological balance is better understood, and hunting is banned within park boundaries.

Roosevelt's memory as a sportsman and conservationist lives on in a limestone and bronze monument at Jacob Lake. A few miles away, the small hunting cabin that he occupied with Uncle Jim has fallen to ruin.

Cougar hunting has long since given way to river running as the most popular canyon sport. Bobby Kennedy, Barry Goldwater, and a hundred-thousand ordinary citizens have been casually drenched for fun and sport in Hance, Sockdologer, Grapevine, Horn Creek and all the other big rapids where Powell and his men struggled for their lives just a century ago. Better boats and improved whitewater techniques provide a safer, faster and easier trip than the early river runners would have ever dreamed of.

The notion of river running as a sporting pastime took root in 1909, when Julius Stone, a gentleman adventurer from Ohio, organized a party that went through from Green River to Needles without difficulty. The commercial tourist trade, taking regular passengers for a fee, was initated by Norman Nevills in the 1930s. The real travel explosion began in the 1950s with the introduction of large rubber pontoon boats by a colorful woman river rat, Georgie White. Today's river trips cater to many specialized interests; one group even provides a professional string quartet to interrupt the solitude at the end of each day's run.

In the second selection, Edward Abbey tells what it is like to row a wooden dory through the rapids in 1976. Abbey effortlessly blends his love of wilderness, and a good time, with physical adventure and an imposing amount of detail about plants, animals and canyon geology. His sense of history is there too—the forlorn ghost of Major Powell keeps intruding into the frivolity, reminding us of the changes that have taken place even here in the last one hundred years.

As a result of just one book, *Desert Solitaire,* Abbey has become the most important writer of the Colorado plateau and canyon country. He has been described as a desert Thoreau, but Abbey rejects the comparison, proclaiming that he is neither a serious naturalist nor a deep thinker. Notwithstanding his disclaimer, the comparison fits, for like Thoreau and Aldo Leopold, Abbey sees detail with poetic clarity and generalizes with great power.

Abbey differs from most environmental writers in one important aspect: his irreverent sense of humor is never far away. For example, his account of his first trip to Havasu Canyon begins:

> One summer I started off to visit for the first time, the City of Los Angeles. . . . On the way we stopped off briefly to roll an old tire into the Grand Canyon. While watching the tire bounce over tall pine trees, tear hell out of a mule train and disappear with a final grand leap into the inner gorge, I overheard the park ranger standing nearby say a few words about a place called Havasu.

Out of the river boats and away from the two mule trails, the only way to see the country is by walking—mostly down and up. Climbing down a desert canyon can be just as dangerous as climbing up an alpine peak. A careless step can cause a fatal fall. Water is hard to find. Summer temperatures in the inner canyon equal the desert extremes of Phoenix and Yuma. Hyperthermia, induced by heat and dehydration, can come quickly and without warning. Almost every year there are new reports of death and injury to careless and unsuspecting hikers.

For those who come prepared, the canyon offers many diverse rewards. Some hike and climb in the canyon for the same reason others scale a mountain peak—because it's there, because some danger is the very essence of adventure, and because it provides a test of endurance and physical skill. For others, canyon hiking simply provides a chance to get away, to relax and discover the natural world.

The selections on inner-canyon hiking are written by two men who exemplify these differing approaches to personal adventure. Colin Fletcher is a compulsive walker who thrives on long-distance and endurance feats. In 1962 he walked the length of California from Mexico to Oregon and wrote of his experience in a book entitled *The Thousand Mile Summer*. Four years later, on a casual first visit to the canyon, he decided to make the first non-stop hike through the length of the canyon. A year later, Fletcher began his trip at Havasu, working his way east along the esplanade, the bench that separates the inner and outer canyons.

Fletcher completed the journey in two months, aided by advance caches of food and water and by three airdrops of supplies at more remote sections. The entire journey is recounted in his popular book, *The Man Who Walked through Time*. The chapter represented here, entitled "Transition," tells of the second week out of Havasu when, adjusted to hard walking and a sixty-pound pack, he begins to awaken to the natural world around him. Adapting to the solitude, Fletcher finds his attention increasingly diverted from the grandiose surroundings to the small, intricate details of the desert life at his feet.

Edward Abbey would rather wander at random than break distance or endurance records. For him, physical exertion is not an end in itself, but rather a necessary means to the desired end of getting as far away as possible from people and motor vehicles. In the next selection, taken from *Desert Solitaire*, Abbey describes five weeks of solitary wandering in Havasu Canyon, inspecting old mine workings, lingering in the blue pools below Mooney Falls, and daydreaming for hours on end. His idyllic interlude ends abruptly with a casual and careless decision that nearly cost his life. Paradise can be very dangerous.

No collection of Grand Canyon writing would be complete without Zane Grey. Grey discovered the Southwest in 1907 on an arduous trip from Flagstaff across Lee's Ferry to the North Kaibab, where he aimed to meet and live with the legendary Buffalo Jones. While in New York, Grey had learned of Jones and his adventures as trapper and Indian fighter and immediately resolved to go West and make his acquaintance. His stay on the North Kaibab with Jones initiated his long romance with the Southwest and provided the material for his two best novels, *Riders of the Purple Sage* and *Heritage of the Desert*.

In *Heritage of the Desert* the heroine, Mescal, spends a year hidden out in a remote canyon oasis to escape danger at the hands of vicious outlaws. As the plot turns in favor of the hero, he rides down to Thunder River to rescue her. The excerpt included here contains all the elements of Zane Grey's universal appeal: a strong story line, romantic interest, good versus evil and authentic description of western scenery. In describing Mescal's canyon hideaway, Grey blends several recognizable scenes from Thunder River and Deer Creek. Finally, the heroine, her rescuer and their good horse Silvermane swim the Colorado and climb out to the rim and safety. The fictional river crossing is as memorable as any scene from the journals of real-life river runners.

Teddy Roosevelt and John Hance (second rider) on the Bright Angel Trail

A Cougar Hunt on the Rim of the Grand Canyon

ON JULY 14, 1913, our party gathered at the comfortable El Tovar Hotel, on the edge of the Grand Canyon of the Colorado and therefore overlooking the most wonderful scenery in the world. The moon was full. Dim, vast, mysterious, the canyon lay in the shimmering radiance. To all else that is strange and beautiful in nature the Canyon stands as Karnak and Baalbec, seen by moonlight, stand to all other ruined temples and palaces of the bygone ages.

With me were my two younger sons, Archie and Quentin, aged nineteen and fifteen respectively, and a cousin of theirs, Nicholas, aged twenty. The cousin had driven our horses, and what outfit we did not ourselves carry, from southern Arizona to the north side of the canyon, and had then crossed the canyon to meet us. The youngest one of the three had not before been on such a trip as that we intended to take; but the two elder boys, for their good fortune, had formerly been at the Evans School in Mesa, Arizona, and among the by-products of their education was a practical and working familiarity with ranch life, with the round-up, and with travelling through the desert and on the mountains. Jesse Cummings, of Mesa, was along to act as cook, packer, and horse-wrangler, helped in all three branches by the two elder boys; he was a Kentuckian by birth, and a better man for our trip and a stancher friend could not have been found.

On the 15th we went down to the bottom of the canyon. There we were to have been met by our outfit with two men whom we had engaged; but they never turned up, and we should have been in a bad way had not Mr. Stevenson, of the Bar Z Cattle Company, come down the trail behind us, while the foreman of the Bar Z, Mr. Mansfield, appeared to meet him, on the opposite side of the rushing, muddy torrent of the Colorado. Mansfield worked us across on the trolley which spans the river; and then we joined in and worked Stevenson, and some friends he had with him, across. Among us all we had food enough for dinner and for a light breakfast, and we had our bedding. With characteristic cattleman's generosity, our new friends turned over to us two pack-mules, which could carry our bedding and the like, and two spare saddle-horses—both the mules and the spare saddle-horses having been brought down by Mansfield because of a lucky mistake as to the number of men he was to meet.

Mansfield was a representative of the best type of old-style ranch foreman. It is a hard climb out of the canyon on the north side, and Mansfield was bound that we should have an early start. He was up at half-past one in the morning; we breakfasted on a few spoonfuls of mush; packed the mules and saddled the horses; and then in the sultry darkness, which in spite of the moon filled the bottom of the stupendous gorge, we started up the Bright Angel trail. Cummings and the two elder boys walked; the rest of us were on horseback. The trail crossed and recrossed the rapid brook, and for rods at a time went up its bowlder-filled bed; groping and stumbling, we made our blind way along it; and over an hour passed before the first grayness of the dawn faintly lighted our footsteps.

At last we left the stream bed, and the trail climbed the sheer slopes and zigzagged upward through the breaks in the cliff walls. At one place the Bar Z men showed us where one of their pack animals had lost his footing and fallen down the mountainside a year previously. It was eight hours before we topped the rim and came out on the high, wooded, broken plateau which at this part of its course forms the northern barrier of the deep-sunk Colorado River. Three or four miles farther on we found the men who were to have met us; they were two days behindhand, so we told them we would not need them, and reclaimed what horses, provisions, and other outfit were ours. With Cummings and the two elder boys we were quite competent to take care of ourselves under all circumstances, and extra men, tents, and provisions merely represented a slight, and dispensable, increase in convenience and comfort.

At is turned out, there was no loss even of comfort. We went straight to the cabin of the game warden, Uncle Jim Owens; and he instantly accepted us as his guests, treated us as such, and accompanied us throughout our fortnight's stay north of the river. A kinder host and better companion in a wild country could not be found. Through him we hired a very good fellow, a mining prospector, who stayed with us until we crossed the Colorado at Lee's Ferry. He was originally a New York State man, who had grown up in Montana, and had prospected through the mountains from the Athabaska River to the Mexican boundary. Uncle Jim was a Texan, born at San Antonio, and raised in the Panhandle, on the Goodnight ranch. In his youth he had seen the thronging myriads of bison, and taken part in the rough life of the border, the life of the cowmen, the buffalo-hunters, and the Indian-fighters. He was by instinct a man of the right kind in all relations; and he early hailed with delight the growth of the movement among our people to put a stop to the senseless and wanton destruction of our wild life. Together with his—and my—friend Buffalo Jones he had worked for the preservation of the scattered bands of bison; he was keenly interested not only in the preservation of the forests but in the preservation of the game. He had been two years buffalo warden in the Yellowstone National Park. Then he had come to the Colorado National Forest Reserve and Game Reserve, where he had been game warden for over six years at the time of our trip. He has given zealous and efficient service to the people as a whole; for which, by the way, his salary has been an inadequate return. One important feature of his work is to keep down the larger beasts and birds of prey, the archenemies of the deer, mountain-sheep, and grouse; and the most formidable among these foes of the harmless wild life are the cougars. At the time of our visit he owned five hounds, which he had trained especially, as far as his manifold duties gave him the time, to the chase of cougars and bobcats. Coyotes were plentiful, and he shot these wherever the chance offered; but coyotes are best kept down by poison, and poison cannot be used where any man is keeping the hounds with which alone it is possible effectively to handle the cougars.

At this point the Colorado, in its deep gulf, bends south, then west, then north, and incloses on three sides the high plateau which is the heart of the forest and game reserve. It was on this plateau, locally known as Buckskin Mountain, that we spent the next fortnight. The altitude is from eight thousand to nearly ten thousand feet, and the climate is that of the far north. Spring does not come until June; the snow lies deep for seven months. We were there in midsummer, but the thermometer went down at night to 36, 34, and once to 33 degrees Fahrenheit; there was hoarfrost in the mornings. Sound was our sleep under our blankets, in the open, or under a shelf of rock, or beneath a tent, or most often under a thickly leaved tree. Throughout the day the air was cool and bracing.

Although we reached the plateau in mid-July, the spring was but just coming to an end. Silver-voiced Rocky Mountain hermit-thrushes chanted divinely from the deep woods. There were multitudes of flowers, of which, alas! I know only a very few, and these by their vernacular names; for as yet there is no such handbook for the flowers of the southern Rocky Mountains as, thanks to Mrs. Frances Dana, we have for those of the Eastern States, and, thanks to Miss Mary Elizabeth Parsons, for those of California. The sego lilies, looking like very handsome Eastern trilliums, were as plentiful as they were beautiful; and there were the striking Indian paint-brushes, fragrant purple locust blooms, the blossoms of that strange bush the plumed acacia, delicately beautiful white columbines, bluebells, great sheets of blue lupin, and the tall, crowded spikes of the brilliant red bell—and innumerable others. The rainfall is light and the ground porous; springs are few, and brooks wanting; but the trees are handsome. In a few places the forest is dense; in most places it is sufficiently open to allow a mountain-horse to twist in and out among the tree trunks at a smart canter. The tall yellow pines are everywhere; the erect spires of the mountain-spruce and of the blue-tipped Western balsam shoot up around their taller cousins, and the quaking asps, the aspens with their ever-quivering leaves and glimmering white boles, are scattered among and beneath the conifers, or stand in groves by themselves. Blue grouse were plentiful—having increased greatly, partly because of the war waged by Uncle Jim against their foes the great horned owls; and among the numerous birds were long-crested, dark-blue jays, pinyon-jays, doves, band-tailed pigeons, golden-winged flickers, chickadees, juncos, mountain-bluebirds, thistle-finches, and Louisiana tanagers. A very handsome cock tanager, the orange yellow of its plumage dashed with red on the head and throat, flew familiarly round Uncle Jim's cabin, and spent most of its time foraging in the grass. Once three birds flew by which I am convinced were the strange and interesting evening grosbeaks. Chipmunks and white-footed mice lived in the cabin, the former very bold and friendly; in fact, the chipmunks, of several species, were everywhere; and there were gophers or rock-squirrels, and small tree-squirrels, like the Eastern chickarees, and big tree-squirrels—the handsomest squirrels I have ever seen—with black bodies and bushy white tails. These last lived in the pines, were diurnal in their habits, and often foraged among the fallen cones on the ground; and they were strikingly conspicuous. . . .

The chief game animal of the Colorado Canyon reserve is the Rocky Mountian blacktail, or mule, deer. The deer have increased greatly in numbers since the reserve was created, partly because of the stopping of hunting by men, and even more because of the killing off of the cougars. The high plateau is their summer range; in the winter the bitter cold and driving snow send them and the cattle, as well as the bands of wild horses, to the lower desert country. For some cause, perhaps the limestone soil, their antlers are unusually stout and large. We found the deer tame and plentiful, and as we rode or walked through the forest we continually came across them—now a doe with her fawn, now a party of does and fawns, or a single buck, or a party of bucks. The antlers were still in the velvet. Does would stand and watch us go by within fifty or a hundred yards, their big ears thrown forward; while the fawns stayed hid near by. Sometimes we roused the pretty spotted fawns, and watched them dart away, the embodiments of delicate grace. One buck, when a hound chased it, refused to run and promptly stood at bay; another buck jumped and capered, and also refused to run, as we passed at but a few yards' distance. One of the most beautiful sights I ever saw was on this trip. We were slowly riding through the open pine forest when we came on a party of seven bucks. Four were yearlings or two-year-olds; but three were mighty master bucks, and their velvet-clad antlers made them look as if they had rocking-chairs on their heads. Stately of port and bearing, they walked a few steps at a time, or stood at gaze on the carpet of brown needles strewn with cones; on their red coats the flecked and broken sun-rays played; and as we watched them, down the aisles of tall tree trunks the odorous breath of the pines blew in our faces.

The deadly enemies of the deer are the cougars. They had been very plentiful all over the table-land until Uncle Jim thinned them out, killing between two and three hundred. Usually their lairs are made in the well-nigh inaccessible ruggedness of the canyon itself. Those which dwelt in the open forest were soon killed off. Along the part of the canyon where we hunted there was usually an upper wall of sheer white cliffs; then came a very steep slope covered by a thick scrub of dwarf oak and locust, with an occasional pinyon or pine; and then another and deeper wall of vermilion cliffs. It was along this intermediate slope that the cougars usually passed the day. At night they came up through some gorge or break in the cliff and rambled through the forests and along the rim after the deer. They are the most successful of all still-hunters, killing deer much more easily than a wolf can; and those we killed were very fat....

When we started on our cougar hunt there were seven of us, with six pack-animals. The latter included one mule, three donkeys—two of them, Ted and Possum, very wise donkeys—and two horses. The saddle-animals included two mules and five horses, one of which solemnly carried a cow-bell. It was a characteristic old-time Western outfit. We met with the customary misadventures of such a trip, chiefly in connection with our animals. At night they were turned loose to feed, most of them with hobbles, some of them with bells. Before dawn, two or three of the party—usually including one, and sometimes both, of the elder boys—were off on foot, through the chilly dew, to bring them in. Usually this was a matter of an hour or two; but once it took a day, and twice it took a half-day. Both breaking camp and making camp, with a pack-outfit, take time; and in our case each of the packers, including the two elder boys, used his own hitch—single-diamond, squaw hitch, cow-man's hitch, miner's hitch, Navajo hitch, as the case might be. As for cooking and washing dishes—why, I wish that the average tourist-sportsman, the city-hunter-with-a-guide, would once in a while have to cook and wash dishes for himself; it would enable him to grasp the reality of things. We are sometimes nearly drowned out by heavy rainstorms. We had good food; but the only fresh meat we had was the cougar meat. This was delicious; quite as good as venison. Yet men rarely eat cougar flesh.

Cougars should be hunted when snow is on the ground. It is difficult for hounds to trail them in hot weather, when there is no water and the ground is dry and hard. However, we had to do the best we could; and the frequent rains helped us. On most of the hunting days we rode along the rim of the canyon and through the woods, hour after hour, until the dogs grew tired, or their feet sore, so that we deemed it best to turn toward camp; having either struck no trail or else a trail so old that the hounds could not puzzle it out. I did not have a rifle, wishing the boys to do the shooting. The two elder boys had tossed up for the first shot, Nick winning. In cougar hunting the shot is usually much the least interesting and important part of the performance. The credit belongs to the hounds, and to the man who hunts the hounds. Uncle Jim hunted his hounds excellently. He had neither horn nor whip; instead, he threw pebbles, with much accuracy of aim, at any recalcitrant dog—and several showed a tendency to hunt deer or coyote. "They think they know best and needn't obey me unless I have a nose-bag full of rocks," observed Uncle Jim.

Twice we had lucky days. On the first occasion we all seven left camp by sunrise with the hounds. We began with an hour's chase after a bobcat, which dodged back and forth over and under the rim rock, and finally escaped along a ledge in the cliff wall. At about eleven we struck a cougar trail of the night before. It was a fine sight to see the hounds running it through the woods in full cry, while we loped after them. After one or two checks, they finally roused the cougar, a big male, from a grove of aspens at the head of a great gorge which broke through the cliffs into the canyon. Down the gorge went the cougar, and then along the slope between the white cliffs and the red; and after some delay in taking the wrong trail, the hounds followed him. The gorge was impassable for horses, and we rode along the rim, looking down into the depths, from which rose the chiming of the hounds. At last a change in the sound showed that they had him treed; and after a while we saw them far below under a pine, across the gorge, and on the upper edge of the vermilion cliff wall. Down we went to them, scrambling and sliding; down a break in the cliffs, round the head of the gorge just before it broke off into a side-canyon, through the thorny scrub which tore our hands and faces, along the slope where, if a man started rolling, he never would stop until life had left his body. Before we reached him the cougar leaped from the tree and tore off, with his big tail stretched straight as a bar behind him; but a cougar is a short-winded beast, and a couple of hundred yards on, the hounds put him up another tree. Thither we went.

It was a wild sight. The maddened hounds bayed at the foot of the pine. Above them, in the lower branches, stood the big horse-killing cat, the destroyer of the deer, the lord of stealthy murder, facing his doom with a heart both craven and cruel. Almost beneath him the vermilion cliffs fell sheer a thousand feet without a break. Behind him lay the Grand Canyon in its awful and desolate majesty.

Nicholas shot true. With his neck broken, the cougar fell from the tree, and the body was clutched by Uncle Jim and Archie before it could roll over the cliff—while I experienced a moment's lively doubt as to whether all three might not waltz into the abyss together. Cautiously we dragged him along the rim to another tree, where we skinned him. Then, after a hard pull out of the canyon, we rejoined the horses; rain came on; and, while the storm pelted against our slickers and down-drawn slouch-hats, we rode back to our water-drenched camp.

On our second day of success only three of us went out—Uncle Jim, Archie, and I. Unfortunately, Quentin's horse went lame that morning, and he had to stay with the pack-train. For two or three hours we rode through the woods and along the rim of the canyon. Then the hounds struck a cold trail and began to puzzle it out. They went slowly along to one of the deep, precipice-hemmed gorges which from time to time break the upper cliff wall of the canyon; and after some busy nose-work they plunged into its depths. We led our horses to the bottom, slipping, sliding, and pitching, and clambered, panting and gasping, up the other side. Then we galloped along the rim. Far below us we could at times hear the hounds. One of them was a bitch, with a squealing voice. The other dogs were under the first cliffs, working out a trail, which was evidently growing fresher. Much farther down we could hear the squealing of the bitch, apparently on another trail. However, the trails came together, and the shrill yelps of the bitch were drowned in the deeper-toned chorus of the other hounds, as the fierce intensity of the cry told that the game was at last roused. Soon they had the cougar treed. Like the first, it was in a pine at the foot of the steep slope, just above the vermilion cliff wall. We scrambled down to the beast, a big male, and Archie broke its neck; in such a position it was advisable to kill it outright, as, if it struggled at all, it was likely to slide over the edge of the cliff and fall a thousand feet sheer.

It was a long way down the slope, with its jungle of dwarf oak and locust, and the climb back, with the skin and flesh of the cougar, would be heartbreaking. So, as there was a break in the cliff line above, Uncle Jim suggested to Archie to try to lead down our riding animals while he, Uncle Jim, skinned the cougar. By the time the skin was off, Archie turned up with our two horses and Uncle Jim's mule—an animal which galloped as freely as a horse. Then the skin and flesh were packed behind his and Uncle Jim's saddles, and we started to lead the three animals up the steep, nearly sheer mountainside. We had our hands full. The horses and mule could barely make it. Finally the saddles of both the laden animals slipped, and Archie's horse in his fright nearly went over the cliff—it was a favorite horse of his, a black horse from the plains below, with good blood in it, but less at home climbing cliffs than were the mountain horses. On that slope anything that started rolling never stopped unless it went against one of the rare pine or pinyon trees. The horse plunged and reared; Archie clung to its head for dear life, trying to prevent it from turning downhill, while Uncle Jim sought to undo the saddle and I clutched the bridle of his mule and of my horse and kept them quiet. Finally the frightened black horse sank on his knees with his head on Archie's lap; the saddle was taken off—and promptly rolled down-hill fifty or sixty yards before it fetched up against a pinyon; we repacked, and finally reached the top of the rim.

Meanwhile the hounds had again started, and we concluded that the bitch must have been on the trail of a different animal, after all. By the time we were ready to proceed they were out of hearing, and we completely lost track of them. So Uncle Jim started in the direction he deemed it probable they would take, and after a while we were joined by Pot. Evidently the dogs were tired and thirsty and had scattered. In about an hour, as we rode through the open pine forest across hills and valleys, Archie and I caught, very faintly, a far-off baying note. Uncle Jim could not hear it, but we rode toward the spot, and after a time caught the note again. Soon Pot heard it and trotted toward the sound. Then we came over a low hill crest, and when half-way down we saw a cougar crouched in a pine on the opposite slope, while one of the hounds, named Ranger, uttered at short intervals a husky bay as he kept his solitary vigil at the foot of the tree. Archie insisted that I should shoot, and thrust the rifle into my hand as we galloped down the incline. The cougar, a young and active female, leaped out of the tree and rushed off at a gait that for a moment left both dogs behind; and after her we tore at full speed through the woods and over rocks and logs. A few hundred yards farther on her bolt was shot, and the dogs, and we also, were at her heels. She went up a pine which had no branches for the lower thirty or forty feet. It was interesting to see her climb. Her two fore paws were placed on each side of the stem, and her hind paws against it, all the claws digging into the wood; her body was held as clear of the tree as if she had been walking on the ground, the legs being straight, and she walked or ran up the perpendicular stem with as much daylight between her body and the trunk as there was between her body and the earth when she was on the ground. As she faced us among the branches I could only get a clear shot into her chest where the neck joins the shoulder; down she came, but on the ground she jumped to her feet, ran fifty yards with the dogs at her heels, turned to bay in some fallen timber, and dropped dead.

The last days before we left this beautiful holiday region we spent on the table-land called Greenland, which projects into the canyon east of Bright Angel. We were camped by the Dripping Springs, in singular and striking surroundings. A long valley leads south through the table-land; and just as it breaks into a sheer walled chasm which opens into one of the side loops of the great canyon, the trail turns into a natural gallery along the face of the cliff. For a couple of hundred yards a rock shelf a dozen feet wide runs under a rock overhang which often projects beyond it. The gallery is in some places twenty feet high; in other places a man on horseback must stoop his head as he rides. Then, at a point where the shelf broadens, the clear spring pools of living water, fed by constant dripping from above, lie on the inner side next to and under the rock wall. A little beyond these pools, with the chasm at our feet, and its opposite wall towering immediately in front of us, we threw down our bedding and made camp. Darkness fell; the stars were brilliant overhead; the fire of pitchy pine stumps flared; and in the light of the wavering flames the cliff walls and jutting rocks momentarily shone with ghastly clearness, and as instantly vanished in utter gloom.

From the southernmost point of this table-land the view of the canyon left the beholder solemn with the sense of awe. At high noon, under the unveiled sun, every tremendous detail leaped in glory to the sight; yet in hue and shape the change was unceasing from moment to moment. When clouds swept the heavens, vast shadows were cast; but so vast was the canyon that these shadows seemed but patches of gray and purple and umber. The dawn and the evening twilight were brooding mysteries over the dusk of the abyss; night shrouded its immensity, but did not hide it; and to none of the sons of men is it given to tell of the wonder and splendor of sunrise and sunset in the Grand Canyon of the Colorado.

CHAPTER
TWENTY

White Water Ramblers

BRIGHT-EYED AND BUSHY-TAILED, we assemble at Lee's Ferry, Arizona, on the banks of a cold green river. Green because of microplankton. Cold (49 degrees Fahrenheit) because this water comes from the bottom of a dam 15 miles upstream—Glen Canyon Dam. We are bound for Pierce Ferry on Lake Mead, 280 miles down-river, through the Grand Canyon of the Colorado.

(We're going to get their stinking dam, by the way. We've got secret plans: underground chemists working on the formula for a new kind of acid that will dissolve concrete underwater; the world's biggest houseboat at Wahweap Marina, above the dam, filled with fertilizer and kerosene; a muralist from Mexico painting a jagged fracture down the dam's face. Long before it fills with mud, Glen Canyon Dam is going to *go*—5,000,000 cubic yards of concrete—down the river. All is ready but the printed announcements.)

I turn my attention to the little boats, the boatmen, my fellow passengers on this suicidal journey down the river of no return.

There are seven dories, bright, gaily painted craft; each is named after some natural feature destroyed or maimed by the works of man. The Peace River (damned in Canada), the Tapestry Wall, the Moqui Steps, the Music Temple (lovely places in Glen Canyon now sunk beneath the waters of Lake Powell), the Vale of Rhondda (mined in Wales) and the Celilo Falls (Columbia River). The boats are seventeen feet long from stem to transom, almost seven feet wide at the beam. Five are made of wood, one of fiberglass, one of aluminum. Closed

"White-water Ramblers" originally appeared in *Playboy*. Copyright 1977 by Edward Abbey. Reprinted by permission of Harold Matson Co., Inc.

hatches at bow, midships and stern make them virtually unsinkable—we are told. I don't believe it for a moment. "Virtually" unsinkable. Virtually, indeed. What sinister ambiguities are contained in that sly equivocation?

I'm looking for a way to creep off unnoticed when my escape is interdicted by the approach of two fellow passengers. Some fellows. One is a dark-brown, exotic wench in a tigerskin bikini; she has the eyes and hair of Salome and breasts like two roebuck gamboling on the playing fields of the Lord. The other is a tall, trim sloop of a girl with flaxen hair, a mouth that promises—well, everything—and elegant thighs emerging from the skimpiest pair of Levi cut-offs I have ever seen.

I pause, hesitate, reconsider. This is a serious assignment. I've been paid real money for this job, money I've already spent, virtually unrefundable. Following my bowsprit back to the beach, I join the crowd around Wally Rist, the head boatman, who is demonstrating—on Salome—the proper way to fasten a life jacket.

An hour later, all too soon, we are launched forth on the mad and complex waters.

Five miles down-river from Lee's Ferry, we glide beneath the bridge, 467 feet above us, that spans Marble Gorge. Some Navaho kid up there, bored with trying to sell clay pots to the tourists, lobs a rock. It crashes into the water ten feet from our boat. Can't blame the Indians, just normal ethnic hatred, but our boatman, John Blaustein, picks up the pace a bit, heaving at the oars, until we are safely out of range.

Entering here over a century ago, Major John Wesley Powell wrote as follows in his diary:

> August 5, 1869—With some feeling of anxiety we enter a new can-
> yon this morning. We have learned to observe closely the texture of the
> rock. In softer strata we have a quiet river, in harder we find rapids and
> falls. Below us are the limestones and hard sandstones which we found
> in Cataract Canyon. This bodes toil and danger.

The Kaibab limestone formation rises on either side of us, forming walls that cut off most of the sky. We float through a monstrous defile one thousand feet deep; two thousand feet deep? From ahead comes the deep, toneless vibration of the first major rapid. Badger Rapid. The sound resembles that of a freight train approaching through a tunnel. On the standard boatman's scale of one to ten, this rapid is rated at four to six. Of intermediate difficulty. Staring, we see the river come to an edge and vanish. Curling waves leap above that edge. Rist, in the first boat, stands up for a good look, sits down, turns his bow forward and slides over the glassy rim of water. His boat disappears. He disappears. Two more dories follow. They disappear. Our turn.

"Buckle up," commands John.

I and the three other passengers in the dory fasten our life jackets. John stands in the center of the boat, reading the water. Pooled behind the wall of boulders that forms the rapid, the river slows, moving with sluggish ease toward the drop. The roar grows louder.

John seats himself, the dory slides down the oily tongue of the rapid, holes and boils and haystack waves exploding all around us. John makes a perfect run down the middle. One icy wave reaches up and slaps me in the chest, drenches my belly, groin and private parts. *Cold!* The shock of it. But we are through, riding the choppy tail of the rapid. John catches the eddy on the right and with a few deft strokes brings our boat to the beach. The other boats join us. Boatmen and passengers clamber ashore. Here we shall make camp for our first night on the river. We haven't gone far, but then, we didn't get started till noon today.

The cooks begin at once preparing supper. Our cooks are two able and handsome young women named Jane and Kenly. Both are competent oarsmen as well, but because of their employer (Martin Litton of Portola Valley, California), they are confined to the role of cook. They don't seem to mind. Good policy, anyway, I'm thinking; after all, if we allow women to do anything men can do, what remains of the ancient dignity of being a *man?* We have to draw the line somewhere. Fair but firm, that's the rule. Keep them down, I say, beat them down with oars and anchor chains, if need be, with vigorous blows about the head and shoulders, but keep them down.

After dinner—pork chops, applesauce, salad, etc., the etc. in my case being a mug of Ronrico 151—the boatman called Sharky digs out his ukulele and his kazoo and announces a party. Darkness settles in, the campfire blazes higher, decorum decays. Salome dances in the sand. The tall slim girl in the cutoff cutoffs stands somewhat aloof, watching us all with a scornful smile on her lovely face. We sing the kind of songs people sing on river trips, we talk, we smoke our long cigars, we watch the fire.

The tall girl leaves us, walking up the dunes into the shadows toward her bed. I resolve to follow. One more nip on the Ronrico and two more songs and then I slink away, unobserved, I hope, and trail her footsteps in the sand. In the dim starlight, I find her lying on top of her sleeping bag, naked as a nymph.

She says nothing as I unroll my bag beside hers, undress and lie down next to her. Two shooting stars trace lingering parabolas of blue fire across the sky. From below rises the sound of rowdy music. Crickets chirp. I reach out and touch the girl, softly, on her warm, rounded hip.

"Took you long enough to get here," she says.

"Sorry, honey."

We wake early in the morning to the sound of Rich Turner, boatman, playing his recorder. *Greensleeves, Foggy, Foggy Dew, Amazing Grace*—sweet, simple tunes that float like angelic voices through the great natural echo chamber under the canyon walls. We pass without trauma from our dreams into the day, the wilderness and desert and river.

Great blue herons rise before us, flap down-river, find another perch and wait until we herd them on again. Ravens croak, canyon wrens sing *a glissando* and, in the thickets on the bank, we spot a blue grosbeak, an ash-throated flycatcher, a sparrow hawk. John rows and rests. Waterdrops fall from his oars and tinkle on the surface of the placid river. An enormous stillness fills the canyon.

Then the sound of motors. "Baloney boats," says John. We look upstream and see a huge silver-gray rubber raft come barging around the bend, bearing down on us. Swarming with people, it looks like a floating anthill. John pulls our dory aside to let it pass. At full throttle, the thing roars by. Followed a minute later by a second and a third. Western River Expeditions, Salt Lake City. The wilderness mass-transit system. The three baloneys swerve around the bend below and vanish. Oil slicks glisten on the water. Gasoline fumes hover on the air, slowly dissipating. Gradually, the quiet returns. We talk about birds, rocks, rapids.

Ah, yes, the rapids. Here they come again. We run Soap Creek Rapid, rated five to six, and Salt Water Wash, where Frank M. Brown was drowned in 1889, surveying for a railroad that was never built. Sheerwall Rapid (two to three). House Rock Rapid (seven to eight). The ratings vary, depending on the volume of river flow. Most rapids are easier in high water; this river is low.

We hit no rocks but plunge through plenty of waves. Soaked with icy water, burning under the sun, we bail out the boat, gaze up at the towering walls and hurry on, borne forward by the hastening current. In the late afternoon, chilled despite the August heat by the water and the shade of the canyon walls, we are glad to see Wally's boat pulled ashore on the beach above the mouth of North Canyon. Second camp: Mile 21 from Lee's Ferry. Sixteen days and nights to go.

Unloading the dories is becoming part of the routine. Most of the passengers help out, scrounging for firewood, carrying water. My wife, Renée, the girl with the legs, has already made herself a member of the crew. Only a few more sensitive types like myself, pained by the sight of toil, sneak away for a walk up North Canyon.

That evening, the wind begins to blow. Dark clouds loom like trouble, lightning crackles in the distance. Will it rain? Renée and I string up our plastic tube tent. It doesn't rain, but all night long the wind howls, the sand swirls in our faces and small green bugs crawl in and out of my ears, seeking shelter.

Today is a good day. John Blaustein lets me row his boat. After getting safely past 24½ Mile Rapid, where Bert Loper died in 1949, and through 29 Mile Rapid, I barely get around the exposed rock at the head of the chute in 30 Mile Riffle and am forced to run the rest of it stern foremost. Backward. The dory does well enough in this attitude, but John is shaken. "Exciting," he says, his knuckles white, "very exciting. Give me back the oars, please."

Well, to hell with him. I thought it was a good run. Any run without loss of boat or passengers is a good run, in my opinion. To hell with him.

Lunch at Redwall Cavern, Mile 33. Lemonade, beer, avocado-cheese-beansprout sandwiches. Redwall Cavern is a huge chamber carved out of the limestone by the old, predamnation river. Major Powell guessed it would seat fifty thousand people. I'd say five thousand. He was off by a digit but assumed, when writing his celebrated report, that no one else would ever come down the river to check up on him. I'm not calling Powell a liar; Powell is a hero of mine. But I will say he had a tendency, now and then, to slightly exaggerate the truth.

The river, brown before, is taking on a rich red-orange color, *muy Colorado*. The good old Paria (a side stream) must be in flood again. So that's where last night's storm was.

We run some modest rapids this afternoon, make third camp at Buck Farm Canyon early in the evening. Much deer sign—thus the name?—and trickling seeps, emerald pools with tadpoles, red and blue and purple dragonflies, cottonwoods, willows, graceful little redbud trees. Soup and salad, steak and sweet corn, plenty of beer for supper. Happiness.

Off again on the river of gold, through a clear, bright, irreplaceable day.

The great Redwall cliffs soaring above, intense and vivid against God's own blue sky. Marble Canyon, Powell called this place, though limestone is not marble and he knew it.

We camp tonight at Nankoweap. "Nankoweap," Wally explains, "is an old Paiute Indian word meaning 'place where scorpions crawl into sleeping bags if not detected by unsleeping vigilance.'"

Onward. We have come only 52 miles in four days. We have many miles, many rapids, many pages to go before this perilous journal is completed.

Kwagunt Rapid (four to six). No problem. 60 Mile Rapid (four). Simple. We pass the mouth of the Little Colorado River, brown with floodwaters, and find new and formidable rock formations rising before us. Powell recorded the approach in these words:

> August 13, 1869—We are now ready to start on our way down the Great Unknown. We have but a month's rations remaining. With some eagerness and some anxiety and some misgiving we enter the canyon below. . . .

Dramatic words. With a little effort of the imagination, we can understand how Powell and his brave men felt. For more than two months they'd been battling the river, all the way from Wyoming—upsetting in rapids, wrecking boats, losing supplies, gambling on Powell's belief that a river so silt-laden would not, as rumors had it, disappear underground or trap boats and boatmen between unscalable walls on the verge of a fatal waterfall.

Above us on the right stands Chuar Butte. Still visible up there, far above the river, are the aluminum scraps of two commercial airliners that collided above the Grand Canyon in 1956. One hundred and twenty-eight went down; all died.

Tanner Rapid. Basalt Canyon, a volcanic region, with grim-looking blue-black cliffs set at a crazy angle to the descending river. We make camp above the roar of Unkar Rapid in the last broad open valley we shall see for more than 200 miles. Not far downstream, the river cuts into the Pre-Cambrian gneiss and schists of the Upper Granite Gorge, the inner canyon. Where the big rapids make their play.

We push on to a river the color of bronze, shimmering like hammered metal under the desert sun. Through Unkar—made it! Then Nevills Rapid (four to seven). Still alive. We pull ashore above Hance Rapid (eight to nine) for study and thought.

Hance is always a problem for the dorymen, especially in low water. Too many rocks sticking up or, even worse, rocks half-hidden near the surface. No clear route through. A zigzag course. Huge waves, treacherous boils, eaters—churning holes that can eat a boat alive. A kind of slalom for oarsmen, with the penalty for a mistake a possible smashed boat.

They run it one by one, not easily but safely. The river carries us swiftly into the Inner Gorge. Like a tunnel of love, there are practically no shores or beaches in here. The burnished rocks rise sheer from the water's edge, cutting off all view of the higher cliffs, all of the outer world but a winding strip of blue sky. We float along as if in a gigantic millstream. Powell called it a gloomy place, but *glowing* is the word. The afternoon sun, hidden by the high walls but reflected and refracted by the water, by the polished cliffs, by the atmosphere, streams upon us with indirect light, from many angles, all radiant.

Two miles below Hance, we crash through the well-named Sockdolager Rapid (six to eight), and two and a half miles later, into and through Grapevine Rapid (six to eight). The boats ride high on the water but not high enough to escape the recoil of the 55-degree waves. Screams of delight, shock, astonishment ring through the canyon as we ride this liquid roller coaster. Unlike the sea, here on the river the water moves, the waves remain in place.

In the early afternoon, we arrive at the ranger station near the Phantom Ranch tourist hostel, the only outpost of civilization within the Grand Canyon. From here, foot and mule trails lead to both the North and the South Rims. Also a telephone line. There is even a heliport for the convenience of visiting dignitaries. The two footbridges across the river at this point are the only bridges on the Colorado from near Lee's Ferry to Hoover Dam, more than 300 miles.

Here we pause for an hour. Some of the passengers are leaving us, having contracted for only the first part of the voyage. Their places are taken by others who have hiked the trail down from South Rim. All is soon ready. One by one the boats move out, down the river, deeper into the Inner Gorge.

This time, my wife and I sit in the bow of the leading dory. Our boatman is young Rich Turner—musician, ornithologist, schoolteacher, rock climber, high diver, veteran oarsman. Two other passengers are on board: Jane, the cook, and a newcomer, 15-year-old Jennie Dear from Henderson, Kentucky. An active, athletic girl, Jennie has never been on a river trip of any kind before. As we drift down the river, Rich plying the oars at a leisurely pace, she asks if we don't get bored sometimes with this effortless sort of travel. We tell her about the birds and the interesting geological formations.

Rich suggests that we buckle life jackets. Horn Creek Rapid (seven to nine) coming up, he reminds us. He says something about The Great Wave. For Jennie's benefit, he reviews routine upset procedures: Take deep breath when entering rapids: hang on; if boat turns over, get out from under and grab lifeline strung along gunwales; stay on upstream side of boat to avoid being trapped between boat and a hard place; climb onto bottom of boat as soon as possible; grasp flip line and assist boatman in righting boat; bail out liquid contents; relax and enjoy the view.

"What was that about a great wave?" Renée asks.

"I didn't say *a* great wave," says Rich. "I said *The* Great Wave."

Not far ahead, the river plays its conjuring trick, pouring off the edge of the known world, disappearing into some kind of grumbling abyss. Above the watery rim I can see hints of a rainbow in the mist, backlit by the westering sun.

What I've forgotten is that Horn, unlike longer rapids above and below, makes its descent abruptly, in one dive, through a narrow channel where the river is squeezed into sudden acceleration. Rich stands up for a last look but sits quickly. The boat slides down the glassy tongue of the current. Into a yawning mouth. I take a deep breath—involuntarily. "Hang on!" Rich shouts.

The dory plunges down into the watery hole, then up the slope of the standing wave. The wave topples upon us, filling the boat in an instant. The force of the river carries us through and toward a second, deeper hole. "One more!" cries Rich. One more, indeed. We drop. The second wave towers above us. Far above. The Great Wave. Our water-laden boat, turned askew, climbs heavily up its face. Never makes it. The wave hits us from the left and the dory turns over with the grave, solemn, unresisting certainty of disaster. No one says a word as we go under.

Below the surface, all is silent and dark. Part of the current, I feel no sense of motion. But before there is time to think about this, the life jacket brings me to the top. The dory, upside down, is only a stroke away. I grab the lifeline. Renée is hanging on beside me. Rich and Jennie cling to the stern, Jane to the downstream side. The wrong side.

The river carries us swiftly toward the canyon wall below the rapid, on the left. Jane seems still a bit dazed. Rich heaves himself onto the flat bottom of the boat and pulls her up. The boat crunches into the cliff. Sound of splintering plywood. The weight of the current forces the upstream side of the boat down, pushing me and Renée underwater again. Down in the darkness, I let go of the boat's lifeline and kick away.

After what seems an unnecessarily long time, I rise to the surface. A wave splashes in my face as I gasp for air. Good God, I'm drowning, I think, choking on a windpipe full of muddy water. Instinctively, I swim toward shore and find myself caught in a big eddy, pulled in a circle by the swirling current. Where's Renée? I see the boat go sailing past, upside down, three people crawling on it, none of them my wife. The eddy carries me to the wall and I make a strenuous effort to find a handhold on the glossy stone. Impossible. The eddy pulls me toward a pile of broken rock fallen from the wall. I succeed in getting onto the rocks, free of the river at last. Renée? I hear her calling me. There she is, below me on an adjoining shelf of rock. Reunited, we watch Rich, Jane, Jennie and the capsized dory float away. Without us. We are relaxing into a foolish despair, feeling abandoned, when good John Blaustein comes charging through The Great Wave, spots us and rows close enough for rescue. With six soaked passengers aboard, he rows hard after Rich. Rich is having trouble getting his boat righted. John and I assist, pulling on the flip lines, and the boat comes right side up.

That evening in camp, as Rich patches up his injured dory with glue and yards of duct tape, it dawns on me why the boatmen sometimes refer to the major rapids as Christian Falls. Why? Because they make a believer out of you.

Today we run a series of rapids, beginning with Granite Falls (seven to eight). Looks bad but proves an easy run down the middle. Then Hermit (six to seven) and Boucher (four to five). From Boucher, I look up and see Point Sublime, far away and six thousand feet above on the forested North Rim. A place of many memories for me, linked with those summers when I worked as fire lookout up there, in another life, another world. We come to Crystal Rapid (eight to ten) and go ashore above it.

Crystal is a problem, with rocks on the right, rocks on the left and a huge churning eater in the middle; below the big hole lies the Rock Garden, extending across the river except for a narrow channel on the far right.

The boatmen start back to their boats. The shutterbugs get out their cameras, sitting on boulders in the sun, half-surrounded by the clamor of the thundering, tormented waters. Out there in the middle of the maelstrom, the eater waits, heaving and gulping, its mouth like a giant clam's, its rage like the 1976 Republican Convention—a horrifying uproar, all things considered. Imagine floating through that nonsense in only a life jacket. You'd feel like a butterfly being flushed down a toilet bowl.

One by one, the dories come through. But Mike Markovich, rowing a heavier boat, gets a stroke behind, is pulled toward the mouth of the eater and caught by the wave that forms the eater's lip. The boat is spun 180 degrees and turned on edge. Mike falls out, vanishing into the waves. The boat dances on the water's crest like a surfboard, is swallowed by the mouth, then spat out, shot downstream. Mike appears, swimming around the rocks and into the narrow channel on the far right. His dory, miraculously still upright, sails sedately down through the Rock Garden without touching a rock. Mike sees the boat, swims to it in the tail of the rapid, climbs aboard.

After Crystal, we pass a series of side canyons with gemlike names: Agate, Sapphire, Turquoise, Ruby. Near Bass Rapid, we see an old rusting metal boat stranded high on the left bank, far above the present water line. Nobody seems to know how it got there. Onward, through Shinumo Rapid, 110 Mile Rapid, Hakatai Rapid and into Waltenberg (five to eight). A sleeper, giant waves shutting out the sun. We plow through, Renée and I now riding in Mike's big boat. Mike's hands are sore, his knees cut up by rocks from his swim at Crystal. I row his heavy, leaky, water-laden boat the last two miles to our camp at Garnet Canyon. Twenty-one miles today—a record. We are wet, cold, tired and murderously hungry.

Onward and downward. Today we run Forster Rapid and Fossil Rapid, then Specter, Bedrock and Dubendorff, and camp at the mouth of Tapeats Creek. Deep in the mantle of the earth.

Sausage and blueberry pancakes for breakfast. I hold out my tin cup, disdaining a plate. An enormous pancake is draped over my cup, hand and wrist. Sharky and Rich, in charge of flipping the flapjacks this morning, begin a game. Who can toss a pancake higher and catch it on his spatula? Higher and higher spin the half-baked pancakes, revolving lazily against the cerulean shore of outer space. One falls in the sand. You lose. But another rises to unimaginable heights, higher and higher, becoming a speck, a mote, a mathematical point, and vanishes forever beyond all human ken. God's pancake.

Time to get out of this awful canyon. Good Christ, we've been lingering and malingering around down in here for ten days—eleven? Twenty-two? Whatever. This claustrophobe's nightmare. This rumbling gulch of iron and stone. This baloney funnel, this motorboat tunnel, this stinking trench of prickly pear and burro shit and Porta Potti fumes.

Speaking of baloneys. I'm tossing another empty Michelob can into the river when three gigantic pontoon barges, 37 feet long if they're an inch, come chugging down the channel. Each is piled high with naked humans blistering under the sun, who wave at us and shout with waning glee as they plow through the cold waves of Tapeats Rapid.

We camp two nights at the mouth of Tapeats. During the day, we hike up Tapeats Creek and visit one of its tributaries, Thunder River, a great gush of frothy water pouring from a cave in the Redwall limestone. (How can a river be a tributary of a creek?) The Redwall formation is full of caverns, partially explored. The whole Kaibab Plateau is full of holes, of which the Grand Canyon happens to be merely the most open and conspicuous.

Late in the evening, returning, Renée and I pause on the rim trail high above the Tapeats and look down at our camp. Twilight down in there. Moon rising on the east. A pillar of blue smoke rises slowly from the cooking fire. Some of the girls are shampooing their hair in the mouth of the clear stream. Wally and Dane Mensik are casting for trout. Others lie about reading, dozing, talking, sipping booze. Murmur of voices. Humans more or less, like us, enjoying the sense of a perfect evening. We hear Sharky and Rich playing a duet with their recorders; the melody of an old, old Shaker hymn floats up toward us on the quiet air:

> *'Tis a gift to be simple,*
> *'Tis a gift to be free,*
> *'Tis a gift to come down*
> *Where we ought to be....*

Onward. We plunge through treacherous Upset Rapid (three to eight), where the motor-pontoon man Shorty Burton got his, back in '67. We doff headgear in his memory. R.I.P., Shorty. We'll join you shortly. We pause for half a day at Havasu Creek. Blue water, full of travertine. This lime solution tends to form hard, stony barriers, like small dams, as it flows down the creek to the river. As a result, Havasu Creek has many falls, cascades and pools.

Here we lounge in the lime-blue water, spouting fountains at the sky, and talk of Phoenix, Arizona, Shithead Capital of the Sunny Southwest, of smog, growth, business, politics and such obscenities. It is Wally Rist who broaches the obvious thought: Suppose all that garbage has ceased to exist. Suppose The Bomb has come and gone and we are the sole survivors. For nearly two weeks, we haven't seen a newspaper, heard a radio or smelled a TV set; how do we know the world is still out there?

Sobering thought. If it's not, I suggest, then the first thing we'd better do is march up Havasu Canyon to the village of Supai and raid the Indians' melon patch. Like Major Powell did.

Sharky shakes his head, looking around at the glistening bodies of the long-haired rosy-bottomed dolphins splashing about in the next pool. No, he says, the first thing we've got to do is start repopulating the earth. First things first.

We camp at National Canyon, Mile 167. The boatmen are somber tonight, thinking of Mile 179: Lava Falls. John takes me down to the beach and shows me a rock close to the river's edge. "See this rock?" he says. "That's oracle rock. If the river is up in the morning high enough to cover the rock, we can go left at Lava. If the water covers only half the rock, we go middle or right. If it doesn't reach the rock, we have to go right."

"What's the easiest run?"

"The slot in the middle."

"What's the worst?"

"Down the right."

In the morning, the river is low. John looks grim. I check the rock. High and dry. (The river level, because of Glen Canyon Dam and its varying peak-power outflow, is constantly rising and falling.)

> August 13, 1869—We are now ready to start on our way down the Great Unknown. . . . What falls there are, we know not; what rocks beset the channel, we know not; what walls rise over the river, we know not. . . . The men talk as cheerfully as ever; jests are bandied about freely this morning; but to me the cheer is somber and the jests are gastly [sic].

Write on, good Major Powell. How prescient you were. I can read your every emotion on the faces of the boatmen.

As Sharky pulls us into the current, lashing about lustily with the oars, I glance back at the beach we are now departing. Only once. A black shadow lies across the unwet rugosities of oracle rock. Well—it looks like a good day to die. All days are OK, but this one looks better than most. Might as well review the scenery.

Some of the highest walls in the canyon rear above our heads. Two thousand feet straight up. With terraces and further higher walls beyond. Toroweap Overlook rises three thousand feet above the river at Mile 176.

The Colorado slides seaward in its stony groove. We'll never make it. Mojave Desert–type vegetation: mesquite, ocotillo, catclaw acacia, barrel cactus, clockface and cow's-tongue prickly pear. All adorn as best they can the talus slopes below the cliffs.

We stop for lunch at Mile 177, not far above *that riffle*. Looking solemn, Wally gives his final harangue of the voyage.

"Listen!" he begins.

We listen. Don't hear a damn thing. Sigh of the river, maybe, swooning round the next bend. Cicadas keening in the dry grass. Faint scream of the sun, 93,000,000 miles above. Nothing significant, right?

"You don't hear it, but it's there," he says. "Lava Falls. Mile 179. It's always there. Every time we come down this river, there it is. Drops thirty-seven feet. The worst rapid in North America. We're gonna need help from you people. Anybody who's hoping to see a disaster, stay out of sight. All passengers will walk around this one except volunteers. Yes, we'll need. . . ."

Hands are rising.

"Not yet," Wally says. "We want everybody to see it first. Anybody who thinks he or she wants to ride through Lava has to get down there and walk below it and look up through the waves. We want people who can handle the oars, who can help right the boat if it flips and can climb around on wet boulders, if necessary. Nobody has to do it, but I'll tell you this much: When you're out there in the middle of Lava, it's nice to hear another heart beating besides your own."

Commander Wally's briefing. You'd think we were in a U-boat about to enter a combat zone. Nobody has to do it, eh? Not even looking at me, he says that. Pretending to talk to everybody but me. But you've tipped your hand, Rist. I can read you like the writing on the wall, Wally. No, thanks. I glance furtively up and down the river, trapped but not yet panicked. Where is that place? That Separation Canyon? That EXIT from this hall of horrors?

Salami on rye, potato salad, peanut butter and Ry-Krisp for lunch. Not half bad. It's all bad. The condemned man revealed no emotion as he ate his lunch. Ironic laughter in the background. No place to hide. All boats shove off onto the shining Colorado.

At Mile 178, a great black basaltic rock appears, standing silent in the middle of the river. Vulcan's Anvil, they call it. It looks like a 40-foot tombstone.

A muttering sound rises ahead, beyond the next bend. Wordless voices grumble in subterranean echo chambers. All boats put ashore on the right bank. Wally leads us, passengers and crew, up a path through the tamarisk jungle and onto a slide of volcanic boulders big as bungalows, high above the river. Lava Falls bellows in the sunlight. He stops. We stop. He waves us on. "Volunteers will assemble here," he shouts, above the tumult from below. *"After* you've looked it over."

We go on, all but the boatmen, who remain clustered around Wally, commencing their usual confabulations. The sad smiles, the solemn headshakings. Same old hype. I smile too, slinking away. See you in hell, boat boys. Chuckling, I join the stockbrokers and sweet old ladies in a safe, shady place near the foot of the uproar. Breathing easily now, I watch the dancing falls, the caldron of colliding superwaves, the lava rocks like iron-blue bicuspids protruding from the foam—here, there, most everywhere, a fiendish distribution of dory-rending fangs. I study the channel on the far left: nothing but teeth. The "slot" in the middle: gone. Hah, I think, they're going to have to run it on the right. Right up against this basalt boxcar I'm relaxing on.

Time passes. Can't see the boatmen from here. But I know what they're doing. They're all squatting in the bushes, taking a last crap. A natural animal reflex. The old phrase "scared shitless" denotes a basic biological psycholophysical reaction. I look back up at the "volunteers' " assembly point. Sure enough, a few suckers have showed up, seven or eight of them.

A red, white and yellow dory appears on the tongue upstream. The Tapestry Wall. There's Captain Rist standing on his seat, one hand shielding his eyes. He looks pretty, all right, heroic as hell. Two passengers ride with him, sunk deep in their seats, white knuckles clenched on the gunwales. Wally lowers himself into the cockpit, takes a firm grip on the oars. Here they come. They disappear. They emerge, streaming with water. Dive and disappear again. Dark forms barely visible through the foam. The boat rears up into sunlight. Wally has crabbed an oar, lost an oarlock. He's in trouble. He's struggling with something. They vanish again, under the waves, to reappear not twenty feet from where I sit, bearing hard upon this immovable barrier. The dory yaws to port. Wally is trying hard to stand; he's got only one oar; looks like he's planning to climb right out of the boat onto my rock. No, he's climbing the high side, trying to prevent the boat from capsizing. Cushioned by a roil of water, the boat and its three occupants rush past me, only inches from the iron rock. Who's that lady in the stern, smiling bravely, waving one little brown hand at me? That's no lady, that's my wife! Renée! The violent current bears her away, out of sight.

Jesus. . . . But they're safe.

One made it. Six more to go. We have to sit and watch this? Too late now, here comes Dane at the control console of the Vale of Rhondda. A passenger in the bow. He makes a perfect run, bow first through the holes, over the big waves, and clears Death Rock by a safe and sane three feet. After him appears Mike Davis in the Music Temple—another good descent.

Three safely past, four to go. Here they come: Sharky Cornell in the Columbia, Mike Markovich in the Moqui Steps, Rich Turner in the patched-up Celilo Falls. Each with a light payload of ballast—one passenger each—they make it right side up, one way or the other way, through the sound and the fury of Mile 179.

One more to go. Poor old John Blaustein in the Peace River. I glance up at the volunteers' assembly point. The slave block. One little girl stands there, clutching her life jacket, hopefully waiting. It's Jennie Dear, the kid who changed our luck at Horn Creek. The Jonah. Now I really feel sorry for Blaustein. Not only are the scales of probability weighing against him—for if six made it through, the seventh is doomed for certain—but he and he alone has to ride with that sweet little jinx we picked up at Phantom Ranch. Tough luck, John. Bad karma. Kismet, you know. (But better him than me.)

Where *is* Blaustein, by the way?

I feel a firm hand on my shoulder. "Let's go," he says.

Oh, shit. Well, of course, I knew it would turn out like this all along. I never had a chance.

We trudge over the rocks, pick up Jennie, trudge through the jungle and down to the lonely boat, hyperventilating all the way. Buckle up. John gives stern instructions, which I don't hear. Pushes off. Me and little Jennie in the bow. The sun glares at us over the brassy water, blazing in our eyes. John is pointing the dory right down into the heart of the madness. The moment of total commitment. This is absurd. We dive headfirst into the absurdity. . . .

Fifteen seconds, twenty seconds, and it's all over. Thirty seconds and we're cruising through the tail of the rapid, busy with the bailers, joining the procession of six boats before us. Nothing to it. Like I always say, running the big rapids is like sex: Half the fun is in the anticipation. The real thrill is in the approach. The remainder is only ecstasy—or darkness.

We still have 100 miles to go. A hundred miles to Pierce Ferry, the hard row against the wind to the dismal mudbanks of Lake *Merde*.

The river goes on and on, but I am going to end this journey where we began, near Lee's Ferry and *that dam,* making the voyage semicircular. I want my tale, like the river, to go to the sea and rise from the sea in mighty clouds, riding the west winds back to the source in the Rockies once again. The river is linear, but its course is the lazy, horizontal figure eight of infinity.

We are going to have our river whole again, someday soon. Glen Canyon Dam must fall. Must soon come tumbling down. Norm Nevills would understand. Bert Loper and Moki-Mac would understand. All old river rats dead and gone and yet to come will understand. The spirit of John Wesley Powell understands, high in his haunt on the rim of Great Thumb Mesa. Listen to his words, still whispered by the wind:

> *We have an unknown distance yet to run,*
> *An unknown river to explore.*

Night and day, the river flows. If time is the mind of space, the Colorado is the soul of the desert. Brave boatmen come, they go, they die, the river flows on forever. We are all canyoneers. We are all passengers on this little mossy living ship, this delicate dory round the sun, that humans call the earth.

Joy, shipmates, joy.

CHAPTER
TWENTY-ONE

Transition

AS I STOOD WATCHING the plane contract to a speck and finally dissolve in the blue distance, I think I already knew that my journey had moved on. It was no picnic yet, let alone a pilgrimage. But I had taken the critical steps. I had crossed the amphitheaters. And by taking my airdrop at the alternate site I had proved beyond all reasonable doubt that I could meet the Canyon's physical challenge.

It was not until evening, though, just after sunset, that I really grasped what the airdrop had meant. I was stretched out on top of my sleeping bag and doing nothing but gaze up into the pale sky when, far overhead, a jet airliner glinted briefly in the rays of the already hidden sun. But the plane was flying so high that its whisper did not really damage the silence. And its remote presence did not even touch the solitude.

And all at once I realized that the airdrop had not touched my solitude either. Had not penetrated my cocoon of peace and simplicity. For there had been no feeling of personal contact. Even on the Cessna's final run I had, curiously, seen no figures in the plane's cabin. And I realized now that I had not really connected the plane and its roar with actual happenings in the outside world. I had seen it as a mere convenience. As an impersonal instrument fulfilling my personal needs. And now, looking up at the remote speck that was the airliner, I saw, in the sudden and overwhelming way you do when the obvious at last forces itself on your awareness, that the important thing was my cocoon of peace and solitude. The fact that a cocoon existed. I had, I saw, finally escaped from the paradox of simple living. The trivia were still there, and would be until the end of my journey. But I had overcome them. Had broken free at last from the din and deadline of the outside world.

I promptly held a celebration: I prefaced dinner with the week's menu-spicing delicacy, a can of smoked sliced lobster, and afterward I tempered the pemmican and dehydrated potatoes with claret. At the meal's end, for a semi-delightful five minutes, I was half-canyons over.*

Yet the turning point that I had sensed did not immediately materialize. I even managed to spend the next three days pressed tighter than ever to the sweaty world of effort.

All through those three days I reconnoitered, hard, in Fossil Canyon. No one, it seemed, had ever found a way down this narrow cleavage in the rock, almost two thousand feet deep. But I knew that if I succeeded I would be able to travel beside the Colorado and avoid the appallingly long and apparently water-less extension of the Esplanade that still separated me from the cache I had hidden just below the Rim near Bass Camp. (As far as I knew this terrace was quite without any natural water source; but halfway along, just below the Rim at Apache Point, I had put out my only other cache, and it included four gallons of water.)

The idea of pioneering a route down Fossil Canyon had attracted me at least as much as the practical advantages, and for three days, based on my air-drop camp, I walked and scrambled and climbed and inched my way down and along and then back and along and then across and up and along an endless suc-cession of terraces and ledges and cliffs. Twice I followed tapering cliff-face cracks until I was out in places I should never have been. And there was one talus slope I hope some day to forget. On the third evening I came back to camp exhausted. My left hand was a throbbing pin cushion: in a sudden moment of fear, on a sloping rockledge strewn with rubble, I had grabbed blindly for a handhold and found a prickly pear. And for the third straight day I had failed to find a break in the Redwall cliff that is Fossil Canyon's major barrier.

It was as I lay in my mummy bag waiting for dinner to cook that I realized that by concentrating on the reconnaissance I had lost sight of why I had come down into the Canyon. Once the idea had occurred to me, the stupidity of the mistake became quite clear. And I decided immediately that I would rest for

---

*Only semidelightful. Although the delicacies were a pleasing change at every cache and drop, the claret never quite seemed to add the final touch I had hoped for. I have since real-ized that you don't really need alcohol in the wilderness. Not when you're alone, anyway.

two days beside the large rainpocket at the head of Fossil Bay—the rainpocket that had been the proper alternate drop site—and then strike out along the terrace toward Bass Camp.

That decision was the real turning point.

I do not mean that I discovered at once the things I had come to find. But from then on I moved steadily toward them. Moved closer to rock and sky, to light and shadow, to space and silence. Began to feel their rhythms.

Of course, the change did not appear clear-cut. If you had asked me at almost any time during that week how the journey was progressing, I would have answered, I think, with reports on water supply and condition of feet and quantity of food left and distance remaining to the next cache. These were still the things I measured progress by. Most of the time, anyway.

On this important and insistent level, the week was a period of steady and straightforward physical progress. I rested as planned for almost two full days beside the deep rainpocket at the head of Fossil Bay, then struck south. The terrace that led to Bass Camp was four times as long as the one I had barely managed to complete on that first Butchart test day to Sinyala Canyon, and even with my halfway cache at Apache Point it looked as if it would be the toughest leg so far. But now I was ten days better tuned, and the operation went off exactly according to plan.

I left the head of Fossil Bay in the cool of evening, as I usually do when a long day lies ahead. I carried three gallons of water and camped barely two hours out. By six o'clock next evening I had crossed the precipitous head of Forster Canyon—a barrier that wild burros cannot pass, and which marks the eastern limit of the bighorn country, just as the amphitheater under Great Thumb Mesa marks its western limit. At nightfall I camped close under Apache Point, on the first map-marked trail since Supai. This Apache Trail, though betraying no hint of human use, turned out to be a busy burro turnpike (the burros are the National Park's unpaid trail maintenance crew) and I made good time along it. By noon next day I had reached and found unharmed the five-gallon can of supplies and the four gallons of bottled water that formed my cache at Apache Point. (I arrived with only 65 cc. of water left, but the situation was much less critical than it sounds: before climbing the steep thousand-foot talus slope below the cache I had lightened my load by drinking most of the quite adequate supply left in my canteens.) In the cool of that evening I carried three gallons of water back down to the terrace and camped. Next day I broke the back of the long, zigzag, burro-trail swing around Aztec Amphitheater.

And by ten o'clock on the fourth morning after leaving Fossil Bay I was standing on Bass Trail with half a gallon of water left in my canteens and luxuriating
in the comfortable knowledge that the Bass Camp cache lay only a thousand
vertical feet above. The week's physical progress was as simple and straightforward as that.

The deeper progress of these days was even more satisfying—but neither so
simple nor so straightforward. It came erratically and hesitantly, so that later I
remembered the week less as a steady stream of events than as a montage of
moments.

They often came, these moments, quite unexpectedly.

About ten o'clock on the morning after I had abandoned the Fossil Canyon
reconnaissance I was breaking my airdrop camp in leisurely fashion for the
move to the head of Fossil Bay when I noticed a small green-speckled lizard
move speculatively out from a crack in the red rock. Jerkily, with many inter-
rogatory genuflections, it investigated my toothbrush. Then it strolled across my
outspread washcloth, mounted the stone that was holding it down, closed its
eyes, and basked. I went quietly about my business. Quarter of an hour, and the
lizard opened its eyes. A minute passed before it moved; but when it did it no
longer strolled. It flicked forward; halted; inspected the world; riveted its attention on a shrub; rocketed toward it; leaped. The leap carried it a full five inches
off the ground. At least, I received the impression of a five-inch jump. But all I
really saw was a blur—and then a re-landed lizard smacking its lips and looking
very pleased with itself and obviously more than ready for another fly if one
should be so ill-advised as to settle within jumping range.

Now, every sunlit desert morning has a magic moment. It may come at five
o'clock, at seven, or at eleven, depending on the weather and the season. But it
comes. If you are in the right mood at the right time you are suddenly aware
that the desert's countless cogs have meshed. That the world has crystallized
into vivid focus. And you respond. You hold your breath or fall into a reverie or
spring to your feet, according to the day and the mood.

The leaping lizard heralded such a moment. I do not mean that anything
very dramatic happened. A waspish-banded fly took a hovering look at my
nylon rope, then snapped away into invisibility. A butterfly landed on one of my
red socks. A hummingbird buzzed the sock and the butterfly flickered, vanished. The hummingbird cased the orange parachute, rejected it, up-tailed away
to a nearby bush, and perched there with constant nervous quiverings of its
violet-banded neck. That was all, I suppose. That, and a sharpening of the sun-

light, a thickening of wind-borne scents, or perhaps a deeper vibration some-where down in the silence. But I know that all at once, standing there on the red rock terrace, still watching the lizard, I was knife-edge alive.

It did not last, of course. They cannot last, these climax moments. In five minutes or ten or thirty the heat begins. Gently at first, then harshly, it clamps down on the desert, stifling the day's vitality. And you sink back from your peak of awareness. In a little while, that sunlit morning on the red rock terrace, I sank slowly and sadly back; but afterward, all through the two days I rested be-side the big rainpocket at the head of Fossil Bay, I remained aware of simple things that the trivia had been smothering. I stood in silence beneath the curving harmony of three huge sandstone boulders. I wondered what lived down a tiny vertical shaft in hot red sand. I even found myself listening to birdsong, which is not, I'm afraid to say, my habit. Found myself really listening—to a piercing intermittent blast so like a referee's whistle that it kept stopping me in my tracks; and to a soft, contemplative warble that repeated, endlessly: "Years and years and years and years and years..."

When I saw another bighorn sheep—clear and sharp this time, in sunlight, and quite close—I realized that I had come to understand something about the lives of these graceful and dignified creatures. I am not talking now about hard zoological facts. Nor even about such practical information as that these nimble-footed individualists are mediocre trailmakers. (Their most heavily used high-way never amounted to much more than a suggestion that a couple of little big-horns might have passed that way in Indian file about the time of Custer's last stand.) I am thinking of less tangible matters.

During my reconnaissance of Fossil Canyon, cloven tracks in rain-smoothed sand pockets had shown me that bighorns travel by preference along the brinks of precipices. I had discovered too that they choose their hideouts, or at least their habitual lying-down places, far out along perilously inaccessible rock-ledges. Most of the heavily patrolled precipices and all the hideouts commanded magnificent, sweeping panoramas of the kind that no man can look at un-moved. After a day or two it occurred to me that the bighorns' choice might be no coincidence; and the more I thought about it, the more difficult I found it to avoid the idea that these dignified animals appreciate scenic beauty.*

---

*For many decades now zoologists have been reacting in justifiable concert against those pur-ple outpourings of the last century which tended to equate simple animal behavior with com-plicated human activity. But perhaps they have leaned backward too far. The incessant and

During the two days' rest at the head of Fossil Bay I even found myself looking differently at inanimate objects. Brooding over the map, I found that instead of worrying only about the way ahead I was reading history. The map—a work of art as well as an astonishingly accurate cartographic document—eased me, step by step, into the past.

The survey which produced the map was begun in 1902 by one François Matthes and was finally completed in 1923. I could grasp this date fairly firmly: I was born in 1922. Stanton Point carried me back around the turn of the century: in 1889 and 1890, Robert Brewster Stanton was first a member and then the leader of two survey parties that investigated a part of the Colorado on behalf of an optimistic railroad company, and lost three men by drowning within six days; not altogether surprisingly, he failed to convince anyone that they should build a railroad through the Canyon. I map-dreamed on, and Bass Trail and Hance Trail took me back another decade: in the late 1880s and early 1890s two miners named William Bass and John Hance, quite independently and in different parts of the Canyon, began to turn from mining to dude wrangling and so begat the local tourist industry. Other place names recalled key figures in the Canyon's white-man history: Powell Plateau honors the one-armed Major John Wesley Powell who in 1869 led the river party that forced the first passage of the Canyon and who later became director of the United State Geological

---

almost automatic accusations of "Anthropomorphism!" are beginning to sound familiar. In other places they shout "Communism!" or "Capitalism!"

There are signs, fortunately, of a corrective swing; but most present-day zoologists would still sniff at my "insight" into bighorn psychology. "Protection from predators," they would intone, "demands inaccessible resting places and maximal visibility." Plausible, of course, but not altogether convincing. What real practical advantage stems from being able to look out over a distant landscape in which any enemy you see is already held at bay by an impassable cliff? And why should aesthetics not have evolved in mammals quite independently of daub-minded monkeys or their more self-conscious successors? We are all made, broadly speaking, of the same flesh and blood and nerve ends.

At the very least, it is pleasing to feel that the zoologists may in the end turn out to be wrong.

(Some time after I had written this footnote I was delighted to find solid support for my suggestion in Sally Carrighar's provocative book *Wild Heritage*. And the trend away from the shibboleth of "Anthropomorphism!" continues. Recently we have had the even more fundamentally challenging *On Aggression* by Konrad Lorenz, a zoologist with a worldwide reputation. Also the more popularly written *Territorial Imperative* by Robert Ardrey. Naturally, both books have been savagely attacked.)

Survey; and Ives Point commemorates the efforts of Lieutenant Joseph Christmas Ives, who in 1857 led the first government exploration of the area.* And Cardenas Butte was obviously named for García López de Cárdenas, one of Coronado's captains, who led the party that "discovered" the Canyon in October 1540.

Other names on the map probed back more deeply, though less obviously, into time. A man who gave buttes and pinnacles such names as Vishnu Temple and Krishna Shrine and Tower of Ra and Wotan's Throne had clearly been moved to feelings beyond the here and now. But religion is not the only mystery that can move a man. Near the head of Bass Trail lay Darwin Plateau. From its northern rim ran Huxley and Spencer Terraces. And between them, sure enough, nestled Evolution Amphitheater. As I brooded over the map, there beside the rainpocket at the head of Fossil Bay, it seemed to me that these last names were the ones that carried the heaviest load of meaning.

Sometimes now I found myself thinking, quite specifically, about the longer time spans.

From the earliest planning days I had expected that as I walked I would ponder a great deal about the rock. After all, the Canyon is above everything else a geological phenomenon. But it had not happened this way. The rock had always been there, but by and large my eye had seen only its surface. Had seen only route and obstacle, shape and shadow, or at the most, magnificent sculpture. Back on the Esplanade, even a striking example of a toadstool rock had seemed little more than an oddity, a chance photogenic freak. I had seen, in other words, only static things, not imprints of a flowing process.

For stimulation along the way I had put in my pack a small paperback book on geology, but in the first two weeks there had been no time to do more than glance at it. But now, resting beside the big rainpocket at the head of Fossil Bay, I began to read.

Perhaps the book was one reason why, as I bathed one morning in water from the rainpocket, standing in warm and soothing sunshine, I noticed that I had a shell-patterned bathroom wall. The big white boulder had broken away

---

*In his report to Congress, Ives perpetrated a masterpiece of malprognostication: "Ours has been the first and will doubtless be the last party of whites to visit this profitless locality. It seems intended by nature that the Colorado River, along the greater portion of its lonely and majestic way, shall be forever unvisited and undisturbed."

Today, over a million people a year visit the Rims of Grand Canyon. And the Colorado is, unfortunately, anything but undisturbed.

quite recently, I saw, from the cliffs above. Less than a million years ago, certainly. Probably no more than a few hundred thousand years ago. Perhaps it had even fallen since that yesterday in which García López de Cárdenas and his party stood awestruck on the Rim. And as I stood wet and naked in the sunshine, looking down at the shells that were now fossils (they looked exactly like our modern cockleshells), I found myself understanding, vividly and effortlessly, that they had once been the homes of sentient, breathing creatures that had lived out their lives on a dark and ancient ocean floor and in the end had died there. Slowly, year after year, their empty shells had been buried by the minute specks that are always settling to the floor of any ocean (specks that are themselves often the shells of tiny creatures that have also lived and felt and died). For a moment I could visualize this drama quite clearly, even though what had once been the slowly building ocean floor was now four hundred feet of solid limestone high above my head, gleaming white in the desert sunlight. I could feel the actuality so clearly that the wetness of that ancient ocean was almost as real to me as the wetness of the water on my body. I could not comprehend in any meaningful way *when* all this had happened, for I knew that those shells in my bathroom wall had lived and died 200 million years before I came to wash beside them; and 200 million years, I had to admit, still lay beyond my grasp. But after the moment of understanding had passed, as it soon did, I knew with certainty that in its own good time the Canyon would show me the kind of geology I had hoped to find.

The evening I struck south from Fossil Bay, the look and challenge of the terrace that stretched out ahead, on and on, inevitably screwed my mind back to the present. Two hours out, as night fell, I camped—because it happened at that moment to become too dark to go on—beside a dead juniper tree. "Damn!" my notebook complained. "Back to press, press, press. Back to Butcharting." But by nine o'clock next morning I had covered half the straight-line distance between Fossil and Apache, and the pressure began to ease. Then, as I swung around an outcrop and for the first time that morning came to the very lip of the terrace, I stopped in my tracks.

Since leaving Supai I had glimpsed the Colorado only briefly, a short segment at a time, framed deep in the V of a side canyon. It had remained remote, cut off from my terrace world. But now there opened up at my feet a huge and unexpected space. On the floor of this space, three thousand feet below, flowed the river. It flowed directly toward me, uninterrupted, down the long and arrowlike corridor of a tremendous gorge.

The whole colossal scene was filled and studded and almost ignited by the witchery of desert sunlight, and the Gorge no longer looked at all a terrible place. Compared with the gloomy chasm in which I had made my reconnaissance, it seemed broad and open and inviting. Now the Colorado no longer swirled brown and sullen; its bright blue surface shone and sparkled. And although the river lay far below me I found that it no longer existed in a totally different world.

Yet because of the size and the beauty and the brilliance of this magnificently unexpected view I felt in that first moment on the lip of the terrace something of the shock that had overwhelmed me when I first stood, a year earlier, on the Rim of the Canyon. It even seemed that, once again, I was meeting the silence—the silence I thought I had grown accustomed to—as something solid, face to face. And just for a moment I felt once more the same understanding and acceptance of the vast, inevitable sweep of geologic time.

The understanding did not last, of course. I was too firmly embedded that morning in the hours and the minutes (though I stayed for almost an hour, gazing at and then photographing that stupendous corridor, which the map calls Conquistador Aisle). But when I walked on eastward again—hurrying a little now, to make up for lost time—I remembered that moment of shock when I first saw the corridor open up in front of me. And I knew that, like the shell pattern in my bathroom wall, the moment had been a promise.

There is something of a gap, then, in my montage of moments. For the next two days, in unbroken sunshine and growing heat, it was all yard and mile, minute and hour; zig and then zag and then zig again along terrace and talus, terrace and talus, terrace and talus; a scrambling, sweaty climb to Apache Point; the long swing around Aztec Amphitheater. But the cool of each evening was an intermission.

The first of these nights I camped—again because that was where I happened to run out of daylight—beside a big juniper tree. As I went to sleep, black branches curved up and over against the stars. The next night I once more camped beside a juniper tree. This time, I camped there because it grew on the brink of a precipice that promised magnificent moonlight vistas. I lit no fire, so that nothing would block me off from the night. And before I went to sleep I sat and watched the promised vistas materialize, gloriously, and felt the hours of sweat and effort sink back and away.

The third night I stumbled on one of those strokes of luck that you seem almost able to count on when things are going well.

I had not actually run short of water, but by dusk I was conscious that I would have to drink a little sparingly until I reached my Bass Camp cache, sometime next day. Then, as the burro trail I was following skirted a smooth shelf of rock, I saw out of the corner of my eye what seemed in the failing light to be the glint of dampness. I stopped, took two paces backward. Nothing more. I drew a finger across the dampness. For a moment there was a causeway of dry rock. Then moisture had welled over again, slowly but without hesitation, and erased it.

I held my breath and listened. A rhythmic rippling of the silence, barely perceptible. I climbed down a few feet of layered rock below the dampness and found, sure enough, a little overhang; and when I put a cooking pot beneath it the metallic and monotonous drip, drip, drip of the single drops of water made beautiful and moving music.

I camped ten feet from the seep, beside a white-flowering bush that over-hung a precipice. From my bedside the bush framed with Japanese delicacy an immense blue-black pit that was filled not so much with shapes as with sugges-tions of shapes—gargantuan shapes that would have been deeply disturbing if I had not known by heart now exactly what they meant.

That night, again, I lit no fire. And as I sat waiting for dinner to cook—cut off from the silence, inside the roaring world of my little stove—I watched the evening sky grow dark. Slowly the darkness deepened. But the blue-black pit below me remained blue-black. Began, even, to ease back from the brink of blackness. For as the last daylight sank away, the moon took over, casting sha-dows at new angles, constructing new shapes, warding off the blackness with a new and cool and exquisitely delicate blue.

When I took dinner off the stove I found myself looking at the fire ring, shining red-hot out of the darkness. Found myself, unexpectedly, appreciating that it too was a thing of beauty and value. And when I turned off the stove I heard all around me, as always happens, the sudden and surprising silence.

While I ate dinner, with the silent blue-black pit opening up below me, I found myself savoring the sense of newness and expectancy that now came with every step of my journey—the always-moving-forward that now filled each day of my life. Soon, I began to contemplate the clock that measured this daily prog-ress; and all at once I was feeling, as if I had never understood it before, the swing and circle of the sun. Sunrise and sunset; sunrise and sunset; sunrise again; and then sunset. It happened everywhere, of course, all over the earth. But now I could detect in the beat of that rhythm an element I had never felt before. Now I could feel the inevitability of it. An inevitability that was impersonal and terrifying and yet, in the end, comforting. And as I sat looking out over the huge and mysterious blue-black space it occurred to me that the pioneers who crossed the American prairies in their covered wagons must have felt, many days out from sight of mountains, the power of this ceaseless rhythm. For them the understanding would have been generated by the monotony of the plains. For me it had something to do with the colossal sameness of the Canyon; but that was a sameness not of monotony but of endlessly repeated yet endlessly varied pattern. A prodigal repetition of terrace mounting on terrace mounting on terrace, of canyon after canyon after canyon after canyon. All of them, one succeeding the other, almost unknown to man, just existing, existing, existing, existing. There seemed at first no hope of a beginning, no hint of an end. But I knew now, more certainly and more easily, that the regularity and the existence were not really timeless. I knew they were echoing reminders of a time, not so very long ago, before the coming of the noisy animal, when the earth was a quiet place.

When I had finished my dinner I lay still and listened to the silence. To the silence and to the music of the water splashing metronomically down into my cooking pot. Before I fell asleep—warm and comfortable inside my mummy bag, passively at ease now inside the silence and the darkness—I knew that at last I stood on the threshold of the huge natural museum that is Grand Canyon.

You cannot, of course, enter such a museum without preparation. It is not a mere place of knowledge. It is not really a place at all, only a state of understanding. As I lay in the darkness, staring up at the stars and hearing how the silence was magnified by the drip, drip, drip of water, I knew that after all my days of effort and silence and solitude I was almost ready at last to move inside the museum.

But a journey is always, before anything else, a physical thing.

By ten o'clock next morning I had begun to climb up Bass Trail toward my cache. In his note with the airdrop Ranger Jim Bailey had said that he might be near Bass Camp on park business somewhere about this date and might be able to check whether I had found the cache. But I knew that he would hardly come down into the Canyon to look for me: it would be like combing Africa for Livingstone, and no natives to question. I climbed up the steep trail, watching the red terrace unfold below, watching it grow less red with distance and more and more orange. I turned onto the last twisting stretch of trail before my cache.

And then, all at once, there was an animal, coming down toward me. A broad, green animal. A large animal, walking upright.

My voice sounded strange. It was the first time I had heard it in two weeks.

"Mr. Stanley, I presume," it said.

"Well I'll be damned!" said Jim Bailey.

CHAPTER
TWENTY-TWO

Havasu

ONE SUMMER I started off to visit for the first time the city of Los Angeles. I was riding with some friends from the University of New Mexico. On the way we stopped off briefly to roll an old tire into the Grand Canyon. While watching the tire bounce over tall pine trees, tear hell out of a mule train and disappear with a final grand leap into the inner gorge, I overheard the park ranger standing nearby say a few words about a place called Havasu, or Havasupai. A branch, it seemed, of the Grand Canyon.

What I heard made me think that I should see Havasu immediately, before something went wrong somewhere. My friends said they would wait. So I went down into Havasu—fourteen miles by trail—and looked things over. When I returned five weeks later I discovered that the others had gone on to Los Angeles without me.

That was fifteen years ago. And still I have not seen the fabulous city on the Pacific shore. Perhaps I never will. There's something in the prospect southwest from Barstow which makes one hesitate. Although recently, driving my own truck, I did succeed in penetrating as close as San Bernardino. But was hurled back by what appeared to be clouds of mustard gas rolling in from the west on a very broad front. Thus failed again. It may be however that Los Angeles will come to me. Will come to all of us, as it must (they say) to all men.

But Havasu. Once down in there it's hard to get out. The trail led across a stream wide, blue and deep, like the pure upper reaches of the River Jordan.

From *Desert Solitaire,* by Edward Abbey. McGraw-Hill, 1968. Reprinted by permission of Harold Matson Co., Inc.

Without a bridge. Dripping wet and making muddy tracks I entered the village of the Havasupai Indians where unshod ponies ambled down the only street and the children laughed, not maliciously, at the sight of the wet white man. I stayed the first night in the lodge the people keep for tourists, a rambling old bungalow with high ceilings, a screened verandah and large comfortable rooms. When the sun went down the village went dark except for kerosene lamps here and there, a few open fires, and a number of lightning bugs or fireflies which drifted aimlessly up and down Main Street, looking for trouble.

The next morning I bought a slab of bacon and six cans of beans at the village post office, rented a large comfortable horse and proceeded farther down the canyon past miniature cornfields, green pastures, swimming pools and waterfalls to the ruins of an old mining camp five miles below the village. There I lived, mostly alone except for the ghosts, for the next thirty-five days.

There was nothing wrong with the Indians. The Supai are a charming, cheerful, completely relaxed and easygoing bunch, all one hundred or so of them. But I had no desire to live *among* them unless clearly invited to do so, and I wasn't. Even if invited I might not have accepted. I'm not sure that I care for the idea of strangers examining my daily habits and folkways, studying my language, inspecting my costume, questioning me about my religion, classifying my artifacts, investigating my sexual rites and evaluating my chances for cultural survival.

So I lived alone.

The first thing I did was take off my pants. Naturally. Next I unloaded the horse, smacked her on the rump and sent her back to the village. I carried my food and gear into the best-preserved of the old cabins and spread my bedroll on a rusty steel cot. After that came a swim in the pool beneath a great waterfall nearby, 120 feet high, which rolled in mist and thunder over caverns and canopies of solidified travertine.

In the evening of that first day below the falls I lay down to sleep in the cabin. A dark night. The door of the cabin, unlatched, creaked slowly open, although there was no perceptible movement of the air. One firefly flickered in and circled my bacon, suspended from the roofbeam on a length of bailing wire. Slowly, without visible physical aid, the door groaned shut. And opened again. A bat came through one window and went out another, followed by a second firefly (the first scooped up by the bat) and a host of mosquitoes, which did not leave. I had no netting, of course, and the air was much too humid and hot for sleeping inside a bag.

I got up and wandered around outside for a while, slapping at mosquitoes, and thinking. From the distance came the softened roar of the waterfall, that "white noise" as soothing as hypnosis. I rolled up my sleeping bag and in the filtered light of the stars followed the trail that wound through thickets of cactus and up around ledges to the terrace above the mining camp. The mosquitoes stayed close but in lessening numbers, it seemed, as I climbed over humps of travertine toward the head of the waterfall. Near the brink of it, six feet from the drop-off and the plunge, I found a sandy cove just big enough for my bed. The racing creek as it soared free over the edge created a continuous turbulence in the air sufficient to keep away all flying insects. I slept well that night and the next day carried the cot to the place and made it my permanent bedroom for the rest of July and all of August.

What did I do during those five weeks in Eden? Nothing. I did nothing. Or nearly nothing. I caught a few rainbow trout, which grew big if not numerous in Havasu Creek. About once a week I put on my pants and walked up to the Indian village to buy bacon, canned beans and Argentine beef in the little store. That was all the Indians had in stock. To vary my diet I ordered more exotic foods by telephone from the supermarket in Grand Canyon Village and these were shipped to me by U.S. Mail, delivered twice a week on muleback down the fourteen-mile trail from Topocoba Hilltop. A little later in the season I was able to buy sweet corn, figs and peaches from the Supai. At one time for a period of three days my bowels seemed in danger of falling out, but I recovered. The Indians never came down to my part of the canyon except when guiding occasional tourists to the falls or hunting a stray horse. In late August came the Great Havasupai Sacred Peach Festival and Four-day Marathon Friendship Dance, to which I was invited and in which I did participate. There I met Reed Watahomagie, a good man, and Chief Sinyala and a fellow named Spoonhead who took me for five dollars in a horse race. Someone had fed my mount a half-bushel of green figs just before the race and didn't inform me.

The Friendship Dance, which continued day and night to the rhythm of drums made of old inner tube stretched over #10 tomato cans while ancient medicine men chanted in the background, was perhaps marred but definitely not interrupted when a drunken free-for-all exploded between Spoonhead and friends and a group of visiting Hualapai Indians down from the rim. But this, I was told, happened every year. It was a traditional part of the ceremony, sanctified by custom. As Spoonhead told me afterwards, grinning around broken teeth, it's not every day you get a chance to wallop a Hualapai. Or skin a pale-face, I reminded him. (Yes, the Supai are an excellent tribe, healthy, joyous and clever. Not only clever but shrewd. Not only shrewd but wise: e.g., the Bureau of Indian Affairs and the Bureau of Public Roads, like most government agencies always meddling, always fretting and itching and sweating for something to do, last year made a joint offer to blast a million-dollar road down into Havasu Canyon at no cost whatsoever to the tribe, thus opening their homeland to the riches of motorized tourism. The people of Supai or at least a majority of them voted to reject the proposal.) And the peach wine flowed freely, like the water of the river of life. When the ball was over I went home to my bunk on the verge of the waterfall and rested for two days.

On my feet again, I explored the abandoned silver mines in the canyon walls, found a few sticks of dynamite but no caps or fuses. Disappointing; but there was nothing in that area anyway that required blowing up. I climbed through the caves that led down to the foot of Mooney Falls, 200 feet high. What did I do? There was nothing that had to be done. I listened to the voices, the many voices, vague, distant but astonishingly human, of Havasu Creek. I heard the doors creak open, the doors creak shut, of the old forgotten cabins where no one with tangible substance or the property of reflecting light ever entered, ever returned. I went native and dreamed away days on the shore of the pool under the waterfall, wandered naked as Adam under the cottonwoods, inspecting my cactus gardens .The days became wild, strange, ambiguous—a sinister element pervaded the flow of time. I lived narcotic hours in which like the Taoist Chuang-tse I worried about butterflies and who was dreaming what. There was a serpent, a red racer, living in the rocks of the spring where I filled my canteens; he was always there, slipping among the stones or pausing to mesmerize me with his suggestive tongue and cloudy haunted primeval eyes. Damn his eyes. We got to know each other rather too well, I think. I agonized over the girls I had known and over those I hoped were yet to come. I slipped by degrees into lunacy, me and the moon, and lost to a certain extent the power to distinguish between what was and what was not myself: looking at my hand I would see a leaf trembling on a branch. A *green* leaf. I thought of Debussy, of Keats and Blake and Andrew Marvell. I remembered Tom o'Bedlam. And all those lost and never remembered. Who would return? To be lost again? I went for walks. I went for walks. I went for walks and on one of these, the last I took in Havasu, regained everything that seemed to be ebbing away.

Most of my wandering in the desert I've done alone. Not so much from choice as from necessity—I generally prefer to go into places where no one else wants to go. I find that in contemplating the natural world my pleasure is greater if there are not too many others contemplating it with me, at the same time. However, there are special hazards in traveling alone. Your chances of dying, in case of sickness or accident, are much improved, simply because there is no one around to go for help.

Exploring a side canyon off Havasu Canyon one day, I was unable to resist the temptation to climb up out of it onto what corresponds in that region to the Tonto Bench. Late in the afternoon I realized that I would not have enough time to get back to my camp before dark, unless I could find a much shorter route than the one by which I had come. I looked for a shortcut.

Nearby was another little side canyon which appeared to lead down into Havasu Canyon. It was a steep, shadowy, extremely narrow defile with the usual meandering course and overhanging walls; from where I stood, near its head, I could not tell if the route was feasible all the way down to the floor of the main canyon. I had no rope with me—only my walking stick. But I was hungry and thirsty, as always. I started down.

For a while everything went well. The floor of the little canyon began as a bed of dry sand, scattered with rocks. Farther down a few boulders were wedged between the walls; I climbed over and under them. Then the canyon took on the slickrock character—smooth, sheer, slippery sandstone carved by erosion into a series of scoops and potholes which got bigger as I descended. In some of these basins there was a little water left over from the last flood, warm and fetid water under an oily-looking scum, condensed by prolonged evaporation to a sort of broth, rich in dead and dying organisms. My canteen was empty and I was very thirsty but I felt that I could wait.

I came to a lip on the canyon floor which overhung by twelve feet the largest so far of these stagnant pools. On each side rose the canyon walls, roughly perpendicular. There was no way to continue except by dropping into the pool. I hesitated. Beyond this point there could hardly be any returning, yet the main canyon was still not visible below. Obviously the only sensible thing to do was to turn back. I edged over the lip of stone and dropped feet first into the water.

Deeper than I expected. The warm, thick fluid came up and closed over my head as my feet touched the muck at the bottom. I had to swim to the farther side. And here I found myself on the verge of another drop-off, with one more huge bowl of green soup below.

This drop-off was about the same height as the one before, but not overhanging. It resembled a children's playground slide, concave and S-curved, only steeper, wider, with a vertical pitch in the middle. It did not lead directly into the water but ended in a series of steplike ledges above the pool. Beyond the pool lay another edge, another drop-off into an unknown depth. Again I paused, and for a much longer time. But I no longer had the option of turning around and going back. I eased myself into the chute and let go of everything—except my faithful stick.

I hit rock bottom hard, but without any physical injury. I swam the stinking pond dog-paddle style, pushing the heavy scum away from my face, and crawled out on the far side to see what my fate was going to be.

Fatal. Death by starvation, slow and tedious. For I was looking straight down an overhanging cliff to a rubble pile of broken rocks eighty feet below.

After the first wave of utter panic had passed I began to try to think. First of all I was not going to die immediately, unless another flash flood came down the gorge; there was the pond of stagnant water on hand to save me from thirst and a man can live, they say, for thirty days or more without food. My sun-bleached bones, dramatically sprawled at the bottom of the chasm, would provide the diversion of the picturesque for future wanderers—if any man ever came this way again.

My second thought was to scream for help, although I knew very well there could be no other human being within miles. I even tried it but the sound of that anxious shout, cut short in the dead air within the canyon walls, was so inhuman, so detached as it seemed from myself, that it terrified me and I didn't attempt it again.

I thought of tearing my clothes into strips and plaiting a rope. But what was I wearing?—boots, socks, a pair of old and ragged blue jeans, a flimsy T-shirt, an ancient and rotten sombrero of straw. Not a chance of weaving such a wardrobe into a rope eighty feet long, or even twenty feet long.

How about a signal fire? There was nothing to burn but my clothes; not a tree, not a shrub, not even a weed grew in this stony cul-de-sac. Even if I burned my clothing the chances of the smoke being seen by some Hualapai Indian high on the south rim were very small; and if he did see the smoke, what then? He'd shrug his shoulders, sigh, and take another pull from his Tokay bottle. Furthermore, without clothes, the sun would soon bake me to death.

There was only one thing I could do. I had a tiny notebook in my hip pocket and a stub of pencil. When these dried out I could at least record my final thoughts. I would have plenty of time to write not only my epitaph but my own elegy.

But not yet.

There were a few loose stones scattered about the edge of the pool. Taking the biggest first, I swam with it back to the foot of the slickrock chute and placed it there. One by one I brought the others and made a shaky little pile about two feet high leaning against the chute. Hopeless, of course, but there was nothing else to do. I stood on the top of the pile and stretched upward, straining my arms to their utmost limit and groped with fingers and fingernails for a hold on something firm. There was nothing. I crept back down. I began to cry. It was easy. All alone, I didn't have to be brave.

Through the tears I noticed my old walking stick lying nearby. I took it and stood it on the most solid stone in the pile, behind the two topmost stones. I took off my boots, tied them together and hung them around my neck, on my back. I got up on the little pile again and lifted one leg and set my big toe on the top of the stick. This could never work. Slowly and painfully, leaning as much of my weight as I could against the sandstone slide, I applied more and more pressure to the stick, pushing my body upward until I was again stretched out full length above it. Again I felt about for a fingerhold. There was none. The chute was smooth as polished marble.

No, not quite that smooth. This was sandstone, soft and porous, not marble, and between it and my wet body and wet clothing a certain friction was created. In addition, the stick had enabled me to reach a higher section of the S-curved chute, where the angle was more favorable. I discovered that I could move upward, inch by inch, through adhesion and with the help of the leveling tendency of the curve. I gave an extra little push with my big toe—the stones collapsed below, the stick clattered down—and crawled rather like a snail or slug, oozing slime, up over the rounded summit of the slide.

The next obstacle, the overhanging spout twelve feet above a deep plunge pool, looked impossible. It *was* impossible, but with the blind faith of despair I slogged into the water and swam underneath the drop-off and floundered around for a while, scrabbling at the slippery rock until my nerves and tiring muscles convinced my numbed brain that *this was not the way*. I swam back to solid ground and lay down to rest and die in comfort.

Far above I could see the sky, an irregular strip of blue between the dark, hard-edged canyon walls that seemed to lean toward each other as they towered above me. Across that narrow opening a small white cloud was passing, so lovely and precious and delicate and forever inaccessible that it broke the heart and made me weep like a woman, like a child. In all my life I had never seen anything so beautiful.

The walls that rose on either side of the drop-off were literally perpendicular. Eroded by weathering, however, and not by the corrosion of rushing floodwater, they had a rough surface, chipped, broken, cracked. Where the walls joined the face of the overhang they formed almost a square corner, with a number of minute crevices and inch-wide shelves on either side. It might, after all, be possible. What did I have to lose?

When I had regained some measure of nerve and steadiness I got up off my back and tried the wall beside the pond, clinging to the rock with bare toes and fingertips and inching my way crabwise toward the corner. The water-soaked, heavy boots dangling from my neck, swinging back and forth with my every movement, threw me off balance and I fell into the pool. I swam out to the bank, unslung the boots and threw them up over the drop-off, out of sight. They'd be there if I ever needed them again. Once more I attached myself to the wall, tenderly, sensitively, like a limpet, and very slowly, very cautiously, worked my way into the corner. Here I was able to climb upward, a few centimeters at a time, by bracing myself against the opposite sides and finding sufficient niches for fingers and toes. As I neared the top and the overhang became noticeable I prepared for a slip, planning to push myself away from the rock so as to fall into the center of the pool where the water was deepest. But it wasn't necessary. Somehow, with a skill and tenacity I could never have found in myself under ordinary circumstances, I managed to creep straight up that gloomy cliff and over the brink of the drop-off and into the flower of safety. My boots were floating under the surface of the little puddle above. As I poured the stinking water out of them and pulled them on and laced them up I discovered myself bawling again for the third time in three hours, the hot delicious tears of victory. And up above the clouds replied—thunder.

I emerged from that treacherous little canyon at sundown, with an enormous fire in the western sky and lightning overhead. Through sweet twilight and the sudden dazzling flare of lightning I hiked back along the Tonto Bench, bellowing the *Ode to Joy*. Long before I reached the place where I could descend safely to the main canyon and my camp, however, darkness set in, the clouds opened their bays and the rain poured down. I took shelter under a ledge in a shallow cave about three feet high—hardly room to sit up in. Others had been here before: the dusty floor of the little hole was littered with the droppings of birds, rats, jackrabbits and coyotes. There were also a few long gray pieces of scat with a curious twist at one tip—cougar? I didn't care. I had some matches with me, sealed in paraffin (the prudent explorer); I scraped together the handiest twigs and animal droppings and built a little fire and waited for the rain to stop.

It didn't stop. The rain came down for hours in alternate waves of storm and drizzle and I very soon had burnt up all the fuel within reach. No matter. I stretched out in the coyote den, pillowed my head on my arm and suffered through the long long night, wet, cold, aching, hungry, wretched, dreaming claustrophobic nightmares. It was one of the happiest nights of my life.

Indian Gardens Camp, 1903

Heritage of the Desert

HE BESTIRRED HIMSELF at the first pale glimpse of day; and when the gray mists had lifted to wreathe the crags, it was light enough to begin the journey.

Mescal shed tears at the grave of the faithful peon. "He loved this cañon," she said softly.

Hare lifted her upon Silvermane. He walked beside the horse, and Wolf trotted on before. They traveled a while under the flowering cottonwoods on a trail bordered with green tufts of grass and great star-shaped lilies. The river was still hidden, but it fllled the grove with its soft thunder. Gradually, the trees thinned out, hard, stony ground encroached upon the sand, boulders appeared in the way; and, presently, when Silvermane stepped out of the shade of the cottonwoods, Hare saw the lower end of the valley with its ragged vent where they would go down.

"Look back!" said Mescal.

Then Hare saw the river bursting from the base of the great wall in two white streams that soon united below, and from there leaped in continuous cascade, white as snow, down through the green grove. Step by step, the stream plunged down through the deep gorge, a broken strip of foam, and at the lower end of the valley it took its final leap into a blue abyss.

"It runs underground to the Colorado," explained Mescal.

"I want to come here again some day."

"You must bring me. Good-by, Thunder River."

From *The Heritage of the Desert,* by Zane Grey. Copyright 1910 by *Popular Magazine.* Reprinted by Zebra Books, 1976.

The fragrant, flower-scented breeze and rumbling of the river persisted long after the valley lay behind and above, but these failed at length in the close, confined air of huge walls. The light grew thick, the stones cracked like deep bell strokes; the voices of man and girl had a hollow sound and echo. Silvermane clicked down the easy trail at a gait that urged Hare now and then to a little trot.

Soon, the gully opened out upon a plateau through the centre of which, in a black split, wound the red Colorado, sullen-voiced, booming, never silent nor restful. Here were distances by which Hare could begin to comprehend the immensity of the cañon, and he felt lost among the great terraces leading up to mesas that dwarfed the Echo Cliffs. All was bare rock of many hues, burning under the sun.

"Jack, this is mescal," said the girl, pointing to some towering plants.

All over the sunny slopes, cacti lifted lofty, slender shafts, unfolding in spiral leaves as they shot upward, and bursting at the top into plumes of yellow flowers. Some were bare and dead, bleached spear points. The blossoming stalks waved in the wind, and huge, black bees circled around them.

"Mescal, I've always wanted to see the Flower of the Desert, from which you're named; and it's beautiful."

Hare broke a dead stalk of the cactus and was put to instant flight by a stream of black bees pouring with angry buzz from the hollow centre. Two big fellows were so persistent that he had to beat them off with his hat.

"You shouldn't despoil their homes," said Mescal, with a peal of laughter.

"I'll break another stalk and get stung, if you'll laugh again," replied Hare.

They traversed the remaining slope of the plateau, and, entering the head of a ravine, descended a steep cleft of black, flinty rock so hard that Silvermane's iron hoofs not so much as scratched it, and, reaching a level, passed out to smooth, rounded sand and the river.

"It's a little high," said Hare dubiously. "Mescal, I don't like the looks of those rapids."

Only a few hundred rods of the river could be seen. In front of Hare, the current was swift, but not broken. Above, where the marble cañon turned, the river sheered out with a majestic roll, and, falling in wide, smooth curve, suddenly broke into turbulent action with its fiercest energy in a wedge-shaped formation, the apex of leaping, reddish waves downstream. Below Hare was a rapid of less magnitude, with the broken water mostly turning toward the near side of the river; still, there were twisting, yellowish swirls and curled, vicious waves and sullen bellow enough to make his flesh creep.

"I guess we'd better risk it," said Hare, grimly recalling the hot rock, the sand and lava and cactus of the desert.

"It's safe, if Silvermane is a good swimmer," replied Mescal. "We can take the river above and cut across so the current will help."

"Silvermane loves the water. I think he used to swim the Sevier River up in Utah. He'll make this crossing easily. But he can't carry us both, and it's impossible to make two trips. I'll have to swim."

Without wasting more words and time in the consideration of an undertaking that would only grow more formidable with every look and thought, Hare led Silvermane up the sand bar to its limit. He removed his coat and strapped it behind the saddle; his belt and revolver and boots he hung over the pommel.

"How about Wolf? I'd forgotten him."

"Never fear for him! He'll stick close to me. . . . Now, Mescal, there's the point we want to make, that bar; see it?"

"Surely, we can land above that."

"I'll be satisfied; I'll be humbly thankful if we get even there. You guide him for it. And, Mescal, here's my gun. Try to keep it from getting wet. Balance it on the pommel—so. Come, Silver! Come, Wolf!"

"Keep upstream," called Mescal, as Hare plunged in. "Don't drift below us."

In two steps, Silvermane went in to his saddle, and in two more he rolled, with a splash and a snort, sinking Mescal to her hips. Nose level with the water, mane and tail floating, he swam powerfully with the current.

For Hare, the water was just cold enough to be delightful after the long, hot descent, but it had the most singular quality of any water in which he had ever swum. Keeping upstream of the horse, and even with Mescal, he swam with long, regular strokes for perhaps one quarter of the distance; then, when they reached the swirling, gurgling eddies, he found that he was quickly tiring. The water was thick and heavy; it compressed his lungs and dragged at his feet.

He whirled round and round in the eddies, and saw Silvermane doing the same. Only by violent force, by literally pushing himself, could he breast his way out of these whirlpools. When a wave slapped his face, he tasted sand, and then knew what was the singular quality of this river. Sand! Sand, as on the desert! Even in the depths of the cañon, he could not escape it.

As the current grew rougher, he began to feel that he could scarcely spread his arms in the wide, long stroke. It was as if they were weighted down. Changing the stroke, he discovered he could not keep up with Silvermane, and he changed back again. Gradually, his feet sank lower and lower, the water pressed tighter around him, his arms seemed to grow useless, strengthless. It was when he realized he could not keep up much longer that he remembered August Naab saying the Navajos did not attempt to swim the river when it was in flood and full of sand. Whereupon, he ceased to struggle, and, drifting with the current, soon was close to Silvermane, and grasped a saddle strap.

"Not there!" called Mescal. "He might strike you. Hang to his tail!"

Hare dropped behind, and, catching Silvermane's long tail, held on firmly. How easily the stallion towed him! The waves dashed over his rump, and lapped at Mescal's waist; and the current grew stronger, sweeping Silvermane down out of line with the black wall that had frowned closer and closer.

Mescal lifted the long rifle, and, resting the stock on the saddle, held it upright. The roar of the rapid that had bellowed in Hare's ears seemed to retreat, to lose its volume, and, presently, it died in the splashing and slapping of broken water closer at hand. Then Mescal turned to him with eyes glancing darkly bright, and, curving her hand about her lips, she shouted:

"Can't make the bar! We've got to go through this side of the rapids. Hang on!"

In a swelling din of watery sounds, Hare felt the resistless pull of the current; and, as he held on with both hands, hard pressed to keep his grasp, Silvermane dipped over a smooth, low fall in the river. Then, Hare was riding the rushing water on an incline. It ended below in a back-lashing, red-crested wave, and beyond was dinning chaos of angry, curling breakers.

Hare had one glimpse of Mescal crouching low, shoulders narrowed and head bent; then, with one white flash of the stallion's mane against her flying black hair, she went out of sight in upspurting waves and spray.

Hare was thrown forward into the back lash of the wave. The shock blinded him, stunned him, almost tore his arms from his body, but his hands were so twisted in Silvermane's tail that the force of the drag could not loosen them. The current threw him from wave to wave, with crash and buffet and pound. He was dragged through a caldron, blind from stinging blows, deaf from the tremendous roar. Then, the fierce contention of waves lessened, the threshing crisscross of currents straightened, and he could breathe once more.

Silvermane dragged him steadily; the roar grew to be a sound, instead of a ponderous weight in his ears; the current ceased to sway his legs upward; and, finally, his feet touched the ground. He could scarcely see, so full were his eyes of the sandy water, but he made out Mescal rising from the water on Silvermane, as with loud snorts he climbed to a bar. Hare staggered up, and fell on the sand.

"Jack, are you all right?" inquired Mescal.

"All right, only pounded out of breath, and my eyes are full of sand. How about you?"

"I don't think I ever was any wetter," replied Mescal, laughing. "It was hard to stick on, holding the rifle. That first wave almost unseated me. I was afraid we might strike the rocks, but the water was deep. Silvermane is grand, Jack. Wolf swam out above the rapids, and was waiting for us when we landed."

Hare wiped the sand out of his eyes, and got to his feet, finding himself little the worse for the incident. Mescal was wringing water from the long, straight braids of her hair. She was smiling, and a tint of color showed in her cheeks. The wet buckskin blouse and short skirt clung tightly to her slender form. She made so pretty a picture and appeared so little affected by the peril they had just passed through that Hare, yielding to a tender rush of pride and possession, kissed the pink cheeks till they flamed.

"All wet," said he, "you and I, clothes, food, guns—everything."

"It's hot, and we'll soon dry," returned Mescal. "Here is the cañon and creek we must follow up to Cononina. My peon mapped them in the sand for me, one day. It'll probably be a long climb, but not steep."

Hare poured the water out of his boots, pulled them on, and, helping Mescal to mount Silvermane, he took the bridle over his arm, and led the way into a narrow, black-mouthed cañon, through which flowed a stream of clear water. Wolf splashed and pattered along beside him. Beyond the black marble rock, this creek cañon opened out to great breadth and wonderful walls.

Hare had eyes only for the gravelly bars and shallow, rocky levels of the creek, and, intent on finding the easy going for his horse, he strode on and on, thoughtless of time. Nor did he talk to Mescal, for the work was hard, and he needed his breath.

Splashing the water, clicking the stones, Silvermane ever kept his nose at Hare's elbow. They climbed little ridges, making short cuts from point to point, and threaded miles of narrow, winding, creek floor, and passed under ferny cliffs, and over grassy banks and through thickets of yellow willow.

As they wound along the course of the creek, always up and up, the great walls imperceptibly lowered their rims. The warm sun soared to the zenith. Jumble of boulders, stretches of white gravel, ridges of sage, blocks of granite, thickets of manzanita, long, yellow slopes, crumbling crags, clumps of cedar and lines of piñon—all were passed in persistent, plodding climb. The cañon grew restricted toward its source; the creek lost its volume; patches of snow gleamed in sheltered places. At last, the yellow-streaked walls edged out upon a grassy hollow, and the great, dark, magnificent pines of Coconina shadowed the snow.

"We're up," panted Hare. "What a climb! Five hours! One more day— then, home!"

Silvermane's ears shot up, and Wolf barked. Two gray deer loped out of a thicket, and turned inquisitively. Reaching for his rifle, Hare threw back the lever, but the action clogged, it rasped with the sound of crunching sand, and the cartridge could not be pressed into the chamber or ejected. He fumbled about the breech of the gun, and his brow clouded.

"Sand! Out of commission!" he exclaimed. "Mescal, I don't like that."

"Use your Colt," suggested Mescal.

The distance was too great for the smaller firearm; Hare missed, and the deer bounded away into the forest.

Hare built a fire under a sheltering pine where no snow covered the soft mat of needles, and, while Mescal dried the blankets and roasted the last portion of meat, he made a windbreak of spruce boughs. When they had eaten, not forgetting to give Wolf a portion, Hare fed Silvermane the last few handfuls of grain, and tied him with a long halter on the grassy bank.

The daylight failed, and darkness came on apace. The old familiar roar of the wind in the pines was perturbing; it might have meant only the lull and clash of the breaking night gusts, and it might have meant the north wind, storm, and snow. It whooped down the hollow, scattering the few scrub-oak leaves, and whirred the red embers of the fire away into the dark to sputter in the snow, and blew the burning logs into white glow. Mescal slept in the shelter of the spruce boughs, with Wolf snug and warm beside her; and Hare stretched his tired limbs in the heat of the blaze.

When he awakened, the fire was low, and he was numb with cold. He took care to put on logs enough to last until morning; then, he lay down once more, but did not sleep. The dawn came with a gray morning shade in the forest; it was a cloud, and it rolled over him soft, tangible, moist, and cool, and passed away under the pines. With its vanishing, the dawn lightened.

"Mescal, if we're on the spur of Coconina, it's only ten miles or so to Silver Cup," said Hare, as he saddled Silvermane. "Mount, now, and we'll go up out of the hollow and get our bearings."

While ascending the last step to the rim, Hare revolved in his mind the probabilities of marking a straight course to Silver Cup.

"Oh, Jack!" exclaimed Mescal suddenly. "Vermillion Cliffs and home!"

"I've traveled in a circle!" replied Hare.

Mescal was enraptured at the scene, as her gaze signified. Vermillion Cliffs shone red as a rose. The split in the wall, marking the oasis, defined its outlines sharply against the sky. Miles of the Colorado River lay in sight. Hare knew he stood on the highest point of Coconina overhanging the cañon and the Painted Desert, thousands of feet below. He sighted the wondrous abyss sleeping in blue mist at his feet while he gazed across to the desert awakening in the first red rays of the rising sun.

Sand—lava—plain—mesa—were mere colored dots and streaks in space, softening aspects of a marginless waste, purple details that led the eye to where a dim horizon merged in the heavens. The same alluring desert, yet how different! He had felt its dry teeth in his life; he had crossed it; he knew its deceiving distances; still was it a mystery.

He followed the Little Colorado winding down through the Painted Desert to join the great river, and his survey brought the chasm directly under his eye. He echoed Mescal's exclamation, and, reaching for her hand, held it while he tried to comprehend the awe-inspiring spectacle. He stood on the edge of a ruined world of stone. Where was the sea that had not been filled by the silt washed from this gap? The huge domes, the escarpments, the pinnacles and turrets were draped in gray. Deep, dark blue marked the clefts between the mesas, and the tips of the crags caught the rose of the sun. There were no sudden changes, no sudden breaks—all the millions of slopes and terraces merged together, enfolded in soft haze, soft mist, soft cloud, in one soft effect of entrancing beauty.

Bibliography

PUBLICATIONS RELATING TO GRAND CANYON have proliferated far beyond the point at which a comprehensive listing would serve the general reader. The purpose of this listing is simply to provide a highly selective and somewhat opinionated guide to further reading.

For readers in search of detail, there are several useful bibliographies. The first, *The Books of the Colorado River and the Grand Canyon* by Francis P. Farquhar (Glen Dawson: Los Angeles, 1953), covers only books published to that date; it is especially strong in description and comparison of the Spanish and nineteenth-century sources. Nineteenth-century magazine articles are exhaustively cataloged and abstracted in *Arizona Odyssey, Bibliographic Adventures in Nineteenth Century Magazines* by D. M. Goodman (Tempe: Arizona Historical Foundation, 1969). Periodical literature after 1900 can be located under the entry "Grand Canyon" in the *Readers Guide to Periodical Literature*.

A recent bibliography of the library holdings of Northern Arizona University, *Grand Canyon and the Colorado Plateau, a Bibliography of Selected Titles in the NAU Libraries,* by K. F. Nutt (Flagstaff: Northern Arizona University Libraries, 1978), includes more recent titles and provides a good list of government documents that have been generated by recent federal environmental planning laws.

The following references are grouped around the subject matter headings used in this anthology:

I. DISCOVERY AND EXPLORATION

The best account of the Coronado expedition is by H. E. Bolton, *Coronado,*

Knight of Pueblos and Plains (Albuquerque: University of New Mexico Press, 1949). Translations of the documents of the Coronado expedition are in Hammond and Rey, *Narratives of the Coronado Expedition,* Vol. II (Albuquerque: University of New Mexico Press, 1940).

The landmark assessment of Powell, his life and his work in the plateau country is in Stegner, W., *Beyond the Hundredth Meridian, John Wesley Powell and the Second Opening of the West* (Boston: Houghton Mifflin Co., 1954). The other important Powell biography is Darrah, W. C., *Powell of the Colorado* (Princeton: Princeton University Press, 1964).

The most readable and accurate overall history of the Grand Canyon area is Crampton, C. G., *Land of Living Rock* (New York: Alfred A. Knopf, 1972). Another good approach to canyon area history, with strong emphasis on the reclamation and conservation movements, is *The Grand Colorado, The Story of a River and Its Canyons,* T. H. Watkins, ed. (Palo Alto: American West Publishing Co., 1969).

A recent study by D. H. Strong, "Ralph H. Cameron and the Grand Canyon," *Arizona and the West,* Vol. 20, Nos. 1 & 2 (1978), gives a scholarly, yet entertaining account of the efforts by Cameron and his friends to corner the canyon for profit.

In the House of Stone and Light, by J. P. Hughes (Grand Canyon Natural History Association, 1967), is beautifully illustrated and well documented.

II. THE VISUAL IMAGE

Since virtually all canyon writers attempt some description, this category is somewhat arbitrary.

Frank Waters's classic account, *The Colorado* (New York: Rinehart & Co., 1946), devotes one chapter to canyon description.

The artists of the Grand Canyon have received little notice. The greatest artist of Grand Canyon, Thomas Moran, is the subject of a full-length biography by T. Wilkins, *Thomas Moran, Artist of the Mountains* (Norman: University of Oklahoma Press, 1966). The most popular canyon painter, Gunnar Widforss, is the subject of a beautifully illustrated monograph by Bill and Francis Belknap, *Gunnar Widforss, Painter of the Grand Canyon* (Flagstaff: Museum of Northern Arizona, 1969).

A good selection of the rather considerable body of canyon poetry, including selections by Carl Sandburg and Edgar Lee Masters, is assembled by McFarland, E. F., "This is Grand Canyon," in *Arizona Highways* (March, 1954).

"The Sound of Silence" by Jack Foster in *Arizona Highways* (June, 1979) is an original approach to prose description.

III. THROUGH TOURIST EYES

Representative pieces by many turn-of-the-century writers including Hamlin Garland, William Allen White, Joequin Miller and Charles Lummis are collected in *The Grand Canyon of Arizona* (Chicago: Santa Fe Railway, 1906). The fascinating entries in John Hance's guest book from 1891 through 1898 are collected and published in G. K. Woods, *Personal Impressions of the Grand Canyon of the Colorado River* (San Francisco: Whitaker Ray Co., 1899).

George Wharton James was a prolific and popular early lecturer and writer on the Grand Canyon; his two canyon books, *In and Around the Grand Canyon* (Boston: Little, Brown & Co., 1900) and *The Grand Canyon of Arizona, How to See It* (Boston: Little, Brown & Co., 1910), still retain the flavor and excitement of early day visits.

The basic reference for place names is *Grand Canyon Place Names* by H. B. Granger (Tucson: University of Arizona Press, 1960).

IV. THE SCIENTISTS

The canyon has been subjected to an enormous amount of scientific study, but good accounts for the lay reader are still rare. *The Grand Canyon Up Close and Personal,* edited by R. Euler and F. Tikalsky (Western Montana College Foundation, 1980) is a useful introduction, with strong sections on biology and archaeology. *An Introduction to Grand Canyon Geology* by Michael Collier (Grand Canyon Natural History Association, 1980) is an appealing mix of science and personal philosophy. *Geology of the Grand Canyon,* edited by Breed and Roat (Flagstaff: Museum of Northern Arizona, 1974) sums up current geological knowledge, but it is tough going for the layman. *Grand Canyon, The Story Behind the Scenery,* written by park naturalist Merrill Beal (Flagstaff: K C Publications, 1967) contains a clearly written and imaginatively illustrated account of the "stream capture" theory of the canyon's origin.

In recent years scientific studies have turned toward assessments of the environmental changes caused by upstream dams, by intensive use of the river, millions of visitors, and thousands of inner canyon hikers. The status of environmental and biological studies is the subject of an entire issue of *Plateau,* Vol. 49,

No. 4 (Spring 1977). The case for the conservationist ethic is stated in different and appealing essays in Leydet, F., *Time and the River Flowing* (New York: Ballantine Books, 1968), and in Sutton, A., *The Wilderness World of Grand Canyon* (Philadelphia: J. B. Lippincott Co., 1971). A recent *National Geographic* article by W. E. Garrett, "Grand Canyon, Are We Loving It to Death" (Vol. 154, No. 1, July, 1978), explores current people-management problems.

Two good biological guides are Hoffmeister, D., *Mammals of Grand Canyon* (Urbana: University of Illinois Press, 1971) and McDougal, W. B., *Grand Canyon Wild Flowers* (Flagstaff: Museum of Northern Arizona, 1964).

The classic early study of the Havasupai Indians is Cushing, F. H., "The Nation of Willows," *Atlantic Monthly* (September–October, 1882).

V. A SENSE OF PERSONAL ADVENTURE

The bible of inner-canyon hiking is Butchart, H., *Grand Canyon Treks* (Glendale, California: La Siesta Press, 1970). A second book, *Grand Canyon Treks II,* published in 1975 by the same author and publisher, extends coverage upriver to Marble Canyon and downstream to the far western reaches of Grand Canyon. A more general and historically oriented description of the trails is found in Peattie, R., editor, *The Inverted Mountains* (New York: The Vanguard Press, 1948).

A guide entitled *Inner Canyon Hiking,* published by Grand Canyon Natural History Association, usefully keys trail descriptions to topographic map sections. Butchart also takes up the relatively new subject of mountaineering in the canyon in "Summits Below the Rim," *The Journal of Arizona History,* Vol. 17, No. 1 (1976).

River books and journals are very numerous. Powell's second canyon voyage is recounted in F. S. Dellenbaugh, *A Canyon Voyage* (New Haven: Yale University Press, 1962). *Through the Grand Canyon from Wyoming to Mexico* by Ellsworth Kolb (New York: The Macmillan Co., 1920) remains a basic river text. *Grand Canyon River Guide* by Buzz Belknap (Boulder City: Westwater Books, 1969) provides mile-by-mile maps, illustrations and commentary useful for first-time river runners.

Index

DESIGNED BY MARK SANDERS
COMPOSED IN LINOTYPE GRANJON
WITH DISPLAY LINES
IN GOUDY CATALOG
PRINTED ON WARREN'S OLDE STYLE
AT THE PRESS IN THE PINES

NORTHLAND PRESS

BOUND BY ROSWELL BOOKBINDING
PHOENIX